Real LOVE and FREEDOM FOR THE SOUL

Eliminating the Chains of Victimhood

GREG BAER, M.D.

Real Love® and Freedom for the Soul - Eliminating the Chains of Victimhood
Copyright © 2007 by Greg Baer, M.D.

Second Edition

All rights reserved including the right of reproduction in whole or in part in any form.

Baer, Greg
   Real Love® and Freedom for the Soul
   ISBN 1-892319-28-4
   1. Relationships 2. Self-help 3. Psychology
Published by Blue Ridge Press PO Box 3075 Rome, GA 30164
   877-633-3568

Also by Greg Baer, M.D.—
Published by Gotham Books, a division of Penguin USA Group:
Real Love® — The Truth About Finding Unconditional Love and Fulfilling Relationships
Real Love® in Marriage — The Truth About Finding Genuine Happiness Now and Forever

Published by Blue Ridge Press:
Real Love® — The Truth About Finding Unconditional Love and Fulfilling Relationships, Unabridged Audio Book — Seven 60 minute CDs
The Real Love® Companion — Taking Steps Toward a Loving and Happy Life
Real Love® in Dating — The Truth About Finding the Perfect Partner — Book and Unabridged Audio Book
Real Love® in Marriage — Unabridged Audio Book, Blue Ridge Press
Real Love® in Parenting — The Truth About Raising Happy and Responsible Children — Book and Unabridged Audio Book
Real Love® in the Workplace - Eight Principles for Consistently Effective Leadership in Business
The Truth About Love and Lies — Three 60 minute CDs
The Essentials of Real Love® — Six DVDs, or Six CDs
The Essentials of Real Love® Workbook for DVDs or CDs
The Essentials of Real Love® Bible Workbook for DVDs or CDs
Real Love® for Wise Men and Women - The Truth About Sharing Real Love

Printed in the United States
10 9 8 7 6 5 4 3 2 1

Contents

Chapter 1: Victimhood and Real Love   1

   The Disease of Victimhood   3
   The Cause of Victimhood: The Lack of Real Love   10
   What We Do Without Enough Real Love: Imitation Love   14
   What We Do Without Enough Real Love (Real or Imitation): Getting and Protecting Behaviors   19
   The Deadly Pitfalls of the Getting and Protecting Behaviors   29
   The Elimination of Getting and Protecting Behaviors with Understanding: The Drowning Metaphor   32
   The Elimination of Getting and Protecting Behaviors with Real Love   35
   Supporting Material for Understanding Real Love   37

Chapter 2: The Foundations of Victimhood   41

   Emptiness   41
   Fear   50
   Pain   54
   The Victim's Disregard for the Law of Choice   67
   The Victim's Disregard for the Law of Expectations   71
   Controlling and Victimhood   75
   Learning Victimhood as Children   78
   What Victims Say   80

Chapter 3: Victimhood and All the Other Getting and Protecting Behaviors — 85

Victimhood as the Foundation of all the Other Getting and Protecting Behaviors — 86
Why Victimhood? — 94
Dancing from One Getting and Protecting Behavior To Another — 97

Chapter 4: The Rewards of Victimhood — 101

Victims Often Hold a Position of Untouchable Self-Righteousness — 102
Victims Make People Feel Guilty, So They'll Stop Hurting Them — 107
Victims Manipulate People for Sympathy and Attention — 109
Victims Manipulate People for Support and Power — 116
Victims Completely Avoid Responsibility — 121
Victims Create a Place in the World Where They Can Belong — 124
Victims of Fate and Self — 127

Chapter 5: The Negative Consequences of Victimhood — 131

We Can't Feel Loved — 132
We Can't Have Intimate Relationships — 133
We Can't Grow in Our Personal Lives — 135
We Can't Be Responsible, Productive Human Beings — 137
We Become Spoiled — 140
We Contribute to a Society of Punishment, Not Learning — 140
We Are Guaranteed To Be Angry — 144
We Are Guaranteed To Lie — 145
We Can't Be Free — 146
We Can't Be Happy — 148
We Raise a Generation of Children Who Will Act Like Victims — 149

Chapter 6: Conditions Caused or Worsened by Victimhood   151

  Marriage Conditions Caused By Victimhood   152
  Dating Conditions Caused By Victimhood   154
  Angry and Rebellious Children   162
  Addiction Caused By or Worsened By Victimhood   162
  Victimhood in the Workplace   166
  Handicapped People   169
  Therapy and Self Help   170
  Infamous Historical Characters as Victims: Adolf Hitler and Saddam Hussein   172
  Civil and International Conditions   172

Chapter 7: Eliminating Victimhood with Understanding   181

  The Law of Choice   182
  The Law of Responsibility   192
  The Law of Expectations   196
  Tell the Truth About Yourself   199
  The Power of Understanding in the Elimination of Victimhood   205

Chapter 8: Eliminating Victimhood with Real Love   209

  Telling the Truth About Ourselves   210
  The Healing Power of Real Love   217
  What Can Real Love Look Like   225
  Getting Real Love When You Need It   235
  The "Power" of Victimhood   238

Chapter 9: Responding to Other People Who Act Like Victims   241

  Victims Are So Irritating - and Captivating   241
  How to Respond To People Who Are Acting Like Victims   245

1. Never Respond with Getting and Protecting Behaviors.	246
2. Tell the Truth About Yourself.	247
3. Listen To What the Victim Wants.	251
4. Offer What is *Needed* and What You Can Give *Freely*.	254
5. Teach the Truth About Human Behavior.	262
6. Occasionally Describe What You Are Doing and the Choices Available.	270
7. Occasionally Impose Consequences.	271
8. Stay Off the Field of Death.	275
1-8. Putting All the Responses Together	276
Responding To Victims in the Workplace	283
Responding To Alcoholics and Drug Addicts	288
Responding To Other Addictions	291
Responding To Victims of Fate	293
Responding To Self-Inflicted Victims	294
Responding To What Victims Say	297
Teaching Children How to Respond To Other People Who Act Like Victims	306
We Are Never Responsible for the Choices Made by Others	308
Our Responsibility To Help Victims	310

Chapter 10: Infamous Characters Created by Victimhood 313

Adolf Hitler	314
Saddam Hussein	348
Conclusion	353
Index	357

≈ Chapter One ≈

Victimhood and Real Love

In our daily, ongoing quest for healthier and happier lives, one powerful tool we have come to enjoy regularly—a tool we almost take for granted, in fact—is the wealth of information available to us literally in the blink of an eye. We can access the Internet, for example, and learn all about the incidence, distribution, and causes of cancer, AIDS, malnutrition, heart disease, crime, and many other diseases or problems that might have a negative effect on our lives. Armed with this information, we can then make much better decisions about where to invest our time, energy, and resources in order to protect ourselves and our families, and even to contribute to the health and happiness of the world as a whole. Over the history of mankind, knowledge has been extraordinarily powerful in our efforts to eradicate disease and other problems.

There are some diseases or disorders, however, that have remained resistant to diagnosis and treatment because they have thus far been "secret." Although I call these disorders "secret" because they carry on their work of injury and death essentially undetected, they are certainly not *silent*, because there's nothing quiet about the wake of devastation they leave behind as they destroy the happiness of individuals and families and even entire nations. You can't go online and read about the incidence and distribution of these secret disorders, nor is there any urgent discussion in the media or in state or national legislatures about identifying or treating them. The damage they cause is every bit as real and painful as that resulting from cancer, AIDS and heart disease, but these secret disorders often spread unchecked and unresisted, because they are poorly understood, often to the point of being completely mysterious.

Let me illustrate the effects of one of the worst of these secret disorders as we observe the following interaction between a man I once counseled, Mark, and his wife, Susan. I do so in the hope that at least by *naming* a scourge—by holding it up to the light to some degree—we might thereby gain some measure of power over it.

With obvious exasperation, Mark walks into the kitchen where Susan is working and throws his keys on the table. They slide across the hard surface with that unique screeching whine, somehow miss every glass and plate, sail into space when they reach the other side, and crash to the floor, where they slide several more feet before coming to a crunching stop against the wall.

"So what's wrong with *you*?" asks Susan.

"Oh, so that's all the thanks I get?" Mark shoots back. "I should have known."

"Thanks for what?" asks Susan with exaggerated irritation. "You expect me to read your mind? What am I supposed to be grateful for now?"

"You can't even remember? Typical. You said you were busy here, so would I please go to the store and pick up some bread for you. Remember *now*?"

"Geez, make a big deal of it. It's just a loaf of bread."

"*Just a loaf of bread*? You didn't think it was 'just a loaf of bread' when you were all in a panic and asked me to get it for you. And then I looked all over the store for you—for that one kind you always make a fuss about—and after all that, now you say, 'it's just a loaf of bread'?"

"So? Did you get it? Did you get the Seven-Grain Nature's Wonder?"

"Like I *said*," Mark snaps at Susan, "I looked all over the place. I did everything I could—except bake it myself—but I couldn't find it. What did you expect I'd do if they didn't have it? So I got the Six-Grain Economy Substitute."

"You're kidding, right? You know I hate that stuff. How many times have I told you that?"

"No, stop, stop, you're killing me with your gratitude. You probably meant to say, *'Thanks so much, Mark, for going all the way to the store—in the hundred-degree heat—finding a parking space, fighting your way through the crowds, hunting all over the store for the one stinking brand I like and doing your very best to find it, even though this stupid brand doesn't seem to exist anywhere in the world. Thanks for doing all you did. I really appreciate it.'* That's probably what you meant to say, right?"

"I ask you to do *one* thing, and it always turns into a big production that you can't handle. Do you *ever* bring back what I ask for? Ever?"

"And no matter how hard I try, when do I ever do *anything* that's good enough for you? Exactly, so why even bother to try?" And then Mark stomps out of the room.

THE DISEASE OF VICTIMHOOD

If someone has a fever, nausea, headache, chills, and a positive microscopic hematological examination for Plasmodium falciparum, we can make a diagnosis of malaria with considerable certainty. It's a disease we're familiar with. We can identify it, label it, and treat it. But the disease that is infecting and poisoning the interaction between Mark and Susan, and which is causing incalculable misery and death all over the world, has largely managed to escape identification, discussion, and treatment for countless generations.

It's time we named this disease. It's time we discussed its causes, its manifestations, its complications, and how we can effectively approach its treatment. The name of the disease is *victimhood*, and this secret killer is causing more unhappiness than almost anyone recognizes—certainly more than cancer, AIDS, and heart disease combined.

It is the disease of victimhood—more than any other single cause—that separates us from one another and causes pain in our individual lives and in our relationships. It is victimhood that

- causes the majority of relationships—friendships, marriages, and so on—to become mired in conflict and even to break down entirely.
- leads to rebellion, anger, and withdrawal in children.
- causes alcohol and drug abuse.
- is the real cause of racism all over the world: whites hating blacks, blacks hating whites, one tribe of any color hating another tribe of the same color, and so on.
- keeps gays and lesbians feeling separated from the majority of the population.
- causes the majority of contention in the world.
- is the real cause of the conflicts between and within nations and other groups: between the Hutus and the Tutsis, the Israelis and the Palestinians, the Islamic world and the West, and so on.

Before we talk about the causes and treatment of victimhood, let's put more of a floodlight on what victimhood is. Let's drag it all the way out of the closet and reveal its hidden secrets.

We've all had conversations that involved some of the elements of the interaction we just witnessed between Mark and Susan, where we have vigorously tried—and failed—to make another person listen to us. We've tried reason. We've tried persistence. We've tried pleading, intimidation, sarcasm, and more. And with these efforts, we've discovered what Mark and Susan found as they tried these elements: that our interactions have been twisted and perverted by *victimhood*, by beliefs we hold deeply, by beliefs that all victims share. Anytime things are difficult, as victims we believe that

- we personally are being inconvenienced.
- we're being injured.
- we're being treated unfairly.
- what we want or need is being withheld from us.
- any mistakes involved are not our fault.

When we feel and act like victims, not only do we always hold some or all of the above beliefs, but we make it one of our primary goals in life to convince the people around us to believe as we do.

Why do we act like victims? Because if we can convince people of the above beliefs we

- gain a position of untouchable self-righteousness.
- can make people feel guilty, and then they'll stop hurting us.
- can manipulate people for sympathy and attention.
- can manipulate people for support and power.
- completely avoid responsibility.
- create a place in the world where we can belong.

I'll be explaining each of the above "rewards" of victimhood in detail in Chapter Four.

As victims we exhibit a pattern of speech and behavior that reflects the set of beliefs and hopes for rewards we described above. When we act like victims, we

- say "Look what you did *to* me."
- say "Look what you should have done *for* me (and didn't)."
- say "It's not my fault."
- often say, "It's not fair."
- make excuses for everything.
- blame everyone but ourselves for our own mistakes and unhappiness.

We've all acted like victims at various times in our lives. We've all made excuses, inappropriately blamed other people, and whined about things that aren't fair. Whenever we're confronted with a mistake we've made and say, "I couldn't help it," we're acting like victims. Some of us make victimhood the primary behavior of our lives, but whether we dabble in victimhood or become fully immersed in it, it has a very negative effect on our lives. It robs us of personal happiness and steals the joy and fulfillment from our relationships.

We need to learn more about victimhood: why it begins, how it grows like a cancer, how it affects us, and how we can prevent and eliminate it. Let's begin our study by examining the real meaning of the words and behaviors used by Mark and Susan in their interaction above.

What Mark or Susan Said or Did	The Real Meaning of What Mark or Susan Said or Did
Mark threw his keys on the table.	1. "Everything has been so inconvenient for *me*." 2. "Nothing is *supposed* to be inconvenient for *me*, because I am the center of the universe." 3. "How *dare* all this have happened to *me*?" 4. "Because you have been such an inconsiderate witch *to me* in the past, I'm going to blame you for how I feel about everything that's going badly right now." 5. "If you cared about *me* at all, you'd know what is bothering me without my having to tell you in words. You'd just *know*. So as I throw my keys on the table, I expect you to figure out why I'm unhappy—or at least ask me about it."
"So what's wrong with *you*?" asked Susan.	"Oh great. Here I had the attention of the world focused on *me*—as it should be—and then you come in having a little fit, demanding that everybody look at *you*. Now, I ask you, how in the world can everyone pay attention to both of us at the same time? Surely you don't expect *me* to figure out what you want and actually *do* something about it, do you?
"Oh, so that's all the thanks I get?" Mark shot back.	"*I* go out of *my* way to do something for you (well, really for *myself*, come to think of it), and what do *I* get out of it? Where's the payoff for *me*? There's no sense my doing anything good unless *I* get paid for it—with gratitude, respect, favors, sex, something."

What Mark or Susan Said or Did	The Real Meaning of What Mark or Susan Said or Did
"Thanks for what?" asked Susan.	"Why should *I* be grateful to *you*? After all you've done *to me*, and all you've failed to do *for me*, why would I owe *you* gratitude? If anything, you would owe *me* service and be glad for the opportunity."
"You expect me to read your mind?" (Susan)	"You big baby. You're such a drag. If you had any sense, and if you understood how incredibly important I am, you'd go out of your way to communicate clearly anything I needed to know. You'd never inconvenience *me* by making me guess what *you* want. In fact, you'd never make me wonder if you wanted anything at all, because only *my* needs really matter."
"You can't even remember?" (Mark)	1. "I keep telling you that you don't care about me, that my needs don't matter, and this proves it. If I were important enough to you—which I am to anybody that has any brains—you'd never forget any conversation we have." 2. "You really are as stupid as I've always told you."
"Geez, it's just a loaf of bread." (Susan)	"You always make everything more important than me, and now here's more proof. You're all upset over having to get a simple loaf of bread, like I'm not worth the effort. Thanks a lot. Thanks for nothing."
"*Just a loaf of bread?*" said Mark. "After I looked all over the store for you?"	"After *I* inconvenienced *myself* for you, how could you possibly fail to give *me* the recognition I deserve? You always demean *my* contributions."

What Mark or Susan Said or Did	The Real Meaning of What Mark or Susan Said or Did
"So? Did you get it?" (Susan)	"After throwing your keys and after all you've said, the answer to this question is pretty obvious, but I have to ask, because there is really only one person here whose needs matter: *me*. I don't really care how much you were inconvenienced. Did you get what *I* want?"
"Like I said," Mark snapped at Susan, "I looked all over the place."	With his anger, Mark screamed that when he looked all over the store he wasn't motivated by a genuine interest in Susan's happiness. His anger proved that he went to the store primarily for his own purposes—in this case to avoid Susan's disapproval—which is a long way from being motivated by unconditional love. (More about this subject later in the chapter)
"You're kidding, right? You know I hate that stuff." (Susan)	"The effort you put into anything is a complete waste if you fail to satisfy *my* needs. It doesn't matter how hard you have to work or how much you are inconvenienced. The real issue is what *I* want, and—pathetically—you failed to supply that."
"No, stop with your gratitude." (Mark)	1. "I simply can't believe that you're actually maintaining here that there is a possibility that you might be the most important person in this relationship. That's insane. It's clear who the most important person is—*me*—and you should live in perpetual gratitude that I even live with you."

What Mark or Susan Said or Did	The Real Meaning of What Mark or Susan Said or Did
"No, stop with your gratitude." (Mark)	2. "You are obviously too stupid to speak the proper words of gratitude, so let me supply them for you. I demand that you recognize what a great charitable act I have performed here, and I demand that you express you gratitude for it right now."
"Do you ever do what I ask?" (Susan)	"Will you ever, ever understand how important *I* am? Will you ever place *me* appropriately on the throne at the center of the world? Until you do exactly what I ask, and recognize *my* importance, nothing you do counts for *anything*. Until that day, you are worthless."
"When do I ever do *anything* that's good enough for you?"	"I kill myself for you, and what do I get? Nothing. I try to give you everything, but if anything isn't perfect, all you do is complain. Without the proper appreciation, why should I bother to try to please you by doing anything at all?"
Mark stomped out of the room.	"When you're this hateful, I can't even stand to be in the same room with you. Who could? I simply can't believe that you could treat *me* in this way. When you can be a decent, civil human being, maybe I can be around you again."

It should be apparent that the core message of everything spoken and done by these two was the same:

- *I* have been inconvenienced, misunderstood, and hurt the most—*I* am the victim here—and therefore have the greatest needs.

- You are not giving *me* enough attention, sympathy, understanding, and support. In short, you are not loving *me* enough.
- You must love *me* right now. I deserve it, and you're doing a lousy job of it so far.
- *Me, me, me.*

Although neither person realized he or she was communicating these central messages, they were nonetheless *felt* by both of them. How can a loving, productive conversation possibly occur in an atmosphere of complete selfishness, where each person is demanding that he or she be the center of attention? In such an atmosphere—which always prevails when people feel and act like victims—the only possible results are wounds and more wounds.

Most of us have been surrounded by victimhood so thoroughly and for so long, that we scarcely notice it. It's so common in our lives—and in our society in general—that we accept it as *normal*, like a kind of background noise, so we don't even see it as a problem or pathology.

Throughout the remainder of the book, we'll be discussing the various manifestations of victimhood, as well as how we can eliminate victimhood, but for now we just need a brief picture of what kind of destruction this disease can cause in a single conversation, like the one above.

THE CAUSE OF VICTIMHOOD: The Lack of Real Love

Where does victimhood come from? Why do so many of us fall into this pattern of behavior that has such uniformly disastrous results? Before we can answer these questions, we must first understand what we as human beings require for our emotional health and happiness.

In order to be happy, what we all need more than anything else is love. I have made that statement as I have spoken to hundreds of audiences—to hundreds of thousands of people—and I have never heard a single objection to it. Intuitively, we know it's true. That's why the majority of our literature, our movies, and even our commercial advertisements use love as a principal or secondary theme. We talk about love, fantasize about it, and search for it as a kind of Holy Grail.

But not just any kind of love will do, and as I say that, again most of us intuitively understand it. Most of us have had a number of negative experiences with what we thought was "love," so we know that everything labeled "love" won't necessarily fill our needs.

The only kind of love that will make us genuinely happy and whole is what I call Real Love.

Real Love is caring about the happiness of another person without any thought for what we might get for ourselves.

It's also Real Love when other people care about *our* happiness in a similar way. Real Love is unconditional. It's not Real Love when I do what you *want* and you like me—frankly, that's worthless. It's Real Love when I'm stupid and flawed and inconvenient, and when I make mistakes, but you're not disappointed or angry. We'll discuss the importance of these two conditions—disappointment and anger—in a few paragraphs.

When I use the word *happiness*, I do not mean the brief and superficial pleasure that comes from money, sex, power, and the conditional approval we earn from others when we behave as they want. Nor do I mean the temporary feeling of satisfaction we experience in the absence of immediate conflict or disaster. Real happiness is not the feeling we get from being entertained or persuading people to do what we want. It's a profound and lasting sense of peace and fulfillment that deeply satisfies and enlarges the soul. It doesn't go away when circumstances are difficult. It survives and even grows during hardship and struggle. True happiness is our entire reason to live, and it can be obtained only as we find Real Love and share it with others. *With Real Love, nothing else matters; without it, nothing else is enough.*

Sadly, few of us have sufficiently received or given that kind of love. From the time we were small children, we observed that when we were clean and quiet, when we got good grades, and when we were otherwise obedient and cooperative, our parents and others smiled at us, patted our heads, and spoke kindly to us. With their words and behavior, they told us what good boys and girls we were.

But what happened when we fought with our sisters, made too much noise, got bad grades, or dragged mud across the clean living room carpet? Then did people smile at us or speak gentle, loving words? No, they frowned, sighed with disappointment, and often spoke in harsh tones. Just as the positive behaviors of other people communicated to us that we were loved, the withdrawal of these behaviors could only have meant that we were *not* being loved. Although it was unintentional, our parents and others taught us this terrible message: "When you're good, I love you, but when you're not, I don't—or certainly I love you a great deal less."

In short, the "love" we were given—perhaps 99% of us—was *conditional*, and to this day we are still "loved" in this way. This conditional love can give us brief moments of satisfaction, but we're still left with a huge hole in our souls, because only Real Love can make us genuinely happy. When someone is genuinely, unconditionally concerned about our happiness, we feel connected to that person. We feel included in his or her life, and in that instant we are *no longer alone*. Each moment of unconditional acceptance creates a living thread to the person who accepts us, and these threads weave a powerful bond that fills us with a genuine and lasting happiness. Nothing but Real Love can do that. In addition, when we know that even one person loves us unconditionally, we feel a connection to everyone else. We feel included in the family of all mankind, of which that one person is a part.

Without sufficient Real Love, we can feel only empty and alone, which is our greatest fear. In any given negative interaction with another person—spouse, lover, child, parent, friend, co-worker—it is the longstanding lack of Real Love in *your* life that determines how you feel, not the behavior of any one person in that moment. In any given moment, you're reacting to the amount of love you feel from everyone, past and present, not just from the person you're interacting with.

Conditional vs. Real Love

Conditional love is distinguished from Real Love by the presence of *disappointment* and *anger*. Let me illustrate this distinction with a hypothetical interaction between you and me. Imagine that I'm your supervisor at work, and you've made a mistake that has cost the company time and money. I come to you and say, "The way you did this task didn't work out very well. It will cost us a couple hundred dollars to fix and will also require that some people work overtime for a few days. But don't worry about it. We can take care of it. Now, let's talk about how you could handle this task in the future. If you'll consider doing it another way—I'll show you how in a moment—the benefits will be considerable:

- You'll find it much easier to do the job.
- It will take less time.
- The job will be done more effectively.
- The task will become more profitable for the company.
- Best of all, you'll *enjoy* it a lot more. It will just be more fun."

Most important, as I describe these benefits to you, you can see, hear, and feel in my words, my tone of voice, my facial expression, my posture, and other mannerisms that even though you've made a mistake, my primary concern here is *your* welfare. How do you feel about my comments regarding your mistake? Almost certainly you feel accepted, relaxed, and even connected to me. There is virtually no stress associated with our interaction.

Now let's suppose that on a different occasion you make another mistake, but this time I immediately respond with impatience and irritation. I sigh with exasperation, frown furiously at you, fuss and fume about the mistake, and criticize you and berate you for inconveniencing me. The instant I become irritated with you, what am I saying with my behavior and my words? I'm saying,

- "Look at what you did *to me!*"
- "Do you not see what you *should* have done *for me?*"
- "How could you have failed to recognize and remember the true center of the universe: *Me!!*"

Notice that when I am disappointed or irritated at you, all my words and behavior essentially boil down to a single expression: *Me-Me-Me*. And while I'm standing over you screaming *Me-Me-Me*, is there any way you can feel my unconditional concern for *your* happiness? No, none at all.

It is imperative that we recognize that the instant we are disappointed or irritated at anyone—a spouse, lover, friend, child, co-worker—that other person hears us say only four words: *I don't love you*. Disappointment and anger are absolutely incompatible with Real Love, and that is the reason so few of us—probably less than

1-2% of us—feel unconditionally loved with any consistency. We have seen disappointment and anger so often on the occasions when we've made our mistakes—from the time we were small children—that we've come to believe that all love is conditional. We've come to believe that this is how "love" is supposed to be. We've come to accept a definition of *love* that is simply not true.

WHAT WE USE WITHOUT ENOUGH REAL LOVE—IMITATION LOVE

Without sufficient Real Love in our lives, the pain and emptiness of many years—even decades—are intolerable, and in order to reduce or eliminate these feelings, we're willing to do almost anything. Everything we use as a substitute for *Real* Love—to temporarily make us feel better in the absence of what we really need—becomes a form of *Imitation* Love, and all these substitutes are one or more variations of four things: *praise, power, pleasure,* and *safety.*

Praise

When people give us their approval, we feel praised and worthwhile, and if we can't get the Real Love we need, we'll do a lot to win that approval. Regrettably, however, we almost always have to *earn* it. In order for people to smile at us, compliment us, and want to spend time with us—all signs that they accept or "love" us—we have to be talented, beautiful, wealthy, witty, cooperative, grateful, successful, or otherwise worthy of acceptance. That kind of acceptance is conditional, because all the signs of it—the smiles and kind words, for example—disappear when we make mistakes, inconvenience people, and fail to live up to the expectations of others.

Because the absence of Real Love is painful, we're willing to do a lot to earn the approval that temporarily makes us feel good, even if it's conditional. For example, we make ourselves look good physically with exercise, clothing, make-up, starvation, and plastic surgery, all in the hope that someone will say, "You're looking good." In another arena, we work hard to succeed at school and in our jobs so we will be complimented for our intelligence, creativity, and diligence.

But consider how you feel—after working hard for hours, days, even years—when you finally get that precious morsel of praise.

How long does it last? In just a moment or two, the feeling is gone, and then you have to work to earn it all over again. Buying praise with our behavior is a lot of work, and because it's usually not given unconditionally, we're left with an empty feeling even when we get it.

Another reason praise is often unfulfilling is that when most people praise us, they're rarely saying something about *us*. They're saying that when we're cooperative and perform according to *their* expectations, they like how we make *them* feel. But we're still quite willing to keep on doing whatever it takes to earn the sensation of praise, gratitude, and acceptance, because these feelings—however superficial and fleeting—are much better than the emptiness that accompanies a lack of Real Love.

Power

Although it's mostly unintentional, any time we successfully manipulate or control someone, we enjoy a sensation of power over that person. We use money, authority, sex, flattery, and personal persuasion to influence, control, and even hurt people. When we do all that, we don't get Real Love, but when we control the people around us, we feel less powerless; we feel less of the emptiness and helplessness that are always associated with a lack of Real Love. In addition, when we control someone, we actually feel more connected to him or her in a brief, shallow way.

We tend to deny our efforts to control people—it's not a flattering behavior to admit—but whenever we try to *get* people to do anything, we're controlling them and using power as a form of Imitation Love. If you doubt that you control people—your spouse, your children, your co-workers—consider how you feel when they *don't* do what you want. Your feelings of disappointment or anger indicate that at the very least you *want* to control the behavior of others—however unconscious your desires or efforts may be.

Pleasure

When we don't feel unconditionally loved, we often use pleasure—food, sex, drugs, shopping, gambling, driving fast, and many other forms of entertainment and excitement—to feel better temporarily.

Certainly there's nothing inherently wrong with pleasure, but when we compulsively seek it, we're using it to fill a deep emptiness.

Safety

Without sufficient Real Love, we're already experiencing an insufferable pain, and we'll go to great lengths to keep ourselves safe from anything that might prolong or worsen our pain. To minimize painful disapproval, we stay away from unfamiliar situations, tasks, and relationships, and then we confuse that feeling of relative safety with real happiness. I've known many couples who believed they had a "good marriage," for example, until they discovered that their "happiness" was only an avoidance of conflict, not a sharing of Real Love.

****

By no means are praise, power, pleasure, and safety always unhealthy. In the presence of Real Love, money, authority, sex, and praise, for example, can all add to our genuine happiness. These things are dangerous only when they're used as *substitutes* for unconditional love.

The Addictive Power of Imitation Love

People who consistently use addictive drugs soon discover that the effects of these drugs become increasingly brief, and more of any specific drug is required in order to achieve the same pleasurable or distracting outcome. All the forms of Imitation Love become like addictive drugs. Despite all the effort required to earn Imitation Love, the beneficial effects of praise, power, money, and sex, for example, become increasingly brief. In addition, we have to work harder to get more and more, and we can tolerate being away from them for shorter periods—all exactly like an addictive drug. Eventually, we discover—exhausted and frustrated by our efforts—that no amount of Imitation Love can give us the effects we once experienced. And no matter how successful we are in obtaining Imitation Love, we never get the feeling of connection with other people that comes with Real Love, so we're still painfully alone.

*Regrettably, Imitation Love **does feel good**, so good that it's easy to confuse that temporary satisfaction with genuine happiness. That self-deception distracts us from pursuing the life-giving steps that lead to Real Love.* The temporary satisfaction—and distraction—of Imitation Love is perhaps its most injurious characteristic.

When we see the role and effect of Imitation Love, we can more easily understand why relationships often fall apart. As I have counseled with thousands of couples, I have been impressed with how consistently and quickly people travel the emotional spectrum from a place of being "in love" to a place where they're willing to disembowel their partners. This same "falling out of love" occurs between friends, family members, co-workers, managers and employees, and even entire countries, and we'll be talking more about that in subsequent chapters.

Let's take a more in-depth look at the relationship between Mark and Susan, the couple we introduced on page 2. When Mark met Susan, he found her physically attractive—which gave him immediate pleasure and suggested the possibility of more physical pleasure in the future—and he sensed that she accepted him and was willing to behave in certain ways to win his approval, which gave him feelings of praise and power. She was attracted to him because he was good-looking, funny, smart, and kind to her, and because he had a good job—all of which gave her feelings of praise, pleasure, and safety. Unwittingly, they were both *trading* Imitation Love with one another. In the absence of sufficient Real Love, we're all strongly attracted to anyone who gives us Imitation Love, and the more the better.

Susan and Mark *fell in love* because they found in their partner the qualities that would entertain them, make them feel worthwhile, and give them safety, not because they unconditionally loved each other. They *married* because they wanted to guarantee that their supply of Imitation Love would continue forever. Most of us pick our partners for the same reasons: We look for someone who has qualities that will temporarily make *us* feel good, and in return we're quite willing to do the same for that person.

In order to get the Imitation Love that temporarily makes us feel better in the absence of Real Love, we *buy* it with whatever forms of Imitation Love we have to offer. As I've said, however, the effects of Imitation Love always fade, and Mark and Susan experienced that.

They really enjoyed the initial exchange of Imitation Love, but it wasn't long before that level of praise, power, and pleasure wasn't as rewarding as it once had been. When people say the "excitement has worn off" in a relationship, they're just describing the fleeting effects of Imitation Love.

As we experience less "happiness" with Imitation Love, we naturally turn to our spouses to supply what we're missing, and understandably our partners feel resentful of our increased demands. They married us based on an unspoken understanding of how much Imitation Love they'd be required to give us to make us happy, and then we changed the rules. As the effects of Imitation Love fade, we begin to demand more attention or praise or sex or time or power or whatever. Understandably, our spouses don't like that.

When they were married, what Mark and Susan both needed was Real Love, but from their childhoods neither of them had ever felt much unconditional love, so there was *no way* they could have loved each other as they needed—we simply can't give what we don't have. But they did offer one another what they had—Imitation Love in its various forms—and they gave as much as they could. Imitation Love does feel good, and because they were both giving it with all their hearts, and because they were both receiving more than they ever had, they were satisfied in the beginning of their marriage. When the effects of Imitation Love wore off, however, they felt enormously disappointed, even betrayed. They were both faced with the horror that they were not going to get the happiness they'd wanted all their lives. That is a terrible moment in any relationship.

This experience where there is an initial peaking of temporary "happiness" from Imitation Love and then a subsequent disappointment when the effects of Imitation Love wear off doesn't happen only in marriages or other intimate relationships. This letdown also happens between family members, friends, business associates, and so on. When we are aware of this phenomenon, we can finally make sense of the disillusionment and even bitterness that have been baffling us in many relationships.

It is common in the corporate world, for example, for a new boss to take over a company or division, and initially the employees are often thrilled with his or her new leadership style. In most cases, however, what they're feeling is only the infusion of a new combination of Imitation Love, which is always exciting. Then when the effects of Imitation Love wear off—as they always do—the employees begin to find fault with the new boss. This initial exhilaration with a new combination of Imitation Love is what motivates a man or woman to have an affair after being married to the same spouse for years. But in the affair, as with the new boss, the new lover loses his or her fresh luster with time. Then the straying spouse or the employees want more of this and less of that from the lover or the boss, not realizing that no amount of Imitation Love will ever make them genuinely happy.

WHAT WE DO WITHOUT ENOUGH LOVE (REAL OR IMITATION): GETTING AND PROTECTING BEHAVIORS

Insufficient Real Love creates an emptiness we cannot ignore, especially when we also don't have enough Imitation Love to make us feel better temporarily. Our subsequent behavior is then often ruled by our *need* to be loved and our *fear* of not being loved. Without Real Love, we do whatever it takes—Getting Behaviors—to fill our sense of emptiness with Imitation Love. To eliminate our fear, we use Protecting Behaviors. The Getting Behaviors include lying, attacking, acting like a victim, and clinging. The Protecting Behaviors include lying, attacking, acting like a victim, and running.

Lying

We're using lying as a Protecting Behavior when we make excuses, shade the truth, or do anything else to avoid the disapproval of others. We don't lie because we're bad; we lie because we've learned from countless experiences that it *works*. People really do disapprove of us less when we hide the truth about our flaws, and we'll do almost anything to keep from feeling that painful withdrawal of acceptance.

We're using lying as a Getting Behavior when we do anything to get other people to like us: when we tell people about our accomplishments but not our flaws, communicate positive feelings that are not true, change our physical appearance to attract people to us, or tell people what they want to hear so they'll like us. We don't think of these behaviors as lying, but they are, because we don't tell other people we're manipulating them. We lie so often that we don't even realize we're doing it most of the time. If you watch almost any two people in conversation, for example, you'll usually see that each of them is carefully and unconsciously studying the other for any hint of disapproval—a forehead wrinkling into a frown, an eyebrow lifting into an expression of doubt, a change in tone of voice—and when that happens, the speaker immediately modifies what he or she is saying until those signs of disapproval disappear. Again, although we do this unconsciously, it's still lying, because we don't tell people we're trying to get them to like us.

From the time we were young, we were told by our parents and others, "Put your best foot forward." That sounds like good advice, but the results are usually undesirable, as illustrated by Mark and Susan's dating experiences, long before they married. When they went out on their first date, they were both nervous about being accepted, so they put their best foot forward. Susan prepared for hours—make-up, hair, clothing—to look good so Mark would like her. Mark too made himself as physically attractive as possible. In addition, they were each careful to talk and behave in a way they thought would be pleasing to the other.

As they each put their best foot forward, they succeeded in winning one another's acceptance, but without realizing it they had then started on a path that often has disastrous consequences. When I show you only my best foot, and you indicate that you like me, I clearly hear, though unconsciously, that you like me *because* of my best foot—and that's almost invariably exactly what you mean. When people tell us *why* they like us, they're also telling us that if we *didn't* have those characteristics, they almost certainly would *not* like us as they do. Moreover, when someone tells you that he or she likes your best foot, there's a strong implication that you must hide the rest of you from that person so you won't lose his or her affection and attention. But despite all the disadvantages of that conditional love, we *still* love to hear people say, "I like you because . . ." Why? Because we're just dying to hear what comes next: ". . . because you're witty, intelligent, handsome, beautiful, strong, responsible, whatever." We really get a high out of that moment of Imitation Love.

Early in their relationship, Mark was careful to project only his good-natured, sensitive, and loving side. And why wouldn't he?

All his life he'd been taught to do all he could to win other people's approval—including his parents' approval—and with Susan he was just applying the lessons he'd learned from childhood. Of course, Susan was delighted to see that side of Mark. We all want our partners to have the positive qualities that would make a relationship enjoyable.

Susan was also trying to buy *Mark's* approval with *her* best foot. That approach really does seem to work in the beginning— Mark and Susan were both thrilled to find someone who "made them happy"—but then they discovered what we all do, that our partners have more than just a best foot. There's that other foot, and often it stinks. We discover that he doesn't smell nearly as sweet after a long day at work as he did on the first date, nor is he as entertaining or accommodating. We learn that her hair and smile don't have quite the same glow after a rough night's sleep, nor is she quite as eager to please after a few years as she was when we first met.

We don't *intend* to deceive one another early in a relationship, but we're willing to do it because we're so anxious to be accepted. If our lies succeed in gaining us the acceptance we want, a serious problem then arises, because our partner *will* eventually discover the rest of us. After Mark and Susan were married, they began to see the qualities they hadn't noticed while they were dating, and they were sorely disappointed.

We often complain that after we get married, our partners change. You may think, He or she is just not the person I dated. Yes, actually, he is, but you didn't see him clearly in the beginning. After you got married, however, you saw more of him, not just the parts he wanted to show you—which were also the parts *you wanted* to see. The real reason relationships fail is not that our partners change. Relationships fail because we came to them without enough of the one ingredient—Real Love—essential to individual happiness and to our ability to participate in a healthy relationship.

Over time in relationships, our partners do change in some ways. They become less willing, for example, to work hard to earn the Imitation Love we gave them initially, because the exchange becomes less rewarding than it once was.

When we lie to a spouse, or potential spouse—however unconscious it may be—we establish a foundation that cannot support a healthy and happy relationship. Later in this chapter, and in following chapters, we'll discuss how we can change that.

The Problem with Lying

Although our "little lies" may often seem innocent, they almost always have a very serious effect on what we all want most, which is to feel unconditionally loved. Let me illustrate this with a simple diagram and brief discussion. This discussion is important to remember throughout the remainder of the book, so take your time as you read it.

What we want is Real Love. We want to feel loved unconditionally, as represented by this part of the diagram:

Loved

Before we can believe that people actively care about our happiness—the definition of Real Love—we need to know that they *accept* us. Feeling accepted precedes feeling loved, which we'll represent in the following way:

Accepted → Loved

We can't know that people accept us as we really are unless we know that they *see* who we really are. We must feel seen, therefore, before we can feel accepted, and we must feel accepted before we can feel genuinely loved, which we can represent as follows:

Seen → Accepted → Loved

Finally, we can't feel seen for who we really are unless we actually *tell* people the *truth* about ourselves. The entire process can be represented in this way:

Truth → Seen → Accepted → Loved

Finding Real Love is absolutely dependent on the first step, which is telling the truth about ourselves. When we lie in any way, we make the entire process impossible. *When we lie, we cannot feel loved.* For most of us lying is almost always an unconscious affair. We're lying when we do anything to get other people to like us or to avoid their disapproval. We're lying when we alter our appearance to earn the approval of others, when we're careful with what we say so that people will like us, and when we change our behavior to win the acceptance of others. One recent study found that the average person lies *four hundred times* a day. That's how eager we are for acceptance, and yet the moment we lie, we *cannot feel loved*. How ironic, how ultimately tragic really, that with our lies we cause the very condition we're trying to cure.

Attacking

Attacking is any behavior that motivates another person through *fear* to behave in a way we want. We're attacking people when we criticize them, physically intimidate them, withdraw our approval, make them feel guilty, or use our positions of authority at work, at home, and elsewhere, all to get Imitation Love—usually in the form of power—and to protect ourselves from fear. With anger, for example—the most common form of attacking—you can often make people sufficiently uncomfortable (afraid) that they'll do whatever you want in the hope that you'll then stop being angry and stop making them feel bad. With your anger, you can get people to give you attention, respect, power, money, flattery, approval, and even sex. But of course, if they're giving you these things not because they're genuinely concerned for your happiness, but simply to avoid your anger, all you're receiving is Imitation Love.

As the relationship between Mark and Susan began to deteriorate, they attacked each other more, which is well illustrated in their interaction on pages 2-3. Attacking involves disappointment, anger, and shaming, all for the purpose—however unconscious—of motivating others with fear. When Mark entered the room and threw his keys on the table, he was attacking Susan with his behavior. Why did he do that, rather than simply discuss with her the results of his trip to the store? Let's look at how Mark's use of anger evolved over time.

Early in their relationship, Susan usually gave Mark what he wanted quickly and willingly, in great part because he gave her what *she* wanted. It was a fair trade, which characterizes relationships where people are in love. But when the effect of Imitation Love began to wear off, Susan responded less quickly and willingly to Mark's desires. If he increased his positive attentions toward her, she was more responsive, but the ever increasing level of attention that Susan unknowingly required of him became inconvenient for Mark, even exhausting.

So he began to experiment with ways where he could get what he wanted—and protect himself—with greater reliability and with less effort.

From past experience, Mark had learned the motivational benefits of anger. As a child, he discovered that when his parents were angry, he could hurry to do what they wanted and thereby avoid more of their displeasure. In time, he learned that he could become angry himself and motivate other people to do what he wanted. In the schoolyard, for example, he noticed that he could persuade his peers to do what he wanted if he raised his voice and physically intimidated them, and in business he discovered that when he became irritated, fellow employees would often hurry to do what he wanted in order to make him happy and thereby cool the fires of his anger.

Having learned the power of anger, Mark increasingly used it to motivate Susan, and that's what he was doing when he threw his keys on the table and when he spoke sharply to her. Although he was not consciously aware of his intentions, on many other occasions he had nonetheless hoped that if he spoke in anger, she would more likely—and more quickly—respond by leaving him alone or otherwise giving him what he wanted (attention, respect, and so on).

Earlier in their relationship, whenever Mark attacked Susan, she had become afraid—afraid that he was withdrawing his love (which in fact he was)—so she did whatever it took to make him happy. Eventually, however, she realized that pleasing him was exhausting and ultimately futile, so she began to protect herself from his anger with the Protecting Behavior *she* had also learned as a child—her own anger. All her life she'd felt the painful emptiness and fear that result from a lack of Real Love. In that condition, Mark's attack in the conversation above was more than she could bear, so when he attacked her—with his overall attitude and with the throwing of the keys—she protected herself by attacking him in return, saying, "And what's wrong with *you*?" To protect himself in turn, Mark then responded with another attack. Had he stayed in the room, they would have continued to attack each other, adding yet more wounds to their bleeding relationship.

Although anger can be an effective way to protect yourself and to manipulate others to do what you want, you need to consider these questions: Have you ever been angry at your spouse and at the same time felt more loving toward him or her? Or felt more loved? Or enjoyed your relationship more deeply? Of course not, and yet we continue to get angry at our partners. Something is terribly wrong with this picture.

Acting Like a Victim

We've already begun a discussion of this particular Getting and Protecting Behavior, and we'll be addressing it a great deal more throughout the remainder of the book.

At this point I do wish to clarify a point of terminology. There is a difference between being actually *being* a victim and *feeling* or *acting* like a victim. Allow me to illustrate this by slightly modifying a metaphor I have used in other Real Love books.

Imagine that you're starving, and you're preparing to go out and get some bread with your last two dollars. So this is a big moment of anticipation for you. Suddenly, I dash into the room, snatch the two dollars off the table, and run away before you can stop me. Almost certainly you'd feel that you were a victim of my behavior, and you'd likely feel hurt and angry.

In this case, are you a victim? *Yes.* Anytime anyone does something to you that inconveniences you or hurts you or frightens you—or threatens to do so—without your permission, you are a victim, what I call a *true victim*. I took money from you without your permission, so you *are* a true victim in this case. *But*—and this is a huge *but*—*your being a victim does not mean that you have to **feel like a victim** or **act like a victim**.* This is a very important concept that requires further illustration with a continuation of the metaphor that we just began.

Now imagine that the day after our interaction above I do exactly the same thing—I steal two dollars off the table as you're getting ready to go out and buy some bread—but this time you have *twenty million* dollars in the bank. You are still a victim—I still took money from you without your permission—but do you *feel* as much like a victim? Of course not. The loss of two dollars matters very little when you have twenty million.

In both situations, you lost exactly the same sum: two dollars. You were *victimized equally* in each situation, but in the second situation you didn't *feel* victimized. It is therefore obvious—and we must always remember—that whether we are victimized, or the degree to which we are victimized, *does not make us **feel like victims** or **act like victims***. In short, we always have a choice about how we feel and behave. No one can make us act like victims. So how do we take control over that choice?

Having sufficient Real Love really is like having twenty million dollars all the time, emotionally speaking. Having twenty million emotional dollars doesn't stop people from taking two emotional dollars from us. In fact, they can still do that rather easily, by lying to us, criticizing us, failing to keep promises, stealing from us, being angry at us, and so on. We simply can't stop people from victimizing us. When we have twenty million dollars, however—when we feel unconditionally loved—we don't *feel* victimized by the loss of two dollars here and there, or by the loss of twenty dollars, or forty. When we have sufficient Real Love, everything else becomes relatively insignificant, so we can easily afford to lose two dollars. That is a powerful way to live, and it is accessible to all of us.

In later chapters, we'll be talking in much greater detail about how to eliminate victimhood with Real Love, but for now the important point to remember is that although we may be victimized—and therefore be true victims—we do not have to feel or act like victims.

For the remainder of this book, then, I'll be using two terms that appear similar but have distinct meanings, as follows:

- Victim: a person who feels like a victim or acts like a victim—as described on page 5—whether or not he or she has actually been victimized.
- True victim: a person who has been inconvenienced or hurt or frightened—or threatened with any of those conditions—without his or her permission by another person.

Other People Can Never Make Us Angry

In our society it is a commonly held belief—almost universally held, actually—that other people make us angry. Look at the language we use:

- "He makes me so mad."
- "She makes me angry."
- "You make me so mad."

Note, however, that the above metaphor about the two dollars and twenty million dollars can be modified slightly to prove that other people *never* make us angry. You might want to review the metaphor, and then we'll modify the last paragraph, which begins with "In both situations . . ."

In both situations, you lost exactly the same sum: two dollars. You were *victimized equally* in each situation, but in the second situation you didn't *feel angry*—or at least not nearly *as* angry as you did in the first situation. There is an important lesson here: We have a tendency to believe that when people do something to us, they *make* us angry, but that couldn't be the case, because if the act of taking two dollars from you *makes* you angry, you would have been equally angry in both situations in the metaphor. But you were not. You became angry in the second situation only because *you* didn't have twenty million dollars. Other people do not make us angry. Our anger is a response to the overall lack of Real Love in our lives, and that is something we can always choose to address. (We'll talk more about how to find Real Love later in this chapter and in greater detail in Chapter Nine.)

Running

If we simply move away from a source of pain, we're less likely to be hurt. Withdrawing from conversations (verbally and physically), avoiding people, and leaving relationships in a state of fear or anger are all forms of running. When people say they're shy, for example, what they're really saying is, "I've felt empty and afraid all my life, and I've learned that when I allow people to see who I really am, they criticize me or laugh at me, making me feel even more unloved and miserable. So in order to minimize that pain, I simply stay away from people or avoid speaking." The use of drugs and alcohol are other ways to run.

After Susan attacked Mark, he briefly attacked her in return, but he knew he'd only experience more pain if he stayed in the room with her and battled it out. So he walked out—he ran.

Not all withdrawing is running. Sometimes withdrawing is actually the healthy course to take, but only under certain circumstances, as I've explained in Chapter Four of *Real Love in Marriage*, amongst other places in the Real Love body of literature.

Clinging

Clinging is obvious when a child grips tightly to his mother's skirt, but as adults we also cling. We cling emotionally to the people who give us attention, hoping we can sometimes squeeze even more out of them. We may do this by flattering the people who do things for us or by being excessively grateful. Sometimes we're clinging to people when we tell them how much we love them and need them, because we hope our words will encourage them to stay with us and return our expressions of love. Effectively, we're begging for more Imitation Love.

Clinging can be demonstrated in—but is not limited to—the following phrases or behaviors:

- "Do you really have to go out tonight? You never stay home with me anymore."
- "Can't you stay a little longer?" This is not always clinging, but it is when it's spoken with a pleading tone, which is quite common.
- "I love you." It is very often the case that when we tell someone we love him or her, we expect to hear a similar expression of affection in return. We all know what an awkward moment it can be if one person says "I love you" and the other person says nothing. If you say "I love you," and your partner *doesn't* say "I love you" in return, or is slow in responding, and you feel disappointed or irritated by that, you can be certain that you were clinging when you said "I love you."
- Excessive gratitude. When we gush with gratitude toward people who have done something we like, very often our excessive gratitude is a way of saying, "I hope you do that for me again."
- Gifts. We often give people gifts—at Christmas, on birthdays, on anniversaries, on Valentines' Day, and so on—for the purpose of earning gratitude, allegiance, appreciation, or something of the sort. That's clinging. It can be difficult *at the time* you give the gift to know whether you're clinging, but if the other person *fails* to adequately acknowledge your gift, and if you then feel disappointed or irritated by that, you can be certain that your gift was a form of clinging.

THE DEADLY PITFALLS OF THE GETTING AND PROTECTING BEHAVIORS

In this chapter we've established why we use Getting and Protecting Behaviors. With these behaviors we protect ourselves and get praise, power, pleasure, and safety, which temporarily fill our painful emptiness to some degree. What then are the *disadvantages* of using these behaviors?

The Central Message of All the Getting and Protecting Behaviors

On page 13 I said that whenever we get *angry*, the people around us hear only four words: *I don't love you*. Now let's consider the message of the other Getting and Protecting Behaviors.

- Lying. When I lie to you, my goal is to protect whom? *Myself.* And to get Imitation Love for whom? *Myself.*
- Acting like a victim. When I act like a victim, my aim is to protect whom? *Myself.* And I act like a victim to get sympathy, attention, and power for whom? *Myself.*
- Running. When I run, I'm protecting whom? *Myself.*
- Clinging. When I cling, the goal is to get attention and praise for whom? *Myself.*

This is not a subtle pattern. We use all the Getting and Protecting Behaviors to benefit *ourselves*, and while we're using them other people really can *feel* that our interests are selfish. They can feel that our primary concern is *not for them*, which means we couldn't possibly be unconditionally loving them.

In short, when we use Getting and Protecting Behaviors other people hear us say *I don't love you*, and in those moments that *is* what we're saying. After communicating that message, how could any conversation possibly go well? Think back on any interaction that went badly for you, or consider any pattern of negative interactions that keeps happening. Most of the time we have been baffled as to *why* these conversations have become so unproductive and why they've kept happening, but now you understand.

The problem is not the *words* we speak. The greatest obstacle in our conversations and in our relationships is the Getting and

Protecting Behaviors we use. If I'm irritated at you—or acting like a victim or running or clinging—it doesn't matter how cleverly I craft my words, because what you'll hear is *I don't love you*, and then you'll likely respond with Getting and Protecting Behaviors of your own. At that point our conversation is doomed.

What We Get from Getting and Protecting Behaviors

If we become skilled at using Getting and Protecting Behaviors, we can accumulate mountains of Imitation Love. We can become the envy of everyone we know. But no matter how adept we become with these behaviors, we can *never* feel loved *unconditionally* as a result. Real Love is never the product of lying, attacking, acting like victims, running, and clinging. Let's examine what we do get from these behaviors:

- Lying. As I said earlier in this chapter, we lie both to earn the approval—the "love"—of others and to prevent the loss of that approval, and yet the moment we lie, we *cannot feel loved*. How ironic, how ultimately tragic, that with our lies we cause the very condition we're trying to cure.
- Attacking. If I use anger in sufficient quantity and with adequate skill, I may be able to intimidate you and thereby gain your respect or cooperation. But will I feel genuinely loved? Of course not, because I know that I *forced* you to cooperate or to give me what I wanted. I know that what you gave me was not freely given, which is required in Real Love.
- Acting like a victim. We act like victims in order to win sympathy and to protect ourselves, all to gain or preserve various forms of "love." But if we act like victims and succeed in gaining sympathy, for example, can we feel loved? Absolutely not, because we know that what we have received is a response to a manipulation on our part—acting like victims—rather than being freely given.
- Running. If I run from you, is there any way I can feel unconditionally loved? Impossible. I can feel only safe, which is a form of Imitation Love.
- Clinging. If I can get your attention only by clinging, I couldn't possibly feel that you gave it to me freely, which is necessary in Real Love.

A Summary of the Effects of Getting and Protecting Behaviors

Let me summarize in the following chart what we have learned about Getting and Protecting Behaviors (G&PBs):

G&PB	Purpose of	Message sent to others by	What we get from
Lying	Get approval	I don't love you	Imitation Love
	Prevent loss of "love"	I don't love you	Imitation Love
Attacking	Get power	I don't love you	Imitation Love
	Prevent loss of "love"	I don't love you	Imitation Love
Victim	Get sympathy, attention	I don't love you	Imitation Love
	Prevent pain	I don't love you	Imitation Love
Running	Prevent pain	I don't love you	Imitation Love
Clinging	Get "love"	I don't love you	Imitation Love

The pattern here is not difficult to discern. With all the Getting and Protecting Behaviors we are trying either to get "love"—praise power, pleasure, safety—or prevent the loss of it. We're trying to create happiness or prevent its loss, and yet the moment we use any of these behaviors we communicate to others that we don't love them, and we make it impossible to feel unconditionally loved ourselves. It is the very tools we use to save ourselves that destroy us.

THE ELIMINATION OF GETTING AND PROTECTING BEHAVIORS WITH UNDERSTANDING: THE DROWNING METAPHOR

You may have noticed that all the Getting and Protecting Behaviors cause a great deal of unhappiness for us at every level, personally and in relationships. First, generally speaking, we really don't like it when people lie to us, attack us, act like victims, and so on. Second, other people don't like it when we use these behaviors with them. Third, we're never happy ourselves when we engage in these behaviors. Considering the harm done by Getting and Protecting Behaviors, therefore, I suggest that as we interact with others—and as we judge ourselves—it can be enormously helpful to see these behaviors from a different perspective.

Imagine for a moment that you and I are in the Bahamas. The weather is delightful: perfect temperature, low humidity, and a slight breeze causing the palm trees to sway. We're eating lunch by the side of a pool, and you're listening to your favorite music from a live band in the distance. As we're enjoying this perfect day, you notice that someone in the pool next to you is splashing you with water—first on your shoes, then higher up on your pants or legs or dress. You can't see who's splashing you because there's a deck chair between you and the person in the pool. At first you ignore the splashing, but you're beginning to get really wet, and finally you become irritated and get up from your chair to say something to this idiot who's being so thoughtless. As you stand up to say something to him, you look over the chair that was in your way, and you see that the man splashing you is . . . *drowning*. Instantly you realize that all this time he hasn't been trying to splash *you* at all. He's just been thrashing with his arms and legs to keep his own head above water.

How do you feel now? Are you still angry at this man? Of course not—who in their right mind could be angry at someone who's drowning? In fact, as soon as you see why he's splashing you, not only do you lose your irritation, but you eagerly extend a pole to help him out of the water. Let's ask some important questions about this event:

- How long did it take for your feelings of anger to be replaced by a feeling of complete acceptance? It happened in an instant.

As soon as you understood that the man was drowning, your anger vanished.
- After seeing the truth of the situation, how much effort did you exert to control your anger? None. When you saw that the man was splashing you only in an effort to save himself, your anger simply disappeared. You didn't have to *control* yourself or *work* to make your anger go away.
- What did the drowning man have to do to persuade you to help him out of the water? Did he have to pay you? Apologize to you? Beg you? Of course not. You offered him your assistance without any conditions.

This is remarkable. With a single moment of understanding, you traveled the emotional spectrum from angry to not angry to unconditional concern for his well-being—the definition of Real Love.

You can achieve this kind of miraculous change in attitude in real life too. Picture for a moment someone in your life who is irritating. Now picture his or her behaviors that annoy you. Can you now see that every one of these behaviors is one or more of the Getting and Protecting Behaviors? Without exception, that is the case. And people use Getting and Protecting Behaviors for what reason? Because they're empty and afraid, a result of not having enough Real Love. Their need for Real Love is just as critical as the need of a drowning man for air.

We can summarize what we have learned from this metaphor by stating that all the people in your life who are behaving badly—your spouse, children, boss, co-workers, parents, other drivers on the road, and so on—are just drowning emotionally, and they're using Getting and Protecting Behaviors only to keep their own heads above water. Their drowning has little or nothing to do with you. It's not personal. Nobody drowns *to you*. As people do their very best to keep from drowning, however, it's inevitable that they will splash the people around them, and the closer you are to them, the more you'll be affected.

With an understanding of Real Love and Getting and Protecting Behaviors, the way you feel toward other people in real life can change just as quickly and dramatically as your feelings changed toward the hypothetical man in the pool. You now realize that without sufficient

Real Love—without the single most important ingredient required for happiness—people feel like they're drowning all the time, and then they'll naturally use the Getting and Protecting Behaviors that allow them temporarily to keep their heads above water. Regrettably, as they're splashing in the water with these behaviors, they often affect the rest of us in negative ways. When you understand this, the effect is powerful:

- Your feelings change immediately. When you understand that every time people use Getting and Protecting Behaviors, they're simply drowning—not trying primarily to annoy *you*—you can't stay angry at them for one moment longer.
- You don't have to *work* at controlling or managing your anger. It just goes away.
- Your negative feelings are actually replaced by a desire to help the people around you. You develop a natural desire to love.

These are remarkable changes in the ways we see people and react to them, especially in the face of how victims usually behave. Remember, victims are drowning, and in that condition they demonstrate two characteristics that usually irritate nearly everyone:

- They are exceptionally arrogant. They think only of themselves, which is simultaneously annoying and also quite understandable. When you're drowning, your own needs are simply overwhelming. There is no room for thinking about the needs of anyone else.
- They are quite irrational. There is no reasoning with victims. They can think and speak only of what *they* want and what was done to *them*. To victims, the universe is only as large as their own skins. When you're drowning, you're not interested in words. You want help, and you want it *now*.

Delightfully, once we see victims as drowning—arrogant, irrational, and all—we can begin to respond to them far more productively. In subsequent chapters we'll talk more about the behaviors of victims and how we can respond to them in ways that are both more loving and more effective.

THE ELIMINATION OF GETTING AND PROTECTING BEHAVIORS WITH REAL LOVE

The simple diagram on page 22

Truth → Seen → Accepted → Loved

reveals how we find the Real Love that makes us whole, that brings us the happiness we have always wanted, and that makes all the Getting and Protecting Behaviors unnecessary. As we tell the truth about ourselves, we create opportunities for people to see us, accept us, and love us. When we find people who are capable of seeing, accepting, and unconditionally loving us as we tell the truth about ourselves, I call these people wise men and women, a term that comes from "The Story of the Wart King and the Wise Man" in the book *Real Love*. In order to find Real Love we must tell the truth

- about ourselves, not everyone else.
- gradually.
- as often as possible—eventually.
- to people capable of accepting and loving us.
- about our mistakes.
- about our lies.
- about the selfishness of our anger.
- about the times when we act like victims.
- about the occasions when we run and cling.
- about our fears.

In Chapter Eight and in other Real Love literature you'll find a great deal more about what it looks like to tell the truth about yourself. If you have a desire to acquire more Real Love—and in the process find great personal happiness and more fulfilling relationships than you ever thought possible—I suggest three approaches that I will describe in ascending order of effectiveness and difficulty.

Before describing these approaches, however, let me compare finding Real Love and genuine happiness to the physical training of an athlete. Suppose you wish to become minimally fit, just a step above couch potato. In that case, if I were your trainer, I would prescribe a minimally rigorous course of physical exercise—perhaps a few trips to the mail box each day. If you wish to become thoroughly fit, however, I would prescribe a strenuous course of exercise. The higher your goal of fitness, the more work will be involved.

The same is true with finding Real Love and genuine happiness. It requires some effort on our part. If you want to eliminate anger, fill your life with happiness, and experience greater joy in your relationships than you can imagine at this point, that will require more effort than if you want to just gain a little intellectual understanding about Real Love as a principle. I hasten to add, however, that the effort required to find Real Love is actually *less* than the effort we now spend on Getting and Protecting Behaviors. Lying, attacking, acting like victims, running, and clinging require enormous effort, to the point that they usually utterly exhaust us.

Now, let me suggest three progressively more challenging and effective programs for finding Real Love and the happiness you want. All these educational materials are described in greater detail at the end of this chapter:

First Level

- Read the book *Real Love—The Truth About Finding Unconditional Love and Fulfilling Relationships.*
- Read *The Real Love Companion.*

Second Level

- Read the book *Real Love.*
- Become a member of RealLove.com at www.RealLove.com, and take advantage of the enormous benefits described on pages 39-40 in the section entitled "Online Resources."

Third Level

- Watch the DVD set, *The Essentials of Real Love.*
- Become a member of Real Love.com at *www.Real.com*
- Form or join a Real Love group.
- Read additional books in the Real Love series: *Real Love in Marriage, Real Love in Parenting, Real Love in Dating*, and so on.

As you apply what you learn from these materials, your life will change in ways you cannot imagine.

SUPPORTING MATERIAL FOR UNDERSTANDING REAL LOVE

Although this book, *Real Love and Freedom of the Soul*, is intended to be understood on its own, you'll gain an even better understanding of Real Love, and of victimhood, as you take advantage of other Real Love educational materials. They are all available at www.RealLove.com, unless otherwise indicated.

Books

Real Love—The Truth About Finding Unconditional Love and Fulfilling Relationships
This is the foundation of any Real Love education, teaching the real meaning of love and giving us the power to consistently choose peace and confidence instead of anger and confusion in our individual lives and in our relationships. Available at retail and online bookstores nationwide. Soft cover, 280 pages, Gotham Books, division of Penguin Group

The Real Love Companion
This workbook amplifies the principles found in *Real Love* and makes that book an intensely personal and transforming experience.
Soft cover, 123 pages, Blue Ridge Press

Real Love in the Workplace
The most important asset in any business is people, and what every human being wants most is to feel loved. This book teaches every manager how to give people what they need most, and with that leadership key, people naturally respond with creativity, communication, collaboration, and increased productivity.
Soft cover, 331 pages, Blue Ridge Press

Real Love in Dating
For most of us, dating is often confusing and frustrating. In this book, learn
- the eight things we do that unconsciously ruin relationships.
- how to find and *become* the perfect partner.
- how to have consistently fun and effective dates.

Soft cover, 227 pages, Blue Ridge Press

Real Love in Marriage
In this book, learn
- the real reasons people fall out of love and have problems in their marriages.
- the secrets for healing all wounds in a marriage.
- the simple but powerful steps for making your marriage consistently more fun and exciting than you can imagine

Available at retail and online bookstores nationwide.

Hard cover, 307 pages, Gotham Books, division of Penguin Group

Real Love in Parenting
Parenting can often be frustrating and exhausting. In this book, learn
- why children are so often angry, disobedient, and otherwise difficult.
- the real reason you get frustrated with your children.
- how you can help your children become loving, responsible, and happy.
- how parenting can be consistently fun and rewarding, instead of tedious and frustrating.

Soft cover, 433 pages, Blue Ridge Press

The Essentials of Real Love Workbook
In this workbook, I greatly amplify the principles of Real Love as found in *The Essentials of Real Love* DVDs (described on next page) and give you many powerful opportunities to practically apply those principles in ways that will change your life.

Soft cover, spiral bound, 447 pages, Blue Ridge Press

The Essentials of Real Love Bible Workbook
This Workbook starts with the material found in *The Essentials of Real Love Workbook* and also adds how the principles of Real Love are taught in the Bible.

Soft cover, spiral bound, 500 pages, Blue Ridge Press

Real Love for Wise Men and Women
After learning in *Real Love* how to *find* unconditional love, learn in *Real Love for Wise Men and Women* how to *share* that love with the people around you. Excellent for teachers, parents, group leaders, counselors.

Soft cover, 303 pages, Blue Ridge Press

DVDs (Video Recordings)

The Essentials of Real Love

This is the centerpiece of your Real Love education! In six hours of video, you'll see and *feel* the power of Real Love as I present the essential principles to a live audience. This engaging and humorous presentation has changed the lives of hundreds of thousands around the world. Six DVDs, Blue Ridge Press

CDs (Audio Recordings)

Much of the Real Love literature is available on CD, or is downloadable from the website at www.RealLove.com.

Online Resources

Become a member of RealLove.com at www.RealLove.com, where you will have access to the following:

1. *The Essentials of Real Love* seminar
   A video recording of the seminar described above as *The Essentials of Real Love* DVDs.

2. Video Coaching with Greg
   Every weekday you'll receive a 3-7 minute video presentation where I explain the principles of Real Love in greater detail, answer questions from members, or tell stories about people who have successfully applied the principles in their lives.

3. The Real Love Live Video Chat
   Each week I host a live video chat, where I answer the live questions of members from around the world. These conversations are endlessly educational and entertaining.

4. Real Love Chat Rooms.
   These are available 24 hours a day, seven days a week, and for specified hours they are monitored by Real Love Coaches.

5. Telephone coaching by Real Love Coaches.
   Real Love Coaches have been personally trained and certified by myself and offer their experience with Real Love on a professional basis over the phone to those who desire it.

6. And more. Many more features are regularly added to the website.

๛ Chapter Two ๛

The Foundations of Victimhood

As we saw in the conversation between Mark and Susan on pages 2-3, when people act like victims they make their relationships very difficult, often impossible. So if victimhood is so counter-productive, why do people cling to it so tenaciously? Why do they continue a practice that is so uniformly harmful? Because they believe they have mountains of justification for doing so, and because the rewards are so great, and that is the subject of this chapter.

EMPTINESS

When I was much younger and even more foolish, I joined with three friends on a hike in a canyon far out in the desert. I had read somewhere that this would be a vigorous challenge, so I was eager to conquer it. But I was afflicted even more than most by two flaws: I tended to create my own way rather than follow directions, and I believed I was invincible. So I ignored the strong recommendations I'd heard that the hike was to be made only *downstream* in the canyon and only in the middle of the *summer*. Under these optimum conditions, the hike should have taken all of one day, from early morning through late afternoon.

We began our journey in late *winter* and walked *upstream*, against the current of the river that flowed in the bed of the canyon. Both of these decisions proved to be most unfortunate. In the summertime, the stream is small, so it's possible to walk along the banks almost the entire distance. Even in the summer, however, there are places where the river must be crossed, and the current is dangerous enough that in most years one or more hikers die in that canyon as they attempt to ford the stream. In the winter, however, the river is swollen, deep, and very cold, so we were forced to cross the river on dozens of occasions, walking and often actually swimming in water so cold that chunks of ice were floating by. I had never been that cold before, nor have I been since.

In many places, the river was frozen over, so we were able to continue only by breaking through the ice with our arms and legs. Our progress was slow and painful, and after pressing on far into the night of the second day, we still hadn't reached our destination.

On the third day, we finally reached the head of the canyon, and from that point we still had a long hike to the main road. By that time we were quite hungry—having brought no provisions—and thoroughly frozen. On our way out, we came upon a cabin that had been sealed up for the winter by the owners. Looking through the windows, we could see cans of food on the shelves.

We did debate for a time—for at least a minute, I'm sure—whether we should take any of the food from the cabin. We avoided the word *stealing*, although obviously it was on everyone's mind. We concluded that in our dire circumstances, it just might be all right if we took only what we *really* needed.

We *stole* that food. In fact, we even broke the lock on the cabin to get in, so in addition to stealing we were also guilty of breaking and entering. None of us had ever been guilty of such crimes before that, and since that time I've never broken into anyone's house and stolen their property. So why did I do so on this occasion? Because I was *hungry*, and I believed that my hunger justified my taking what wasn't mine. I felt that my personal *need* justified disregarding the rights and needs of others.

And *that* is the rationale of everyone who feels like a victim. Such people do not have a sufficient supply of Real Love, and in that condition they feel empty and alone. They are emotionally and spiritually hungry—even starving—all the time, much as I was after working my way up the icy waters of that canyon for three days. But their condition is actually much worse, because they have endured their pain for a lifetime. When they judge that their needs are great enough, they

- become increasingly insistent that their needs be filled by the people around them.
- become increasingly insistent that their needs be filled *right now*.
- begin to ignore the usual constraints of civility as they make their demands.
- lie in order to get their needs filled.
- attack people with anger and guilt and criticism in order to get what they want.
- no longer care whether they injure others in the filling of their needs.
- rarely consider their selfish actions to be morally wrong.
- are often willing to break the law and risk serious consequences to get what they want.

We must understand that when victims don't get their needs filled, they feel victimized in just as real a way as though they were robbed, attacked, or otherwise violated. These feelings quickly and easily turn into sufficient justification for almost any action they take to get their needs filled, which makes victims potentially very dangerous people.

It should also be noted that victims usually make these judgments almost entirely without being aware of them.

The Fields of Life and Death

When people don't have enough Real Love, their emptiness is intolerable. Understandably, then, their pursuit of Imitation Love to fill that emptiness—and their use of Getting and Protecting Behaviors—is no casual affair. Their pursuit of relief becomes desperate. In the absence of Real Love, every scrap of Imitation Love seems monumentally important, even though long experience has taught all of us that no amount of Imitation Love will ever make us truly happy.

On many occasions I have visited men and women in prison. On one visit to a maximum security prison in Illinois, I spoke with Robert, an 82-year-old man who was serving a sentence that guaranteed he would never see freedom again. He was also not in the best of health. No matter how many times I visit a prison, I am sobered by the experience of being thoroughly searched, giving up everything in my possession, passing through one locked gate after another, and being surrounded by razor wire and armed guards.

I had corresponded with Robert on well over a hundred occasions, so our conversation was not impeded by a lack of familiarity.

As I sat down with Robert, he said, "I'm at the end of my life."

"That just might be true," I replied. Few conversations benefit from sugar-coating the truth.

"Being in this position, having essentially lived my life, has given me quite a perspective on what really matters. I didn't realize it at the time, but I have spent an entire lifetime trying to fill an emptiness that was gnawing at my guts. It was literally tearing me up, so I was running around trying to fill that emptiness as though I was possessed by demons."

"What did you find?"

"In the beginning, praise worked pretty well. I was brilliant, and I got a lot of praise for my successes academically and in other arenas. But after a while, that got old, so I started using sex. That became an addiction for a long, long time. In fact, that addiction eventually got me sentenced to prison. I was a physician for forty years, so that helped me get a great deal of praise and power at the same time. I really enjoyed that. In fact, now I look back, and I can see that I was like a human vacuum, sucking up all the praise, power, pleasure, and safety I could find—everywhere. I was good at it too. I accumulated *piles* of Imitation Love, more than most people could ever hope to have."

"How'd that work out?"

He smiled wryly and said, "Look at where we are. We're in a maximum security prison out in the middle of nowhere. My idea of a great moment is when you go to the snack machines over there and buy me a bottle of cranberry juice. I'm going to die here. Other than you, I have no friends. Overall I'd say it didn't work out very well, wouldn't you?"

"What happened to all those piles of Imitation Love?"

"Garbage, all garbage. Everybody I knew thought I was a brilliant man, a physician, making lots of money, influential in the community, the whole deal. But I couldn't see that I was wasting my entire life. With my every breath I was focused on the pursuit of *garbage*, accumulating things that just didn't matter. Everything I pursued didn't last and never made me happy—even in the short term. No matter how much Imitation Love I got, I was slowly dying, and it got worse by the year. It was pathetic, but I just didn't know any better. I didn't know that Real Love existed. Now I believe all those mistakes and all that pain—including my coming to prison—have been the price I had to pay to discover Real Love. And, strange as it sounds, it's been worth it. Even though I'm pretty old now, Real Love has changed my life. I'm happier now than I've ever been. I do wish I had discovered this a bit sooner, but there's nothing I can do about that."

In the absence of sufficient Real Love, we *will* pursue Imitation Love. We *will* use Getting and Protecting Behaviors. People who feel like victims do this. And some of us are better at accumulating Imitation Love—and better at using Getting and Protecting Behaviors—than others.

Imagine, however, that life is one great game. Everyone who uses Imitation Love and Getting and Protecting Behaviors is playing with rules and tools that can lead only to disappointment and frustration and misery. As a human family we have proven these outcomes trillions of times without exception. Because these conditions are in direct opposition to our highest purpose in *life*—to become loving and happy—it is appropriate that we regard them as the *opposite of life*. It is appropriate that we regard these conditions as a kind of death.

In short, going back to our comparison of life to a game, everyone who uses Imitation Love and Getting and Protecting Behaviors is playing on the Field of Death, and no matter how cleverly and effectively they use these behaviors, everyone on that field *dies*—emotionally, spiritually, and often physically. If you choose to play on that field, you might acquire more points—more toys, praise, power, money, sex, and so on—than the other players through the use of more effective trading and manipulating. You might inflict more wounds on others than they can inflict upon you. But in the end *you still die*—every time.

People who feel and act like victims are playing on the Field of Death. In view of their emptiness, it's quite understandable that they pursue Imitation Love, but the end result is fatal. We'll discuss the results of victimhood in greater detail in Chapters Four, Five, and Six.

There's only one way to find genuine happiness: Get completely off the Field of Death and play on the Field of Life, where Getting and Protecting Behaviors are not the means of survival. On the Field of Life, the game is played by the guidelines of truth and Real Love. There are still ups and downs, to be sure, and life is still a struggle at times, but on the Field of Life the end product is happiness. Everyone lives. We'll discuss this way of living in Chapters Seven, Eight, and Nine.

How Victims Compete for Imitation Love

Let's observe another conversation between Mark and Susan, whom we met in Chapter One. One evening while Mark is watching television, Susan states, "We never go *anywhere* anymore."

"We went to your mother's house two weeks ago," Mark snaps testily.

"You call that *going somewhere?*" she says.

"Would it matter where we went? No matter what I do, it doesn't count with you, so what's the difference?"

Is there any doubt where their conversation will go from here? They exchange accusations and defend each other for several minutes, and then they withdrew into a stony silence for two days.

It is helpful to understand, once again, the true meaning of what was said and done:

What Mark or Susan Said or Did	The Real Meaning of What Mark or Susan Said or Did
Susan said, "We never go *anywhere* anymore."	1. "You're a lousy husband." 2. "You have broken your promises to me." 3. "You have robbed me of the joy I had always hoped to find in marriage."

What Mark or Susan Said or Did	The Real Meaning of What Mark or Susan Said or Did
Susan spoke while Mark was watching television	1. "I don't care what your needs are. If I really cared, I would have waited to talk to you until you were finished with what you were doing." 2. "I care only about what I want, and if that inconveniences you, too bad."
"We went to your mother's house two weeks ago." (Mark)	1. "I am not listening to you." 2. "What you want is not important to me." 3. "I'd rather defend myself and try to be right than listen to you."
Mark snapped at Susan.	1. "I don't love you." 2. "If defending myself means that you will be hurt, I don't care."
"You call that *going somewhere*?" (Susan)	1. "Your efforts to do what I want are pathetic." 2. "Again, you are such a failure as a husband."
"No matter what I do, it doesn't count with you." (Mark)	1. "I try so hard to please you, but it's useless." 2. "I'm much more concerned with your seeing *my* pain than I am with trying to see yours." 3. "Since it's impossible to please you, I give up."

In a relationship without Real Love, the participants don't *relate* to each other. They're *combatants*, fighting over every morsel of Imitation Love, which seems so very important to them. Now let's look at the same interaction between Mark and Susan in terms of the Imitation Love they were trying to gain or preserve, and how they were using various Getting and Protecting Behaviors to accomplish that.

What Mark or Susan Said or Did	The Imitation Love or Getting and Protecting Behavior Used
Susan said, "We never go *anywhere* anymore."	1. Acting like a victim ("Look at what you don't do for *me*.") 2. Lying (She exaggerated considerably.) 3. Attacking (She was angry and critical.) 4. Clinging (She was begging for his attention.) 5. Power (She was trying to make Mark do what she wanted.) 6. Praise (She wanted to re-create the sense of acceptance she enjoyed early in their relationship.) 7. Pleasure (She wanted him to create a pleasurable distraction for her.)
Susan spoke while Mark was watching television	Power ("I will control this situation and get what I want, no matter what your desires are in this moment.")
"We went to your mother's house two weeks ago." (Mark)	1. Lying (Mark knew she was talking about going out on a *date* with only the two of them, not just going *somewhere*, like her mother's house, but he purposefully ignored the real meaning of her statement.) 2. Acting like a victim ("You never appreciate me.") 3. Power ("I am not going to allow you to draw me into this discussion where I'd have to admit I'm wrong and where I'd look foolish. I will insist on being right.") 4. Safety (He was protecting himself.)
Mark snapped at Susan.	1. Attacking 2. Acting like a victim 3. Power

What Mark or Susan Said or Did	The Imitation Love or Getting and Protecting Behavior Used
"You call that *going somewhere?*" (Susan)	1. Attacking 2. Acting like a victim 3. Power
"No matter what I do, it doesn't count with you." (Mark)	1. Acting like a victim 2. Attacking 3. Power 4. Safety

Because both Mark and Susan were consumed with emptiness, they felt justified in acting like victims and could think only of *themselves*. They could only fight for praise, power, pleasure, and safety. In that condition, they couldn't possibly think of the well-being of their partner. Victims are absolutely trapped by their selfishness. They don't *intend* to be selfish. It's just that in their emptiness they can see no other way to behave, just as I—when I was hungry from the hike through the canyon, as described on pages 41-2—could see no choice available to me other than to break into the cabin and take the food I found there.

The Demands of Victims

Because victims feel empty almost all the time, they feel justified in making demands of virtually everyone around them, and they can become very insistent about it. We've all seen examples of people making such demands:

- The woman whose husband neglects her. Feeling victimized, her demands for attention become increasingly sharp and insistent.
- The customer who has been wronged. Certain that the scales of justice have been deliberately unbalanced—or even thrown away—he or she feels justified in doing whatever it takes to make them right again.
- The man whose wife won't have sex with him. Feeling wrongly deprived, such a man believes he is justified in demanding that

which has been "taken" from him, even though the effect of his demands is almost always the opposite of what he wants.
- The elderly man or woman who has not been visited by his or her children. After all she has done for her children for all those years, how could they possibly neglect her now? She then feels justified in requiring her children to repay at least some of that attention to her in her old age.
- The neglected child. Children who are insufficiently loved feel victimized—and they *are*, because they are being deprived of the love they need most—even though they couldn't put it into words. Their demands then come in the form of anger, rebellion, tantrums, and demands for time, attention, money, the freedom to do what they want, and so on.
- The student who has been treated unfairly. Have you ever seen a student complain about a test when it has been graded incorrectly? He doesn't *request* that his grade be changed. He *demands* it, fortified by the horrifying injustice that he must correct.
- The recently divorced woman who demands that her friends sympathize with her as she vilifies her ex-husband.

FEAR

In the absence of Real Love, not only are we consumed by emptiness, but we are also riddled with fear, a fear that we'll never experience the love and happiness and sense of wholeness we really want. Fear is the most instantly distracting and even paralyzing force in the universe. It twists us and envelopes us in a kind of darkness that nothing but Real Love can penetrate.

Reports of fear's physical effects alone are legion. To name just a few:
- Elevation in blood pressure
- Heart arrhythmias
- Heart attacks
- Gastrointestinal upset
- Skin rashes
- Nervous tics
- Headaches
- Hysterical blindness

- In the prelude to the Iraq war, some clinics in the United states reported a six-fold increase in the number of people seeking help for anxiety.
- As threat alerts were implemented during the war on terrorism, health officials reported, "Kids are acting out, and adults don't know what to do or who to talk to about the terror alerts. People are reporting headaches, insomnia, back pain, neck pain, disorientation. But after a physical exam, we can't find a physical cause."
- Israel recorded 100 excess deaths during the 1991 Scud missile attacks by Saddam Hussein, not from bomb injuries but from heart attacks presumably triggered by fear and stress.
- Heart patients around New York City suffered life-threatening heart arrhythmias at more than twice the usual rate in the month following the World Trade Center attacks.

We've all experienced the racing heart, the sweaty palms, the trembling hands, the stuttering tongue, and other physical signs of fear. But aside from the physical signs, fear has an astonishing power over our minds and souls. It distorts our perception and thinking, and it can even paralyze us completely.

For many years I was a Boy Scout leader, and I often took young men on expeditions that involved an activity called rappelling, where they descended on a rope from the top of a high cliff, sometimes from as high as two hundred feet. It is not the natural inclination of most people to even approach the edge of a cliff two hundred feet high, much less go off the edge, so considerable instruction was required before these young men were prepared to descend the face of the cliff.

On top of the cliff, I hooked each young man into a climbing harness, which enclosed his waist and both legs. Then I ran the rope through a metal loop—which was fastened to his harness—then around the left side of his body, around his back, and to his right hand. If he properly used the loop, the position of the rope around his body, and the position of his right hand, he could completely control the rate of his descent down the cliff, even stopping whenever he wished.

When you're hanging from a cliff, however, the *natural* tendency is to grab hold of the rope above you with both hands. That works very poorly, because then when you get tired and loosen your grip, you have none of the advantages of the rope being controlled by the loop, your body, and your right hand, and you drop very quickly—sometimes disastrously. It is critical that you *never* release the loose end of the rope with your right hand and reach up and grab hold of the rope above you with that hand.

The other trick to rappelling is body position. The safest technique—though certainly not the most natural—is to walk off the edge of the cliff *backward*. In addition, the upper body remains vertical (parallel to the cliff), while the legs are horizontal (parallel to the ground), thereby separating the body from the face of the cliff. In that position, properly using your hands, you can literally walk down the cliff. When done correctly, the whole process is rather easy and enjoyable.

Over the years I instructed many young men in this technique, and I also observed the effect of fear on their performance. If the young men felt connected to me and confident, they usually found it easy to listen carefully to my instructions and descend the cliff. If fear overwhelmed them, however, their connection to me was instantly severed, and immediately they forgot everything I had taught them. Instead of doing what *worked*, they did what was *natural*. Instead of carefully controlling their descent with the balance of the rope, the loop, and the right hand, they immediately let go of the rope with the right hand and grabbed hold of the rope above them with both hands.

At that point they found themselves hanging two hundred feet above the canyon floor *without* the benefit of all that sophisticated equipment and technique that were designed to keep them from falling to their deaths. I didn't usually bother to tell them ahead of time that there was yet another safety measure in place that made their falling quite impossible, even if they became completely unconscious, because I wanted them to experience a greater measure of reliance on their own wits.

As fear overtook their reason, not only did they let go of the loose end of the rope with the critical right hand, but they almost always straightened out their legs, so in addition to hanging by their own strength, they no longer had the advantage of their legs separating their body from the cliff. At that point, they immediately swung into the cliff, usually face first. That was only a distance of about three feet, depending on the length of their legs, but at a height of two hundred feet it's terrifying—and a little painful—to swing three feet face-first into a wall of rock.

At this point terror took over completely, and the air was filled with heart-rending screams for help. Of course I was prepared for this and had already hooked myself up to another rope, so I could then descend to their location to help them. They were always most grateful for the assistance.

When these young men became afraid, they no longer chose to do what was *effective*. Under the influence of fear, they did what came *naturally*, which was also least effective, and if I had not provided additional safety measures for them, they could easily have died. We respond in similar ways in our emotional lives. When we become afraid, we don't tend to respond naturally with what is most effective—with Real Love. Instead, we respond with Protecting Behaviors, which uniformly cause terrible unhappiness, both for us and for others.

Think about the last time you lied to someone, or blew up at someone, or acted like a victim, or ran. When you engaged in those behaviors, did you *ever* feel more unconditionally loved or more unconditionally loving? Did these behaviors ever result in a richer and more fulfilling relationship? Not a single time. So why do we use them? It makes no sense to keep using behaviors that are so consistently harmful. We use them because when we're afraid, we don't think clearly, we don't see clearly, and we don't respond sensibly. Fear paralyzes us. It pushes us into a form of insanity.

People without sufficient Real Love are terrified that they'll lose any piece of Imitation Love that might briefly relieve their pain. If anyone threatens to compete for one of these morsels of Imitation Love, they become frightened. They feel victimized, and then they often act like victims. In their interactions above, both Mark and Susan acted like victims, because they were afraid that the other person was about to take a little power from them. In the absence of Real Love, we can't allow other people to take *any* Imitation Love from us. None at all.

PAIN

Above I have described emptiness and fear as the two conditions that naturally follow a lack of Real Love, but both of them share a single characteristic: pain. Emptiness and fear are painful, intolerably so, and that pain is what victims use more than anything else to justify their behavior.

Victims reason like this—usually without thinking about it—and usually in this sequence:

- I am in pain.
- My pain is intolerable.
- What could possibly be more important than my pain? Is there anything you're doing that could compare in importance to the relief of my unbearable pain? Surely you could not make such an insensitive proposal.
- Because the relief of my pain is so important—centrally so—you are obligated to do whatever you can to help me eliminate it. You must drop everything to help me.
- If you are not willing to help me, this would be absolute proof that you have no morals, no sense of right and wrong, and no decency. You are a monster, and I would be justified in taking whatever steps I deem necessary to take from you what I need to lessen my pain—or to protect myself from your evil.

With this kind of reasoning, a victim can justify almost any behavior, as we will discuss in this chapter and again in Chapter Three. This reasoning is also easy to understand. When you are in pain, what do you focus on? What in the world could be more important? In the moment that you have a headache, or in the moment you've just hit your thumb with a hammer, does it occur to you to wonder whether the children in Somalia have sufficient food and shelter? No, because in the moments we're in pain, our pain becomes the absolute center of our attention. When we're in pain, we naturally become *selfish*, and the pain that victims feel is simultaneously severe and longstanding.

Victims find it especially easy to use the pain in their lives to justify their behavior, because they can point to virtually endless sources of pain. In this world, pain is everywhere. People are always getting in our way, failing to meet our expectations, neglecting our needs, and sometimes even behaving in unkind and malicious ways toward us. What victims don't understand is that pain is the price we *all* pay for simply being around other people. Because other people always have their own needs, it is an absolute certainty that at times—usually many times a day—their needs will unavoidably conflict with ours. Other people will compete with us for attention, money, space, time, promotions, positions on the highway, praise, power, and so on. As they do that, they will inevitably get in our way, take some of the bits of Imitation Love we want, and otherwise inconvenience us. When we're starving for Real Love, each of these losses is painful. In short, being surrounded by needy and flawed people means that we *will* experience endless occasions to feel pain.

Victims are characterized by the pain they feel—almost constant pain, from a lack of Real Love and usually an additional lack of Imitation Love—and their behavior is devoted primarily to diminishing that pain. In Chapter One, we discussed the *beliefs* victims share, *why* they act like victims, and *what* victims *say and do*. Now let's examine those beliefs, whys, and whats, and let's see how they relate practically to the victim's primary goal of reducing pain.

The Beliefs We Share As Victims

1. *We personally are being inconvenienced.*

This attitude of the victim can be illustrated by a call I received one evening from a woman, Sylvia, who was furious with her husband, Brad.

"He is so selfish," she said. "He never thinks of anybody but *himself*, and I'm sick of it."

"Really?" I asked. "Give me an example."

"There are so many."

"Pick one."

"Okay, the toilet seat. I've asked that man to put the toilet seat down at least a thousand times, but has it made any difference? No, it's like he's never heard me."

"I have a question. Why *should* he put the toilet seat down?"

There was a long pause before Sylvia said, "So you're defending him?"

"Heavens no," I said. "I'm only suggesting that you honestly examine what you're asking him to do. I'm not making an *accusation*. I'm asking a genuine *question*. So again, why should he put the toilet seat down?"

"It's just considerate. Have you ever sat on a toilet where the seat was *up*?"

"Oh, I understand the physical implications of the position of the *seat*. My question is really about *him*. Why should *Brad* feel obligated to put the seat down? If *you* want the seat down, why wouldn't it be *your* job to put it there?"

"Well, like I said, because it would be considerate on his part."

"So you're saying that Brad is *required* to be thoughtful. He doesn't really have a choice."

"No, he has a choice."

"Not really. If he really had a choice, you'd let him *make it* and then leave him alone, but you don't. In your own words, you've bothered him about this 'at least a thousand times,' right?"

Sylvia was clearly uncomfortable. "Well . . . "

"What you're saying with your behavior is that Brad has to change *who he is* before you'll accept him. How unconditionally loving is that on your part?"

"Hmmm."

"So let's set that aside for a moment, and let me ask you another question. Do you put the toilet seat *up* for *him*?"

I could have taken a nap during this pause. "Uh, no."

"Interesting. How is it that he should put the toilet seat *down* for you, but you feel no obligation to put it *up* for him?"

"Ummm . . ."

"Wouldn't it make more sense for each of you to adjust the seat for your own needs? I mean, if he does what you want, he'd have to put the seat up to use it, put it down for you, and then if he uses the toilet next, he has to put it up again and down again. That's a lot of work for nothing, don't you think? Instead, couldn't you just put it down for yourself when you need it?"

"I guess I'd never thought of it like that."

"But all this is just *details*. The *real point* here is that whenever you're inconvenienced, you think it's about *you*, and I really understand why it would seem like that. Over a period of decades, people have failed to love you and have ignored you and hurt you so many times, that you are one huge open wound all the time. Then when anything happens that inconveniences you, it's more painful than you can stand, and you think it's being done *to you*, when in truth little inconveniences just happen around us all the time as a result of being in a world where stuff just happens."

"Stuff happens all the time," I continued. "It rains. Tires go flat. Equipment breaks. People are late for their own reasons, without intentionally inconveniencing *us* at all. Stuff just happens, and we are often affected in negative ways. But when you're in pain all the time, every little thing becomes intolerable, and then it's only natural that you'd think it was about you, after which you'd feel like you'd been *victimized*. And you've been feeling like that with Brad for almost your entire marriage. He does some little thing without meaning to bother you in any way, and you think he's done it to *you*. Then you feel victimized and unloved, and in that condition how could you possibly feel close to him or be loving toward him?"

Sylvia's recognition of her victimhood was a huge step toward changing the way she behaved in her relationship with Brad.

Variations on "I personally am being inconvenienced" would include

- "Why do *I* have to wait?" (So often we think waiting is an inconvenience or injustice inflicted on us personally.)
- "You promised me you'd have this done by four o'clock!" (We act as though people go out of their way not to keep their promises so that *we* are inconvenienced.)
- "How many times have I had to tell you to _____?" (We make the assumption that people fail to do as we've asked just to inconvenience *us* or so that we'll have to ask them again.)
- "What is this stuff all over the floor?" (Again we assume that if something is in our way, this was done *to us*.)

2. *We're being injured.*

Victims believe that pain is directed *at them*, as illustrated in the following interaction between me and a woman named Elise.

One day Elise called and said, "I've had it with my mother-in-law. I try to be patient with her. I try to be nice for my husband's sake, but she is so rude and hurtful."

"What does she do?" I asked.

"Like today, she came over to visit while my husband was gone, and she never stopped talking, and most of it was to say something critical: The house isn't clean enough. The kids aren't well-behaved. The furniture doesn't match. The bathroom smells funny. She was constantly asking me, Why don't I do this or do that? I think she enjoys hurting my feelings."

"Have you ever seen your mother-in-law be *unconditionally* loving toward *anybody*?"

"Well, she's a lot nicer to her daughter."

"Let me guess. Does her daughter do everything her mother tells her to do?"

There was a pause. "How did you know that?" Elise asked. "That's exactly what she does. It's like she's her mother personal slave. She doesn't dare contradict her mother about anything."

"That's why her mother accepts her. Her daughter does everything she wants, which gives her mother a feeling of power, and in exchange her mother gives her acceptance or praise. It's just a mutual trading of Imitation Love. That's not Real Love. So back to my question: Have you ever seen your mother-in-law be *unconditionally* loving toward *anybody*?"

"When you put it like that, no, I guess not."

"So it's pretty obvious, isn't it, that your mother-in-law doesn't have any idea how to be loving?"

"I suppose so."

"And why does she criticize you?"

"Because she wants to get power over me, just like she does with her daughter and her husband and just about everybody in her life."

"Of course. And why would somebody settle for power, which is just a form of Imitation Love?"

"Oh, I see what you're saying now. Because she's empty and afraid. Because she doesn't feel loved."

"Right. To put it in a single word, your mother-in-law is just *drowning* (page 32), and it actually has *nothing* to do with you. Now, when you're in the room, it's true that she splashes *you* with her drowning, but it's nothing personal. She's not drowning *to you*. She's just desperate to keep her own head above water, and she *believes* the only way to do that is to fill herself up with Imitation Love at the expense of others—including you."

"But what she does is still hurtful."

"What she does seems hurtful to you *only* for two reasons: First, you believe she's doing this *to you*. But again, she's just drowning, and you get splashed only because you happen to be around her. If you were not around, she'd be splashing somebody else. Second, you're hurt because *you* are empty and afraid too, just like your mother-in-law. When you're empty yourself, every little thing that woman does has a big impact on you."

Then I explained to Elise the metaphor on pages 25-6 about how two dollars being taken from us means nothing if we have twenty million.

"When you have enough Real Love in your life," I said, "you won't be bothered *at all* by what your mother-in-law does, because you'll already be full and happy. You won't need her to give you two dollars, and it won't bother you if she actually *takes* two."

3. *We're being treated unfairly.*

Most of us are obsessed with the idea of justice. We want things to be fair all the time. Our sense of "fairness" itself, however, is rarely genuinely fair, as demonstrated by the following conversation I had with my friend Andy.

As I walked into the room, it was obvious that Andy was unhappy about something, so I asked him what was wrong.

"My boss is such a @#%& jerk," he said.

"In what way?" I asked.

"I really try hard to do a good job at work. I don't just put in my time. I really work at helping the department and the company, but my boss does nothing but criticize and be demanding. Even though I do good work, he treats me badly all the time, but there are other people who do a lousy job, and he treats them better. It's like he plays favorites, and it's not fair."

"One question."

"What?"

"Do they pay you at work?"

"Sure."

"Do you accept the paycheck they offer?"

"Yes."

"When you do that, you agree to do the work they give you in exchange for what they pay you. Is there *anything* in your contract that says anyone has to be kind to you or respect you or appreciate you or be grateful to you?"

"Well, no, but—"

"Now, it's a fact that it would be *nice* if your boss treated you with more appreciation and understanding, but he doesn't. And he doesn't *have* to."

"But he treats some people pretty well, and that's not fair."

"Actually, *fair* means that you receive what you were promised. Do you receive the check you were promised?"

"Yes."

"Then you were treated fairly. Now let's look at how you treat your boss. You don't like it that he treats some people better than he treats you. Would it be *fair* if you had the authority to choose his friends for him?"

"Well, no."

"So he gets to choose his own friends. He *gets* to treat some people better than others. That's *his choice*. It's actually *fair* that he gets to make that choice. Certainly *you* can't. Now, why do you suppose that he treats some people better?"

"I'm not sure."

"Are you irritated by your boss?"

"Well, sometimes."

"It's pretty obvious that you are, and that's just here with me, when he's not around. I'm guessing that when he's being difficult, and you're around him, you're even more irritated. I can tell you for a fact that when we're irritated at people, they really do *feel* our irritation, whether we mean to communicate it or not. When you're around him, you're angry and you act like a victim. I'm guessing you also tend to avoid him, right? We do tend to avoid people we don't like."

"That's probably true. I don't like being around him."

"So you use at least three Getting and Protecting Behaviors with him, and each one of them conveys to him the message *I don't love you*. I *promise* you that he feels those messages, whether you mean to express them or not. By comparison, some of the people at work are not angry at him. I'm guessing that they even kiss up to him, right?"

"Yes, and it's disgusting."

"Perhaps, but you need to understand it for what it is. It should be obvious that your boss is not filled with Real Love, yes?"

"Very obvious."

"So if he doesn't have enough *Real* Love it's only natural that he would *like* the people who give him the greatest quantity of *Imitation* Love. When people kiss up to him, they make him feel worthwhile and important. They give him praise, power, and also a sense of safety. You, on the other hand, are irritated by him and avoid him, so not only do you not give him Imitation Love, but you tell him you don't like him. Is it any wonder that he likes them better than he does you? I am *not* saying you should change your behavior, just explaining why things are as they are. You see all this as unfair only because you're in pain yourself and because you need your boss's acceptance, which you're not getting."

As Andy saw that he was acting like a victim, and that his concept of *unfair* was selfish, he was able to change his perspective regarding his boss's behavior. There were, however, yet other insights he needed and steps he could take to respond more productively to his boss, and we'll talk about those in Chapter Eight.

4. *What we want or need is being withheld from us.*

As victims we believe that if we don't get what we want, it's intentionally being withheld from us, as illustrated in the following conversation between me and a woman named Linda, who was eager to complain about her husband, Joel.

"When Joel comes home from work, all he does is watch television," Linda said.

"And why does that bother you?" I asked.

Linda looked at me as though I were stupid. I had asked the question not because I didn't know the answer, but so she would really think about the answer.

"Because we never talk," she said.

"And why does that bother you?"

"Because he never pays me any attention."

"You're getting warmer with each answer. What is the real reason it bothers you that he comes home and watches television?"

Linda gave me a puzzled look. Most people have a hard time getting to the root issue of any conflict, and the root issue is the same almost every time: It's always about Real Love, not about television or socks on the floor or money or sex or whatever.

"Each time he sits and watches television without talking to you," I said, "don't you feel like he doesn't care about you? Don't you almost hear him saying with his behavior that he doesn't love you?"

"Yes!" she said instantly.

"So when he comes home, *why* doesn't he talk to you? Why does he watch television instead? Have you told him you'd like to talk to him?"

"Sure I've told him, but he doesn't listen. He won't do anything I like to do."

"Do you feel like he's *withholding* his affection from you?"

"Of course. Isn't it obvious? I've talked to him about this one subject a hundred times, and he refuses to change his behavior, so it's obvious that he's withholding from me what I want."

Linda's anger alone proved her belief that Joel was intentionally withholding his affection. If she didn't believe he was withholding it intentionally—if she believed he was completely unaware of what he was doing, for example—she would not have been irritated.

"Linda," I said, "everything between you two would begin to change if you could see the *truth* about what's happening here instead of seeing it from the skewed perspective of a victim. You believe he's withholding his attention *from you*. That's not true."

"It sure *feels* like he is."

"Of course, but only because *you* are empty. But he's not doing this *to you*. He's simply empty and afraid and alone himself, and he just has no clue how to interact with you in a loving way. When you get angry, he becomes frightened. When you place demands on him, he feels utterly incompetent. He has no idea how to love you. So how does he respond to his fears? He withdraws from you, but it's not about *you*. He's withdrawing from *his pain*. He's running away from any source of pain *to him*. Watching television is running. It makes him feel safer than talking to you would. It's all for *him* and has little to do with you."

As victims we believe everything is about us, and we see everything we can't have as being withheld from us personally. For example, as victims we believe that

- if we don't get a promotion, it's being *withheld* from us.
- if someone takes our parking space, they did it so *we* couldn't

have it. We don't see that the other person was motivated by entirely selfish reasons and didn't think about us at all.
- if the guy we dated once doesn't call as promised, he's deliberately failing to keep a promise *to us*, rather than simply manifesting a selfish character that's been in development for decades.
- if people don't return our calls, they're deliberately being inconsiderate *to us*.

5. *Any mistakes involved are not our fault.*

When mistakes are made, as victims we are very quick to take one or both of two courses:

- Make excuses
- Blame others

In our defense, as victims we *have* to do this, because we simply *can't* be wrong. The essence of victimhood is that something has been done *to you* or is being taken *from you*. Victimhood is all about being *wronged*, so as a victim if you admit that you might be wrong yourself, you would likely lose your position as a victim.

Following are some examples of victims making excuses or blaming others:

- "But there wasn't time."
- "But he hit me first."
- "I had no choice."
- "He yelled at me first."
- "She started it."
- "My alarm clock didn't go off."
- "I didn't know about the meeting."
- "The traffic was bad."
- "One of my kids wouldn't get dressed."
- "I thought you meant _____."
- "But I *tried*."
- "But he (or she) is impossible to talk to."
- "I didn't say that!"

In following chapters we'll be discussing in greater detail what victims get from saying such things, what we can do to eliminate victimhood from our own lives, and how we can respond when other people act like victims.

What We Say and Do As Victims

It should be no surprise that as victims what we say and do is focused on the potential for pain in our lives. As we discussed on page 5, when we're victims we say

- "Look what you did *to* me."
- "Look what you should have done *for* me (and didn't)."
- "It's not my fault."

On page 257-8 there is a long list of the more common things victims say, as well as what we might say to them in response.

As victims we also demonstrate characteristic behaviors. To name just a few:

- We make excuses for everything. We talked about this above.
- We blame everyone but ourselves for our own mistakes and unhappiness.
- We're selfish. As victims we're too focused on our own emptiness and pain to care about the needs of others (page 43).
- We're rude. As victims, we use our pain to justify making demands of the people around us, and if they don't respond in the ways acceptable to us, we become increasingly insistent, to the point of rudeness.
- We're angry. As victims we don't hesitate to use anger to protect ourselves and to get the Imitation Love we need.
- We're often late. As victims we're the center of the world—justified by the sacredness of our pain—so we don't care about deadlines, punctuality, and other such courtesies. We don't care if other people have to wait for us.

A Special Kind of Victim: The Victim of Fate

Within the culture of victimhood, there is one kind of victim—the Victim of Fate—whose song is a bit different from that sung by all the other victims. Whereas most victims talk about what *other people* did to them—or did not do for them—the Victim of Fate feels victimized by

- genetics.
- the weather.
- time.
- their bodies (their health).
- their own lack of talent, skill, or intelligence.
- God.
- circumstances.
- luck.
- fate.

Victims of Fate don't blame other *people* for their difficulties and pain. They blame circumstances, influences, and "things." So, whereas most victims say things like "Look what you did *to* me" and "Look what you should have done *for* me (and didn't)," Victims of Fate tend to bemoan their condition with words like the following:

- "I'm just too stupid."
- "I can't do anything right."
- "I was never meant to succeed."
- "Nothing goes right for me."
- "I never have any luck."
- "I never get a break."
- "It's all because I'm too short/tall/fat/stupid."
- "If only I were prettier/taller/smarter."

There is a clever—albeit mostly unintentional—kind of irresponsibility and cowardice involved in choosing to be victimized by fate. Why? Because "regular" victims have to blame other people for their pain, and those people eventually get tired of being blamed. If I blame you for hurting me, for example, you might allow me to do that the first few times, but eventually you'll become weary of my blaming:

- You'll get tired of my making you feel guilty.
- You won't like it that I make you look like a monster to other people.
- You won't like the burden of my making you feel responsible for eliminating my pain.

And when you do get tired of my doing all that to you, you'll respond with your own Protecting Behaviors. You might, for example,

- lie. You might deny any responsibility for your behavior in our relationship, which—if I'm feeling like a victim—I'll find annoying.
- attack me. After I repeatedly attack your character, you might well get fed up and attack me in return. That could be a distinctly unpleasant experience for me.
- act like a victim yourself. Tired of my blaming you, you might respond in kind by saying something like, "All you ever do is blame me. You never appreciate anything I do for you." Of course you'll say this with a whine of pain in your voice, all of which will make me feel responsible for hurting you.
- run. Sick of my blaming, you could just avoid me as much as possible.

If you choose any of the above Protecting Behaviors, I'll feel less loved and more alone, which I will have brought upon myself by acting like a victim with you. Throughout the process I will discover that there is quite a negative *price* for acting like a victim with other people.

People who are Victims of Fate, however, don't blame other people. They blame inanimate objects or forces or circumstances, so they don't tend to irritate people as much or experience the negative repercussions that "regular" victims do.

In Chapters Four and Five we'll talk about the rewards and negative consequences of victimhood, and then in Chapter Nine we'll discuss how to respond to Victims of Fate.

Guilt and a Sense of Worthlessness:
A Self-Inflicted Victimhood

As we have discussed, victims feel as though people and circumstances

- treat them unfairly.
- fail to give them what they want.
- beat them down and oppress them.

Guilt and a sense of worthlessness are forms of self-inflicted victimhood, because people who suffer from guilt feel that they are beaten down and oppressed by the effects of their own mistakes or flaws or sins. We're all quite familiar with guilt in our own lives, but we might benefit from seeing how there is an element in this condition. Following are some of the victim-oriented utterances of those who feel guilty or worthless:

- "Nothing I ever do is good enough." People who say this are implying that they are so flawed that they could never succeed. They are victimized by their own weaknesses. They're saying, "I'm so flawed, how could I possibly succeed? Who I am makes success impossible."
- "I'm a terrible mother." Translation: "I'm such an awful person—I'm such a monster—that I could never succeed as a parent."
- "I often just feel worthless." "I've made so many mistakes that I'll never crawl out of this hole I've dug." It's a self-inflicted victimhood.
- "How could God ever forgive me for what I've done." When people feel excessively guilty, they beat themselves up for their mistakes. "How could God accept someone who has made the mistakes I have made?"

In Chapters Four and Five we'll talk about the rewards and negative consequences of victimhood, and then in Chapter Nine we'll discuss how to respond to guilt and worthlessness.

THE VICTIM'S DISREGARD FOR THE LAW OF CHOICE

When people do bad things to us, it's quite understandable that we wonder—silently or aloud—"How can they be allowed to do that to me? It's so unfair. It's just not right." People—especially victims—have been asking this question from the beginning of time, and I suggest that we may be asking the wrong question.

Let us ask instead, What would it be like if we *could stop* people from doing things to us? Really, let's imagine that. Imagine that every time I did something you didn't like, you could push a button on your Fairness Enforcing Device (FED for convenience), which emits a force field that stops me from hurting you, inconveniencing you, or being unfair in any way. The FED, in effect, freezes me. Ooh, that is a seductive thought, isn't it? We could sell these devices for more than a few dollars on eBay, couldn't we? But think this through. Remember that your goal is to be *fair*, so you couldn't possibly object to *my* having the same device, so that I could freeze *you* if you should do something I didn't like. And, to be ultimately fair, we'd have to allow everyone else to have a FED, so before long everyone would be freezing everyone else who did anything they didn't like.

Now, what would the world be like? The world would become a popsicle. Effectively, no one could make their own decisions. We'd all be at the mercy of everyone around us. We'd all become objects in the hands of everyone else. In that condition, would it be possible for any of us to be happy? *No, it would not.* Happiness can exist only when we make our own choices and learn and grow from them—including the foolish, stupid, and inconsiderate choices, the ones that affect other people in negative ways.

We now have at least one answer to why other people must be allowed to make choices that inconvenience us, that are unfair, that are unkind, and so on. The answer is this: The alternative—a world where all choices are controlled and where no one can ever be happy—is *much worse*. The price we pay for being allowed to make *our* choices, and to learn from them and to grow and become happy, is that other people must be allowed to make *their* choices too—including the ones we don't like. We're all learning together as we make our choices, and in the process it is simply unavoidable that we will get in each other's way. We will inconvenience each other, sometimes hurt each other, and occasionally even cause each other's deaths. There is no other way to learn and be happy.

Let's formalize the importance of this idea. Let's call it the Law of Choice: *Everyone has the right to choose what he or she says and does.* It is the single most important principle in any relationship and very likely the most important principle in the universe. It is discussed in greater detail in the books *Real Love* and *Real Love for Wise Men and Women*, as well as in other books in the Real Love series.

As victims, however, we're more than willing to violate the Law of Choice, and we demonstrate this willingness with our behavior. Let's examine how some of our utterances and behaviors as victims—as listed on page 64—indicate our willingness to violate the Law of Choice for others:

What We Say or Do	What It Means in Terms of The Law of Choice
We say, "Look what you did *to* me."	"I believe in the Law of Choice, but it must be amended. It should read, 'Everyone has the right to choose what they say or do *until they make a choice that inconveniences or hurts me*. Then I get to limit their choices.'"
We say, "Look what you should have done *for* me (and didn't)."	"I believe in the Law of Choice, but it must be amended. It should read, 'Everyone has the right to choose what they say or do *unless they refuse to give me what I* really, really *need*. Then I get to make them do what I want.'"
We're selfish.	"Everyone gets to make their own choices, but they must remember that my choices are always more important than theirs."
We're rude.	"If other people fail to recognize that my choices are more important than theirs, I am allowed to remind them in whatever terms I choose."
We're angry.	"I'm angry that sometimes other people *don't* modify their choices to suit me. I really do *want* to control them."
We're late.	"I don't mind a bit if the choices I make interfere with the ability of other people to make their choices."

When we are in pain, we immediately become selfish. We tend to think only of our own pain. In fact, we become utterly consumed with our pain. The elimination of pain becomes the central preoccupation of our lives. If we're in enough pain, in fact, we're willing to disregard the welfare of everyone else, and in order to diminish our pain we're often willing to ignore what is right and moral and even legal. In general, we're not selfish because we're evil. We become selfish because our pain causes us to focus on ourselves.

The poet W. H. Auden once penned these lines (in the poem, "September 1, 1939"):

> I and the public know
> What all schoolchildren learn,
> Those to whom evil is done
> Do evil in return.

In the case of a victim an actual offense—or evil—need not even have been committed against him. He needs only to *believe* that an offense has occurred, or to believe that some benefit has been withheld from him, and at that point he feels entirely justified in committing any number of retaliatory acts against those who have wronged him.

The Downside of Violating the Law of Choice

As attractive as it might seem on occasion to violate the Law of Choice and control people, there is an immediate downside. If you control me in any way, I'm no longer truly myself. Instead I become an extension of you, like your shoes or gloves. The problem with that is, when you're in the company of your shoes or gloves—or anything else you control—you're *still alone*, the worst condition of all.

You might sometimes think you want to control what another person does, like a spouse, for example, but if you succeed in that effort—if you make all the decisions and do all the thinking—you'll only guarantee your own loneliness. You won't have a partner but a prisoner. Is that what you really want? To be in control but alone? Or do you want to have a richly fulfilling relationship with a real person as you allow your spouse or anyone else to make his or her own choices?

What you truly want is a real relationship with people, and *a relationship is the natural result of people making independent choices.* In the process of making independent choices, we all make mistakes, and as we do, it is simply unavoidable that the people around us will be inconvenienced, even hurt. If *you* expect to make mistakes, how could you expect that *other people* would not make mistakes too, including those that inconvenience *you*?

In Chapter Seven we'll discuss the effect on ourselves and others of violating the Law of Choice.

The Law of Responsibility

Connected irrevocably to the Law of Choice is the Law of Responsibility, which states, *I'm always responsible for the choices I make.* Without responsibility, the freedom to make our own choices becomes nothing more than an excuse to be selfish. Victims violate the Law of Responsibility as much as they violate the Law of Choice. They love to make their own choices, but they don't like taking responsibility—or being held accountable—for the choices they make.

THE VICTIM'S DISREGARD FOR THE LAW OF EXPECTATIONS

A natural corollary to the Law of Choice is the Law of Expectations, which states that we never have the right to expect anyone to do anything for us. If we understand that other people really do get to make their own choices and mistakes—the Law of Choice—how could we possibly expect them to change their choices to please us?

Regrettably, we expect people to make the choices we want all the time. Consider how often we do this:

- Whenever we're disappointed in the behavior of other people, we're saying that they haven't met our *expectations* for their choices. We're saying that we wish they'd make choices more like the ones *we'd* make.
- Whenever we're angry, it's always because people have failed to meet our expectations. Without expectations, anger is pretty much impossible. You wouldn't get angry if the *mailman* didn't give you a kiss in the morning, but you might if your *spouse* didn't. The difference? Expectations. You have no expectations of the mailman. Also remember the example earlier in this chapter (pages 55-7) of Sylvia, who was angry because Brad didn't fill her expectations of behaving as she wished.
- We feel like victims when people don't meet our expectations that they'll do what we want: when they don't cooperate with

us, when they fail to give us the gift we expected, when they're not grateful for something we've done, when they treat us unfairly, and so on.

If expectations are selfish on our part, why do we have them so often? For the same reason we feel like victims: need. Imagine that you're starving to death in the middle of the desert. Just when you've given up all hope of living, a man walks by holding a submarine sandwich in his hand. What would you notice about the man? Would you see *him*: his talents, needs, and fears? No, almost certainly you'd focus mostly on what *you needed*, the sandwich, and in no time you'd ask him if he'd be willing to share some of it with you. In fact, you'd make more than just a *request*. Out there in the desert, starving, you'd *expect* him to share with you. After all, in your moment of dire need, how could he possibly refuse you?

In order to further demonstrate the effect of neediness on our expectations, let's make a few changes to the above scenario. Imagine that again you're in the desert, but this time you've just eaten a full meal, you have a table next to you heaping with food, and you have access to a Humvee that can take you out of the desert whenever you'd like. Again a man walks by holding a submarine sandwich in his hand. This time what would you notice about the man? Would you focus on the sandwich? You probably wouldn't even notice it, and you certainly wouldn't expect him to share it with you. What's the difference? Why the expectations in the first situation and not in the second? In the first situation your attention was ruled by *need*, and so it is in our personal lives and in relationships.

Being without Real Love is like being without food. Without sufficient Real Love, we have enormous expectations of other people—for Real Love if they have it and for Imitation Love if they don't. It's from the people *closest* to us—often our spouses and our families—that we usually have the greatest expectations of all, and for two reasons: First, it's very likely that these people actually did fill our expectations for "happiness" in the beginning of our relationships with them, even though it was accomplished temporarily and superficially with Imitation Love. On the whole, *that* is why we chose to have relationships with these people—because they temporarily made us feel good.

The second reason we have huge expectations of our spouses and others is that they actually *promised* to make us happy. Regardless of the words actually spoken at the wedding ceremony, for example, what we *hear* our spouses say is this: "I promise to make you happy—always. I will heal your past wounds and satisfy your present needs and expectations—even when you don't express them. I will lift you up when you're discouraged. I will accept and love you no matter what mistakes you make. I give to you all that I have or ever will have. And I will never leave you."

Neither partner is consciously aware of making this bushel of impossible promises, but each partner still hears them and insists that they be fulfilled. When both partners lack sufficient Real Love, however, they can't possibly make one another happy, and then their efforts to do that yield only disappointment and anger, no matter how hard they try.

Although expectations are quite understandable in the presence of emptiness, they can only kill the potential happiness in a relationship, as illustrated by Rachel, a woman who came to me with quite a list of complaints about her husband, Kevin: He never gave her flowers anymore, didn't look at her with affection as he once did, and didn't talk to her when he came home from work. She was in the process of listing more of his failings when I said, "It sounds like you expect Kevin to do a lot of things."

She looked at me like I was stupid. "And why *wouldn't* I?" she asked. "He's my husband."

"What if I *expected* you to give me a dozen roses on my birthday," I said, "and you only gave me nine? I'd only have one thing on my mind, wouldn't I?"

"The three roses you *didn't* get," she said.

"Right," I said. "Even though you gave me a great gift—nine roses—I ruined the gift with my expectations, just as surely as though I had thrown them in the garbage. On the other hand, if I expected *nothing* from you, if you gave me even a single rose, I'd be delighted. I'd feel like you really cared about me. Ironically, even if you did give me a dozen roses, I wouldn't be thrilled by them—I'd only be *satisfied* that you filled my demand, kind of like filling an order. It can't feel like a gift when I'm essentially *making* you give me something with my expectations."

"With your expectations," I continued, "you make it impossible for anything you get from Kevin to feel like a gift. Everything he does seems like nothing to you. He can never do enough to please you. In addition, he *knows* he can never do enough, and eventually he gets to the point where he doesn't *want* to do anything with you or for you."

The Law of Expectations states that we never have the right to expect anyone to do anything for us. That makes sense when we understand the Law of Choice. If we understand that other people really do get to make their own choices—and mistakes—how could we possibly expect them to change their choices to please us? Rachel didn't have the right to demand (another word for expect) that Kevin give her what she wanted.

After I explained the Law of Expectations, Rachel said, "But if I don't have any expectations, Kevin won't do anything. How do I get what I want?"

"You can always *ask* Kevin for what you want—nothing wrong with that—but you haven't been making *requests* of Kevin. You've been making *demands*."

"How do you know that?" she asked.

"When Kevin doesn't give you what you 'ask' for, do you feel either disappointed or irritated?"

Throughout our discussion, Rachel had made it clear that she was experiencing both of these feelings, so she could hardly deny it. "I guess I do," she said, "but isn't that natural?"

"Sure, it's natural, but it also shows that you're making demands and having expectations. The hallmark of an expectation is that we're disappointed when we don't get what we expect, and your expectations are killing your happiness and your marriage. Kevin is empty himself, so he feels your expectations as a huge burden for him to carry and as an accusation that he's not acceptable. Then he responds with Getting and Protecting Behaviors, and those never make the two of you feel closer."

With our families, actual vows aren't spoken as they are in a wedding, but they are still powerfully *implied*—our expectations of a "mother's love," for example, are deeply ingrained—so we have strong expectations that our families will love us, respect us, support us, and so on. When they fail to do so, we are deeply disappointed and very likely to feel like victims.

CONTROLLING AND VICTIMHOOD

One of the most common harmful behaviors seen in relationships is *controlling*. We've all seen people who like to control the people and circumstances around them, and most of us engage in this behavior many times a day ourselves. Following are some examples of controlling behaviors:

- Your spouse is on the way out the door, and you say, "Are you going to wear that?"
- You tell your spouse or girlfriend what route to take when driving somewhere, when he or she already knows the way.
- When someone is telling a story to a third person or to a group, you butt in to correct the inaccuracies in the details they are communicating. Your partner—husband, wife, boyfriend, whoever—might say, for example, "We went to Atlanta this past Wednesday—" and you feel compelled to interject with, "No, it was Thursday." He or she continues, "And the traffic was awful. We didn't move on the highway at all for half an hour," and you can't resist saying, "Actually, it was only for twenty minutes, and it wasn't a complete standstill, just stop and go."
- People who are obsessive-compulsive, who engage in excessive hand washing, house cleaning, organization of objects or people, and repetition of words, to name a few examples.
- When you get in arguments, you just have to be right. You can't let the other person win an argument.
- When you go out to dinner or a movie or wherever, you usually get your way about where you go and what you do.
- You make the decisions about how the money is spent in your relationship.
- You demand or withhold sex in your relationship.
- You give an employee or child an assignment, and then you stand over him, giving detailed instructions about exactly how you want it done, instead of letting him complete the assignment in his own way.
- I was in a restaurant one day, and I heard a mother at an adjacent table say to her son—within a period of less than five minutes and all with a tone of considerable impatience—

- "Sit up straight."
- "Wipe your face."
- "No, put your napkin over there when you're done using it."
- "No, that's not how you open your milk. Let me show you how to do it."
- "When you're finished drinking your milk, put the carton over here, not there."
- "No, not like that."
- "That's too much ketchup."
- "Don't take such big bites."
- "Your mouth is too full. You can't chew when it's that full."
- "Oh my (said through an enormous sigh of exasperation), now you've spilled on your shirt. Come here, and I'll clean up that mess. How many times have I told you to be careful not to slop food on your shirt when you eat? Are we going to have to put a bib on you?"
- "Look how you've pushed those peas off your plate. Pick them up and put them back where they belong."
- "You don't need that much butter on your roll."
- "Did you finish drinking your milk?"
- "Sit still. Quit fidgeting while you eat."
- "Eat your french fries one at a time. Don't be a pig about it."
- "Don't eat so fast. You can't digest your food when you eat that fast."
- "Now hurry up. We don't have all day here."

So why are we talking about controlling in a chapter about victimhood? When people are controlling they are both (1) anticipating the condition of victimhood and (2) planning to prevent being victimized. In order to illustrate this controlling-victimhood relationship, let's use one of the examples from above:

Why did the mother in the restaurant control everything her son did, with the possible exception of the way he breathed? Is it possible that she was only trying to teach him some valuable table manners? No, not really. Children learn everything better while they're being unconditionally loved, which means in an atmosphere where there is a complete absence of disappointment and irritation. Intuitively this is obvious. If I gave you an assignment to learn anything, would you prefer that I calmly gave you instructions and then just hung around to offer support as needed, *or* would you rather that I taught you as I rolled my eyes, sighed, tapped my feet, told you to hurry up, and perhaps yelled at you? There's no doubt whatever about which choice you'd make, so we can never claim to nag and hound our children for *their* benefit.

So if the mother wasn't entirely motivated by a desire to teach her son manners, what was her true motivation? Can we relate it to her feeling victimized? Yes, we can. For ease of description, let's call her Vicki and her son Lewis:

- Vicki knew from past experience that if she said nothing to Lewis, he would almost certainly spill liquids, drop food on his clothes and on the floor, and otherwise make messes that she'd feel obligated to clean up. Vicki regarded any additional mess as an inconvenience directed *at her*. She felt *victimized* by virtually every inconvenience in her life, and she hoped that by bombarding Lewis with a constant stream of instructions, she might minimize his mistakes and the subsequent problems she would have to deal with.
- Whenever Lewis made a mess in public, Vicki was certain that other people looked at her and made harsh judgments about what a negligent mother she was. She hated that feeling—she felt *victimized* by the judgments of others—and hoped that she might minimize Lewis's mistakes by controlling his every motion.
- Perhaps most importantly, Vicki had experienced a lifetime of consistent emptiness and fear already, and she hated the additional pain she felt whenever she was in situations where she felt out of control, because it was in those situations that people tended to inconvenience her, hurt her, and fail to fill her needs. Whenever Vicki felt out of control, she felt *victimized*, and she learned that if she took control over people and situations, she felt somewhat less out of control, less fearful, and a little stronger. Being in control—even with her own son—gave her a feeling of power that felt better than having no control at all.

When we attempt to control other people, it should also be obvious that we are also disregarding the Laws of Choice and Expectations. As

I control your behavior—in the ways listed above or in others ways not listed—I'm declaring a belief that you don't deserve to make your own choices. I'm saying that the Law of Choice should be repealed, allowing me to make your choices for you. I'm also declaring that I have a right to have expectations of you, that you should do as I wish. The act of controlling people is quite selfish and unloving.

LEARNING VICTIMHOOD AS CHILDREN

One day I watched a toddler trip and fall as he ran. Although his outstretched hands made a loud noise on the floor, he wasn't hurt. He looked around to see if someone was watching, and when he saw his mother's anxious face, he burst into tears. She rushed over, picked him up, and made quite a fuss over him.

Minutes later, the same child fell again, in a virtually identical manner. As before, he looked around for a possible source of attention, but this time he saw no one. Without a sound, he got up and continued running.

We don't intend to do it, but we encourage our children to act like victims when we're quick to give them sympathy and when we rescue them instead of satisfying their real need for simple acceptance and guidance. When they use victimhood as a Getting Behavior, we tend to give them what they *want* instead of what they *need*. In Chapter Nine I'll describe how a parent could handle the above situation—and other situations—in a way that a child is not encouraged to act like a victim. Children who are loved and taught to be responsible don't need to act like victims to protect themselves and get what they want.

Children Learning Victimhood by Observing Us

Children often learn to act like victims by watching us. When a child behaves in ways we don't like, we commonly say things like, "I'm disappointed in you," or "How could you do such a thing?" Or, perhaps more often, we indicate our disappointment without words—when we silently spear a child with a disgusted expression, for example. We act like they've hurt us, because we know that then they'll feel guilty, and they'll be more likely to do what we want and not do the things we disapprove of. The message we communicate to our children is "How could you possibly do this—*to me!!*" Without realizing it, we often act like enormous victims with our own children, thereby making them responsible for our happiness.

In the presence of our children we whine and complain about many things: the boss, our co-workers, our spouses, the government, the neighbors, the traffic, the weather, and so on. We blame other people for being monsters that treat us unfairly, instead of taking responsibility ourselves for how we feel and behave. Our children see us do this and thereby learn to act like victims themselves—especially with us. Children who act like victims, however, can get only Imitation Love as they manipulate us and others for attention and safety, and then they still feel unloved and alone.

Let's watch while one mother, Rebecca, manipulates her son, Justin, by acting like a victim, and in the process teaches him how to act like a victim.

On several occasions today Rebecca has instructed Justin to clean his room, but he has ignored her each time. Now he's sitting in front of the television when Rebecca comes into the room and says, "Justin, I've told you to clean that room. Please get up and do it now."

"Okay, Mom, I will," he says, but he doesn't move.

Rebecca has done this dance with Justin hundreds of times before, and it has never produced positive results. So she changes her tactics a little. "Justin," she says with a choke in her voice, "I've been working hard all day, and I just don't have time to beg you to do this. I'm tired, and after all I've done for you, the least you could do is clean your room without me having to ask you over and over."

Justin shrugs and sighs. "Okay, Mom, I'll do it."

Rebecca wasn't conscious of her ploy, but she was saying

- "Look at my pain." ("I've been working hard all day." "I'm tired.")
- "How could you add to my pain?" (I don't have time to beg you to do this.")
- "Look at all I've done for you."
- "How could you not help me?"

These are classic victim techniques and are entirely inappropriate for a parent to use with a child. It is the responsibility of parents to teach their children to be responsible, but the moment parents act like victims, what a child learns is not responsibility but obligation and guilt. To learn much more about how to properly teach a child responsibility, see the book *Real Love in Parenting*.

There are many ways we can act like victims with our children:

- We can say, "After all I've done for you, how could you . . ."
- We can say, "How could you talk to me like that?"
- We can quietly act hurt when they disappoint us, with or without tears.
- We can say to an adult child, "Why do you never call?" or "You haven't visited in months."

As we act like victims with our children, we can often persuade them to behave in ways we desire, but—as with all the Getting and Protecting Behaviors—our selfishness makes it quite impossible for our children to feel loved.

WHAT VICTIMS SAY

Victimhood is so widespread as to be nearly universal. It is important that we see how we act like victims, because if we don't see this behavior in ourselves, we are condemned to repeat this unproductive behavior over and over again. It can be helpful for us to review some of the common phrases and behaviors used by victims:

- "I couldn't help it." Victims always have an excuse. To be sure, there are often circumstances beyond our control, but only victims emphasize these, while non-victims freely admit and discuss the factors they *did* have control over.
- "Why do *I* have to do that?" When a task has to be done, it can't be given to *everyone. Somebody* has to do the job, which means that in that moment everyone else "gets out" of doing the job. Victims don't mind when *other people* get an assignment, but they have a tantrum in the moments when the "wheel of fortune" falls on their number.
- "You did *what*?" We say this when something is particularly distressing to us, and our real meaning is, "You did *what* to *me*?"
- "But you *said*_____" We say this when we perceive that people aren't doing exactly what they've promised to *us*. How dare

anyone fail to keep his or her promise to people as important as ourselves.
- "There wasn't time." Oh, the excuses we think up. We choose to put off doing a job day after day, and then at the last minute—surprise!—there isn't enough time. Then we blame it on the *clock* rather than taking responsibility for our own choices to procrastinate.
- (Sigh) How many times have we done this? Something happens that inconveniences us, or someone gives us an assignment we don't like, and we react by rolling our eyes and letting out a long, exasperated sigh. In that one action we communicate so many victim thoughts.
- "How could you do this?" The implication, of course, is "How could you do this *to me?*"
- "How could you say that?" Translation: "How dare you have said something accusing or inconsiderate to *me?*"
- "Did you see what he gave me for Christmas?" Most of us don't give genuine Christmas—or birthday or anniversary—*gifts*, which are given unconditionally. Instead we make Christmas *investments*, giving to people with an expectation that we'll get something in return: gratitude, appreciation, loyalty, a return gift, and so on. We prove the existence of our expectations on the occasions when we *don't* get what we expect and we become disappointed or irritated, as in the phrase above.
- "*But* _____ " How quickly we protest what we don't like, certain that our rights have been violated, that justice has been offended in some way. When we're given a task to do, the first word out of our mouths is often *but*. We say that word when we feel *we* have been victimized, but how often do we employ it in the defense of others?
- "Why does *he* get to have that?" Heaven forbid that someone else would ever get to have more of something good than we do. That would be unfair. Only a victim sees the world in this way.
- "Look at this mess!" Message: "How could you make a mess and inconvenience *me!*"
- "There's so much to do." Translation: "I carry such a burden. Woe is me. Does anyone do as much work as I do?"

- "I never get any help around here." Message: "No one appreciates me. I do so much for everyone else, but I never get any help in return. It's so unfair."
- "She didn't even remember my birthday." Translation: "I am so giving and thoughtful toward her—and everyone else, for that matter—but does anyone ever return my graciousness? Oh no."
- "My son never calls." Message: "After all I've done for him—I brought him into the world, nursed him, changed his diapers, took him to school, tucked him in at night, and so on—he is completely ungrateful. How could he do this to me?"
- "How many times have I had to tell you_____?" Translation: "Do you not understand who I am? If you did, you would never require that I ask for anything more than once. In fact, I shouldn't have to ask at all. You'd just *know* what I want."
- "You always have a headache." Translation: "Why did we even get married? You promised to love me, and yet you ignore me all the time. I never get what I want."
- "All he ever wants is sex." Meaning: "All he ever does is use me."
- "We never do anything together anymore." Translation: You never pay attention to *me*. You promised to love *me*, but you don't. You never keep your promises to *me*."
- "But you *promised*." Translation: "Breaking a promise to *me* is utterly unthinkable, because there is nothing in the world more important than I."
- The whining child. Children are born into this world with a right to expect one thing above all else. They have a right to be loved, and when they don't get that—when they are not loved unconditionally—they truly are victimized, and they *feel* like victims. In that condition, they respond with whining, complaining, resisting, and so many of the activities we abhor in children.
- "That's not fair." Victims are not talking here about true justice at all, only about their not getting what *they* wanted.
- "You have to go out of town again?" As a victim you don't consider the behavior of other people in terms of what *they*

need. You see their behavior only in terms of how it affects *you*. Victims see everything that way.
- "If only you would _____." Message: "Everything would be fine if only you would do your job better. Certainly I am doing my job just fine."
- "If it weren't for you _____." Message: "Everything would be fine if only you hadn't made that mistake. You're the problem. Certainly I'm not."
- "You *should* _____" or "People *should* _____" Should has purpose of keeping people in line, reminding them of their duty to do exactly what we want as victims.
- "So you're on *his* side?" Victims make everything about *them*, so everything is either *for* them or *against* them.
- "You're saying this is *my* fault?" Heaven forbid you should ever imply that a victim could be wrong. Victims simply can't admit that.
- Anger. Victims are almost always angry. It's a second language for them, because that's how they get what they want.
- "I'm so disappointed in you." If you do anything other than what a victim wants, you become a huge disappointment, an unacceptable blight on the face of the earth.
- "I'll remember that." Victims usually say this silently. If you disappoint a victim sufficiently, then you deserve any manner of revenge you'll ever receive.
- "You'll pay for that." Same as above.
- "I can't forgive him for that." Victims are so self-important that crimes against them are simply unforgivable. Besides, victims *need* their monsters to blame for everything that's gone wrong in their lives. If they forgive a monster, they have one less person to blame, and that would not be acceptable.

Following are some examples of children acting like victims:

- When we talk to them about a mistake they've made, they say, "I couldn't help it." They're claiming they had no responsibility for their own choices and were helpless victims of circumstance or of the actions of other people. That is rarely a true claim.
- When we tell them they can't buy something, they say, "But all my friends have one; it's not fair." They're claiming to

be victimized by us in the hope that we'll feel obligated to eliminate this grave injustice by giving them what they want.
- When we tell them they can't go somewhere, they counter with, "But everybody else is going."
- When we tell them they can't do something, they get that pathetic look on their faces as they say, "Pleeease." They imply that if we continue to ignore their pleas, we are unbelievably selfish and cruel.
- When we ask why an assigned task isn't done, they say, "I didn't have time," or "It was too hard."
- When children act hurt, and when they sulk, they're acting like victims. They've learned that the more wounded they appear, the less likely we are to punish them, and the more likely they are to get what they want and get away with unacceptable behavior.
- Children often choose to wait till the last minute to study for a test in school. Then when they're poorly prepared and get a bad grade, they blame the teacher for giving a "hard" or "unfair" test. They falsely portray themselves as victims.

🗫 Chapter Three 🗬

Victimhood and All the Other Getting and Protecting Behaviors

Imagine that you're in the kitchen, and you casually pick up a pot that's sitting on the counter, intending to put it on the sink. What you don't know is that someone else took that pot off the stove just moments ago, so the handle of the pot is still quite hot. As soon as you wrap your hand around that handle, the searing heat stimulates pain fibers in your skin that transmit neurochemical signals with impressive speed to your brain and spinal cord, after which you can react before you even consciously put together what has happened.

How would you react? You *could* run through the following reasoning in your mind: *I'll be darned, I had no idea this pot was hot. If I leave my hand here, this could have some really negative consequences, so I'd probably better unclench my hand and move it back at least a few inches.* Then you could pull your hand away—only your hand.

You *could* react in that way, but you won't. You won't *think* about it at all, and you won't pull just your hand away. No, in a single instant

- you'll holler like you've been shot. You might even say a word or two that under normal circumstances you wouldn't utter.

- your entire arm—not just your hand—will jerk back as far as possible in a single move. If someone happens to be standing immediately behind you, you might actually injure him or her with your exaggerated and violent motion.
- both your legs will stiffen involuntarily and cause you to jump back.
- your face will contort in a dramatic way.
- your other arm will also pull back rapidly, even though the hand on that side wasn't burned.
- muscles all over your body will contract: in your neck, chest, abdomen, and elsewhere.

When we're in physical pain, we react with every means available to us to eliminate or diminish our pain. Similarly, when we're in emotional pain, we also have a natural tendency to use all the Getting and Protecting Behaviors we're familiar with in order to achieve relief from our emptiness and fear. That's why victimhood almost never exists in isolation. It's usually accompanied by combinations of lying, attacking, running, and clinging.

When we're in pain, we don't think clearly. We become focused only on our pain, to the point, in fact, that we're often willing to hurt other people in the process of protecting ourselves—as in the case of jerking back from the stove above—or limit their right to make their own choices (the Law of Choice). On page 69 we discussed a few examples of how we indicate our willingness to violate the Law of Choice.

VICTIMHOOD AS THE FOUNDATION OF ALL THE OTHER GETTING AND PROTECTING BEHAVIORS

Victimhood is not only a powerful Getting and Protecting Behavior in its own right but is also the insidious root of all the other Getting and Protecting Behaviors. We would not lie, attack, run, and cling without also experiencing some sense of victimhood.

We use Protecting Behaviors, for example, only when we are afraid. Afraid of what? Afraid that someone—or some *thing*, in some cases—might do something to us. In other words, we're afraid of a perpetrator, a monster, an evil-doer, which puts us in the position of *victim*, the one who will be injured. Having put ourselves in that position, we then become afraid and must defend ourselves with one or more of the Protecting Behaviors.

In most cases we use Getting Behaviors for a similar reason. We lie, attack, act like victims, and cling because we believe that what we need is being *withheld* from us. This is classic victim reasoning, and with that belief we feel justified in doing almost anything to fill our emptiness.

Lying

One day I was visited in my office by a man named Wayne. He never stopped talking. I'm convinced I could have sat there for hours, and Wayne would not have paused except to breathe. People do this only when they're trying to get you to like them. They're literally building a case for themselves, proving to you beyond all possibility of denial that they are likable, so you couldn't possibly fail to accept them.

Finally, I interrupted. "Wayne, why are you here?"

"My minister just suggested that it might be nice to meet you."

This was his first obvious lie. Why would his minister send him just to chat with me? I knew his minister, and I knew he wouldn't send someone just to shoot the breeze with me, so there had to be a *reason* he sent Wayne. There were also a number of things Wayne had said before I interrupted him that didn't quite seem truthful. He had talked about his job, his hobbies, and other things, and on several occasions it seemed that he was exaggerating his accomplishments and positive qualities.

We need to remember two important characteristics of liars before we consider confronting them about their lies: First, they rarely *realize* they're lying. They lie to get Imitation Love and to protect themselves, and they usually engage in these activities quite unconsciously. Second, they don't usually welcome having their lies pointed out to them. Their lies protect them, and they're not eager to give up a tool that protects them from pain.

Understanding the above, I proceeded slowly. "How's your marriage?" I asked.

"It's good, good."

"Your job?"

"Great."

"Your kids?"

"They're fine."

Using the subject of children as a relatively safe starting point, I described my own children. Then I asked him to describe what his childhood was like. Initially he insisted that it was great, but as I questioned him about the details, it became obvious that his childhood was not a loving experience. His father was a very angry and critical man who was quick to find fault with Wayne, so Wayne learned at an early age to hide his mistakes from his father. He also learned to exaggerate his accomplishments to earn his father's praise, which was slow in coming. Wayne laughed about the occasions when he had deceived his father and gotten away with mistakes.

We talked about the definition of Real Love and about how rarely people get it in their lives. "When you were born," I said, "you wanted one thing from your father more than anything else. What was it?"

"To be loved."

"And did you get it? Did your father love you *unconditionally*?"

"After what we've talked about today, I'd say no, not even close."

"Let's be clear that we're not blaming him, just establishing the effect he had on your early life. We're just trying to better understand *you*. I'm sure he loved you as well as he knew how, but no, he did not love you unconditionally. Instead, he attacked you and criticized you and told you in hundreds of ways that he did *not* love you, and that hurt you more than anyone could ever know. You hated those *I don't love you* messages more than anything, so you learned to hide your mistakes from him, and you learned to exaggerate your accomplishment so that at least he'd give you praise temporarily. You did that because in the short term, Imitation Love feels better than nothing at all. You learned to *lie*."

"I guess I did. I never thought about it like that."

"And your father wounded you so many times that you were determined—quite unconsciously—that nobody else would do to you what he did. So you learned to lie to other people too—teachers, friends, bosses, whoever—both to protect yourself and to earn their praise. What's important is that you're still doing it. You're still lying to the people around you all the time, and you don't even realize it."

"How do I lie?"

"Let me emphasize again that you don't *realize* you're lying. You lie *only* because you believe that people won't accept you if you tell the truth. You believe they'll criticize you and not love you. And considering your past, you have plenty of reason to believe that. Here today, though, you have an opportunity to change your entire world. No kidding."

"I don't understand."

"A little bit ago, I asked you why you came to see me today, and you said you didn't know. Then I asked about your wife, your children, and your job, and you said everything was just fine. It is an absolute certainty that if you were talking to your minister, and he thought you and I should speak, something is wrong in your life. Has to be. He didn't send you here so you and I could talk about football. Now, it's entirely understandable that you'd be reluctant to talk about whatever is really going on, because you've been wounded and victimized so many times in the past, and now you protect yourself without even thinking about it. You lie to everyone, whether you need to or not. Why take a chance, right? You believe that if you protect yourself with everyone, then you won't ever get hurt. The problem with that is that then you're always alone."

"You don't have to discuss *anything* with me," I continued. "I'm only extending an opportunity here for you to do something different. I don't care what mistakes you've made. I don't care if your life is all put together or not. I won't be critical of you in any way. And you don't need to be successful in any way for me to like you."

There was a long pause as Wayne decided what he'd do next, and then he told me that his wife had left him, he was about to lose his job, and he had no friends. As he told the truth about himself, he could see and feel and hear from my words, posture, facial expression, tone of voice, and other signs that I didn't feel the slightest criticism of him. By his telling the truth, he had created an opportunity to feel seen, accepted, and loved, a pattern we discussed in Chapter One:

Truth → Seen → Accepted → Loved

I didn't do anything dramatic with Wayne. I didn't hug him or kiss him or tell him I loved him. I simply accepted him and cared about him, and he *felt* that. Real Love is a genuine power, and we really can feel it. As Wayne told the truth about himself, he felt as though a mountain had been taken off his shoulders, and that was the beginning of his changing the rest of his life.

We lie only to protect ourselves from pain and to fill our emptiness, and that's how victims live most of the time. They see the world as filled with perpetrators who are determined to hurt them and to take acceptance, respect, attention, praise, power, pleasure, and safety from them. If lying will prevent some of that injury, victims will not hesitate to do that.

To further illustrate the foundation of lying, imagine that you know for a certainty that I love you. You have previously shared with me every mistake in your life, and I have accepted you completely, without reservation. I have never hurt you nor given you any indication that I ever would. In that scenario, why would you ever lie to me? Lying wouldn't even make sense, because it would *serve no purpose*. Only when we feel like victims—when we suspect we'll be injured—do we lie to others.

Attacking

We can learn a lot about how victimhood is the foundation of attacking as we observe a man named Gary, who came to see me because he was having problems with his self-owned business. I soon learned that Gary motivated people with anger and intimidation, at work and everywhere else. Even his wife and children were afraid of him. He was a classic attacker, and no one would have thought of him as a victim. We tend to think of victims as mousy people who whine and complain a lot, and Gary certainly didn't fit that profile.

I discovered that Gary had been abandoned by his father at an early age and that his mother had been verbally and physically abusive toward him. He was large for his age, of average intelligence, and he soon learned in school that he could get what he wanted by physically intimidating his classmates. So he became the class bully.

As he got older—late in high school and especially in college—he found that being a bully had distinct disadvantages. People who were physically bullied would sometimes call the police, for example, and that proved to be a most unpleasant consequence. He did discover, though, that he could bully people emotionally with his anger, with criticism, and with guilt, so he continued to use these techniques for the rest of his life.

As we discussed Gary's approach to people, and as I put words to his aggressive, intimidating style of motivating people, he provided quite a number of excuses for his behavior:

- Referring to his employees: "But if I don't push them, I don't get a lick of work out of them."
- Referring to his wife: "But she doesn't listen to me until I finally raise my voice. Otherwise, she just ignores me."
- Referring to his children: "They're so irresponsible. I *have* to yell at them to get them to do anything at all."
- Referring to other drivers on the road: "But if I don't yell and honk my horn, they'll think they can just run me over and do anything they want to me."

Everyone saw Gary as a monster, as primarily an attacker. But look at the language above. In every one of these expressions, Gary is declaring that he is a victim. He believes he *has* to be angry and intimidating—he *has* to be an attacker—because otherwise no one pays attention to *him*. No one listens to *him*. No one helps *him*. People are trying to take advantage of *him*. Poor *him*. He believes that he's entirely justified in being angry and even in hurting people because, after all, *they hurt him first*. He is such a victim.

This is the key to understanding almost all attacking behavior. First we believe that someone has injured *us*, or taken something from *us*, and then we feel justified in lashing out to protect ourselves or to get something we want.

Gary often spoke harshly to his wife, Ellen, and then she in turn thought, "How could you talk to me like this? Look how you're hurting me"—a question and an accusation typical of victims—after which she felt entirely justified in attacking Gary with her own anger. We can't act like victims until we've first identified a perpetrator who's doing something *to* us—or is wickedly refusing to do something *for* us—and then we feel justified in responding however we want. When you believe someone is hurting you, defending yourself—even harshly—can seem like the only effective response. Gary and Ellen then competed for position as #1 Victim, each further justified by the anger of the other, and these conversations were always disastrous.

The familiar phrase "Hell hath no fury like a woman scorned" is really most useful as a statement about victimhood, *not* women.

Once we feel that someone has hurt us, we can rationalize almost any behavior as a defense. Imagine, for example, that I'm hitting you with a baseball bat. There's a very real possibility that I could injure you seriously, maybe even kill you. Would you feel justified in grabbing a stick and hitting me back in order to defend yourself? Almost certainly you would. But what if you hit me and broke my arm? It would be so easy for you to reason that I had brought the injury upon myself by attacking you, and that you were only defending yourself.

Victims feel that way about their anger and other attacking behaviors. They feel that once you've injured them, you've given up all rights as a human being and deserve whatever happens to you.

At the core of most of the terrible events and monsters in our history is victimhood. I have studied history for most of my life, and I am impressed with the consistency of how wars begin, for example. One country does something that the second country finds offensive. The second country judges that it has been injured in some way and then attacks the first country in righteous indignation, to wipe away the injury, real or perceived. This pattern can also be seen between individuals, families, tribes, and so on. In Chapter Six I'll present some examples of how victimhood causes or worsens many of the conditions we struggle with as individuals and groups: unhappy marriages, conflict at work, racial prejudice, and war, to name a few. I'll also demonstrate how victimhood is at the root of the behavior of those we view as monsters: Adolf Hitler and Saddam Hussein, for example.

Running

Earlier in this chapter we met Gary and Ellen, a married couple. Gary's elderly mother lived about a mile away and depended upon her son in a number of ways: trips to doctors' offices, some of the shopping, repairs around the house, and so on. Gary tended to foist these responsibilities on Ellen, feeling justified because he worked full time, while Ellen had a part-time job.

At dinner one evening, Gary asked, "Did you go over to my mother's place today?"

"Yes, I did," said Ellen. "I saw her this afternoon."

Although Ellen's answer was technically correct, she was actually lying. Gary's mother was quite demanding and had wanted to spend time talking with someone that day. She was lonely. Gary had promised her, in fact, that Ellen would drop by and spend time with her, and Ellen knew that both Gary and his mother expected her to spend some significant time with his mother that day. What Ellen did, however, was pass by the older woman's house for about two minutes to drop off some groceries. She didn't especially like spending time with her mother-in-law, and she resented Gary's essentially "dumping" his mother on her, so she often did as little as possible in that regard.

"She tells me that you were hardly there for a second," said Gary with considerable accusation in his voice.

"Then maybe *you* should spend more time with her. How about that? She's *your* mother, and you hardly ever see her." In the world of a victim, one good accusation certainly deserves another. Ellen felt victimized by Gary's comment—and certainly he was attacking her—so she defended herself with an attack of her own. Regrettably, as we discussed on pages 6-10, this amounts to two people shouting *I don't love you* at each other. The conversation was absolutely doomed.

"I work full time," Gary said. "You don't." This was a combination of attacking—because he was angry—and lying, because his work schedule didn't begin to explain why he didn't spend more time with his mother. He simply didn't like being around her anymore than Ellen did.

"A handy excuse for you," said Ellen. "Is that the one you use for not spending time with me too?" Ellen was now in full-blown attack mode.

"Geez, all I did was ask you if you'd been over to visit my mother," Gary said, and then he walked out of the room in a huff. Gary was an expert attacker, but on occasion Ellen got fed up and really turned her guns on him. Bullies are looking for relatively easy, defenseless prey. They're not eager to be wounded in return, so if their victims turn and attack them, they will often run. Gary chose to play the part of the victim here as Ellen attacked him for being a lousy husband, and then he responded by running.

Clinging

As I said in Chapter One, clinging is obvious when a child is holding tightly to his mother's skirt. As adults we cling emotionally in other ways:

- Gifts. If we give someone a gift with any expectation of something in return—a gift, recognition, gratitude—we are clinging. We're trying to get some kind of affection. Sometimes we don't realize we're clinging until *after* we've given the gift and then the other person doesn't give us what we'd expected. Our subsequent disappointment or irritation are sure signs that we had expectations and were clinging.
- Bragging. When we broadcast the good things we do—sometimes subtly, even "humbly"—we often do so for the purpose of gathering recognition and praise, which are forms of Imitation Love.
- "I love you." When we say this to a partner, we almost always have strong expectations that he or she will say something like it in return. In that case, we said "I love you" to get something for ourselves. We were clinging.
- Begging. Your partner gets up to leave and you say, "Do you have to go now?" Or your partner tells you his or her plans for the weekend, and you say, "Do you have to play golf again?"
- Gratitude. A simple *thank you* can be an expression of healthy gratitude. When we go on and on, however, describing how *very, very* grateful we are, that's usually an indication that we're manipulating that person to repeat the action we enjoyed.

Even clinging has its roots in victimhood. We wouldn't have to cling if other people recognized *our* needs, if they put *us* appropriately high in their list of priorities, and if they didn't withhold from *us* what we needed.

WHY VICTIMHOOD?

Although we all tend to use various combinations of all the Getting and Protecting Behaviors from time to time, each of us also has a tendency to use one or two of these behaviors more than the others. Some of us are primarily attackers, others primarily victims, and so on. Why is that? What makes someone primarily a victim, for example? The answer to this question has many potential facets—genetic, hormonal, sociological, and behavioral—but here I will deal only with how we *learn* to use one Getting and Protecting Behavior over another.

Children tend to mimic the behaviors they've seen in their parents. If one or both parents are experts at acting like victims, for example, it's very likely that their children will use the same behavior. Within the same family, however, each child tends to use one Getting and Protecting Behavior more than the other children do. We can begin to see one reason why this happens as we observe a young child named Mike.

When Mike was a baby, much of what he did—his smiles, his first steps, his first words—was the subject of praise and admiration. He was too cute for words, and he loved the attention he received. On the other hand, being a young child has significant drawbacks: You're always being told what to do; you're pulled here and there; you're buckled in, tucked in, and wiped off; you have no say in anything; and things are always being put on you, taken off you, poured down you, and stuck in you or up you. That can get to be a real drag.

So one day when Mother was putting Mike's coat on him, he'd had enough. He stomped his little feet and shouted *No!* Instantly his mother stopped putting on his coat, and suddenly he was the object of a great deal of attention. In that moment Mike had discovered the power of anger, or attacking. The next day, when he didn't get something else he wanted, he furiously demanded it, and his flustered mother gave in to his demands. Understandably, Mike began to repeat these behaviors often, and his parents were utterly baffled by the transformation of this child who had once been their "little angel."

There was nothing mysterious about this metamorphosis. He had simply learned that anger is a powerful tool, and he continued to use it because *it worked*—to protect himself and to get what he wanted. Ironically, he continued to use anger—and to get much better at it—in great part because of his parents' example. He noticed that when he was resistant to what he was told, his parents often became irritated, and that attitude then highly motivated him to do what he was told. When they became angry, he was afraid of losing their approval, so he quickly changed his behavior to conform to their wishes. Children are not stupid. Increasingly, Mike figured out that he could use the same motivating behavior—anger—to persuade other people to do what *he* wanted. He learned that he could do unto others as had been done unto him. Two-year-olds are not malicious, just practical. We all tend to do what we've learned and what works.

When Mike was two, his sister Amanda was born. One day when Mike was four, he grabbed a toy from Amanda, now two, and she made one of her first attempts to use attacking as a Getting and Protecting Behavior—much as Mike had done at the same age. Angrily, she shouted *No!* and tried to take the toy back. But Amanda was about to discover that *her* world at age two—with Mike in it—was quite different from the world *Mike* had known at age two. At age four, Mike had been practicing for two years using anger and other forms of attacking, and he had become an expert.

So Amanda was badly outmatched, her ability to attack being severely limited by her size and experience. Mike found Amanda's feeble counter-attack laughable, and he responded by yelling at her and pushing her down. Amanda couldn't begin to compete as an attacker, and in the process she learned an indelible lesson: Attacking is not an effective way to get what I want.

Learning that attacking was ineffective, Amanda nonetheless could not settle for no Imitation Love at all. That would have been intolerable. So she ran to her mother, screaming as though someone had stuck a knife in her leg. Her mother came and severely chastised Mike for his behavior, and Amanda experienced her first delicious taste of the rewards that come with acting like a victim. It was great, and it helped to motivate her to use this behavior for the rest of her life.

All children have a tendency to use attacking, because it's such an effective tool and because they've seen their parents use it often. Second and subsequent children, however, are at a real disadvantage in attacking, so they tend to become more proficient at the use of other Getting and Protecting Behaviors. Several books have been written about the characteristics of children based on their birth order. They describe firstborns as more aggressive, and the other children as more "social." It would be more accurate to say that second and subsequent children are better at lying, acting like victims, and clinging. This description of birth order characteristics is, of course, a generalization.

In some families, for example, the second child is the attacker—perhaps because the firstborn is a girl, or for other reasons.

DANCING FROM ONE GETTING AND PROTECTING BEHAVIOR TO ANOTHER

At various times in my life, I've been quite an outdoors person, and in my adventures with others we have used canoes, motorcycles, buses, trucks, cars, rappelling equipment, scuba gear, boots, zip lines, spelunking equipment, tents, and other gear in the accomplishment of our goals. We changed the equipment we used according to the terrain we were in and the activities we were engaged in.

People who are empty and afraid use Getting and Protecting Behaviors in a similar way, like tools they pick up and use according to what they need in any given situation. Moreover, we all have a certain *pattern* of Getting and Protecting Behaviors we tend to use. To illustrate this, let's look at a conversation between Kate and her husband, Scott.

From Victimhood to Attacking

"You never touch me anymore," said Kate, acting like a victim.

"You might remember," said Scott with a real bite in his voice, "that two nights ago I tried to touch you, and look how that turned out." Scott hated it when Kate acted like a victim. It made him feel small and powerless, so he often reacted by attacking her, which made him feel stronger, more in control, and less powerless.

"Oh come on," she said, "that wasn't *touching*. You just wanted *sex*. That's all you ever want. You never think about *me*." Kate was escalating her victimhood here, hoping to make Scott feel guilty and give her some sympathy. It didn't work.

"Oh, heaven forbid I should ever want sex. Why would a healthy married man ever want sex anyway? For all the sexual attention I get from you, I'd just as well have a roommate. Most men would just go out get what they needed." As Kate increased her victimhood, Scott retaliated with increased attacking, including a veiled threat here.

On some occasions, Kate could manipulate Scott with her victimhood to stop attacking her, but on this particular occasion she sensed that this contest of victimhood versus attacking was producing no clear winner. So she decided to change her tactics, from acting like a victim to attacking.

"Maybe if you ever paid me any attention, I'd *feel* like having sex with you. As it is, you're no great wonder as a husband either."

They exchanged insults for several minutes, during which they didn't hesitate to exaggerate the offenses of their partner or minimize their own, which of course is the Getting and Protecting Behavior of lying. Eventually Scott began to feel overwhelmed. He finally stomped out of the room, running from the whole situation. In the space of just a few minutes, they had employed the tools of acting like victims, attacking, lying, and running in their dance of relationship death.

From Attacking to Victimhood

On another occasion, Scott and Kate had exchanged unkind comments with one another for several minutes when finally it became apparent that neither of them had a superior ability to wound the other. At some point Kate realized that if she continued in this exchange, although it would give her the considerable enjoyment of cutting live chunks of flesh from Scott's quivering body, it would also result in considerable pain of her own. Not eager to continue this one-for-one trading of pain, Kate changed her approach:

"Sure," Kate said. "You just keep it up. Just keep being unkind to me. You've never really cared about me anyway," she said while squeezing tears from her eyes.

As attackers they were well matched, but in a single moment Kate changed the game completely by successfully labeling Scott as a monster. If he continued speaking in an unkind tone for another second after that, he knew he would be seen as the villain in their conversation, even though nobody else was watching their interaction.

From Infancy to Prison

In order to illustrate even further how the use of Getting and Protecting Behaviors can evolve over time, let me tell you about my visit in prison with Jack, who was serving a very long sentence for his third violent felony. He had treated a number of people very badly, and in return society had pretty much thrown him away as an unredeemable and worthless object. To most people he had ceased to be a human being at all. His family—ex-wife, children, parents, and siblings—would have nothing to do with him. His appeal attorney wouldn't answer his letters. He had become utterly alone in the world.

I visited him on several occasions and learned that he had been treated abominably as a child. His father left the family before he was born, and his mother was far too occupied with her drug addiction to spend much time with him. On the occasions when she was sober, she was demanding and critical. He remembers being beaten whenever he didn't do what she wanted, which was several times a week. The horror stories of his childhood went on and on. As a very young child, therefore, he learned that the world was a harsh and lonely place, where there was no hope of support or compassion. I can't begin to overstate what a damaging wound that is.

So, understandably, Jack withdrew from the world. He withdrew from the pain. He ran. He was quiet and shy as a child. He never spoke in class, which his teachers actually thought was a good quality, because he never caused them any problems. No one ever took an interest in him, so his grades steadily slipped until he was failing all his subjects and eventually left high school. He moved from one poorly paid job to another, frustrated at the lack of income, acceptance, and respect.

Eventually, simply running wasn't enough. He was tired of the lack of everything—Real and Imitation Love—in his life, so he began to drink and use drugs more and more. One night he and his friends got drunk and robbed a convenience store, and he found that very exciting. For a few moments, he experienced an infusion of power that he'd never known before. Partially fortified with alcohol, he began to experiment with anger and violence as Getting Behaviors, and he enjoyed the power he derived from them.

He became increasingly violent, to the point that even his friends became afraid of him. He had to do something to finance his drug habit, so he dealt in drugs, and finally he was caught for assaulting someone while under the influence of cocaine. He served his sentence, but he was imprisoned twice more for other violent crimes while intoxicated.

Like the rest of us, Jack began his life as a cute, innocent child. And then he was tragically victimized. He was what I described in Chapter One as a true victim. Then, as he got older, he began to *act* like a victim. Then he learned to run, yet another Protecting Behavior. Then he discovered attacking and lying. By the time I met him in prison, he was a poster child for all the Getting and Protecting Behaviors.

We all tend to use the Getting and Protecting Behaviors that we're taught and the ones that work, and we also tend to use combinations of all of them.

☙ Chapter Four ❧

The Rewards of Victimhood

In previous chapters we discussed somewhat the terribly negative effects we see on our personal lives and on our relationships when we act like victims. So why do we continue to use this Getting and Protecting Behavior? Because the immediate rewards are great.

We don't engage in our Getting and Protecting Behaviors for no reason. We *get* something from them. So what is it? What do we get in return for acting like victims, for example? When we act like victims, we

- often gain a position of untouchable self-righteousness.
- can make people feel guilty, and then they'll stop hurting us.
- can manipulate people for sympathy and attention.
- can manipulate people for support and power.
- completely avoid responsibility.
- create a place in the world where we belong.

Each of these is a powerful reward, but none of them is Real Love, which is the only thing that can make us genuinely happy.

Now let's discuss each of these "advantages" to acting like victims.

VICTIMS OFTEN HOLD A POSITION OF UNTOUCHABLE SELF-RIGHTEOUSNESS

Can you remember what it was like when you were in grade school and one of your classmates came into the room with a cast on his arm? Instantly he was the center of attention, wasn't he? Everybody gathered around to ask, What happened? Did you have to go to the hospital? Does it hurt? When does the cast come off? Does it itch? And so on. Then everybody signed the cast, each person thinking of something especially clever to say while looking for a place of prominence for his or her signature.

There has always been a certain degree of glory attached to being injured. Our wounds set us apart, and if our wounds were *inflicted upon us* in some *good cause* or in some *unjust way*, we are elevated to an even higher plain of righteousness. Witness, for example, the deaths of those involved in the terrorist attacks of September 11, 2001. Between the World Trade Center, the Pentagon, and the four planes involved, 2,976 people died. The outpouring of sympathy for those who died and their families was exceptional—in letters, phone calls, emails, prayers, visits to the sites, memorials erected, radio and television tributes, and millions of dollars contributed.

By contrast, 450,000 die every year as a result of using tobacco, which means that tobacco kills as many people *every 2.4 days* as the terrorists killed on September 11. And these deaths *continue to occur every day*, every year, not to mention the associated sickness and disability. But where is the outcry over these deaths? They are virtually unnoticed on the social radar, in great part because they rank lower on the Victim Scale. When something is done *to us*, we become rather caught up in the process of crying foul, and we expect a great deal of attention, while our right to do so is greatly limited when we participate in the causation of our own injuries.

In no way am I diminishing the pain of those who directly suffered or of those families who lost loved ones because of the events of September 11, but loss is loss, and death is death. The survivors of September 11 feel their pain no more keenly than do thousands of others who suffer or lose family members every day. In our society, however, victimhood inappropriately confers a much greater *value* on the loss of someone who was treated unjustly—the truly "deserving victim"—and everyone else is then *expected* to devote greater attention and sympathy to those who were victimized in that way. Note, for example, how angry some families of 9/11 victims became that they didn't get *more* sympathy, attention, and monetary compensation than they thought they deserved as victims. The "deserving victim" myth is not serving us well, as we shall discuss in Chapters Five and Six.

As victims we treasure the badges of honor we have earned by being inconvenienced and injured. In order to earn these badges—and our official social status as victims—we feel obligated to provide endless lists of evidence that prove our worthiness:

- We tell people about the many virtuous and saintly things we have done for others, proving that we deserve to be treated better than we have been.
- We describe in exquisite detail the events that prove we have been treated unfairly. As victims we talk a great deal. On the whole, people who talk a lot are either defending themselves or convincing others that they are worthy of acceptance.
- Without being asked, we eagerly bring up our wounds, past and present, and we very much enjoy discussing them.
- We love to talk about the flaws of other people. The more mistakes other people make—and therefore the more flawed they are—the more proof we have that other people must be the cause of our pain.

As victims we display our wounds with pride and *expect* people to give us the attention and sympathy we have earned. We *demand* it. In a way, we actually hold people hostage with our victimhood. How, we reason, could anyone possibly question our right to whatever we want while we are in such pain, especially if it has been unjustly inflicted upon us? Other people *dare not refuse* to give us the sympathy we deserve.

As an illustration of how victims hold everyone else hostage, let me share an account of an experience I had in a Real Love group I once visited in a state far from my home. One woman in the group, Julie, began to tell a story of many sorrows, mostly about how her husband was a thoughtless, uncaring, inconsiderate human being who had no appreciation for her whatever. As she spoke, three things became clear:

- Julie had told these stories many times before.
- She was just getting warmed up on the beginning of a list that would go on and on, perhaps for the entire time of the group.
- No one in the group had the slightest intention of interrupting her tale. How could they? She was in such pain that no one had the heart to interrupt.

After Julie had spoken for five minutes, I interrupted. "It's clear that your husband has no idea how to love you."

"I'll say he doesn't. He can be such a—"

Again I interrupted what was about to become a long and unproductive tirade. "And his inability to love you must be quite painful to you. But in all the times you have complained to him about his behavior, and in all the times you have described his behavior to the people here in this meeting and everywhere else, has he ever changed? Even a little?"

There was a pause. "No."

"So after trying to *change him* roughly several thousand times now, it should be pretty clear that you're not likely to succeed, wouldn't you say?"

"Well..."

"I'm not giving *my* opinion here. You've proven with *your* experience—over a period of many years—that your efforts to change *him* are doomed. So let's try something different instead. Let's talk about *you*. What do *you* do in your relationship that makes your marriage unloving? How are *you* unloving?"

Julie looked almost like she'd been slapped, and there was a wide-eyed reaction from the people in the room too. This woman had held the group hostage for a long time with her victimhood. They had been held captive by her pain, and it had never occurred to them to question what part *she* played in her situation. That is how thoroughly victims seduce and imprison the people around them. We don't *dare* question a victim, because we don't want to be the one person in the room who appears to be unsympathetic, heartless, and perhaps even cruel. And because we're all afraid to speak up, the victim continues unquestioned in his or her victimhood forever.

As a victim I am in a powerful, almost unassailable, position. And, ironically, the more you try to attack or undermine me, the more you actually *serve* my cause. You see, if I can demonstrate how you are treating me unkindly, unfairly, or hurtfully, you become a real monster—in my eyes and often in the eyes of others—which further confirms my position as a victim. As a victim, I actually love monsters. I *need* them to justify my victimhood. Having proven yourself to be a monster, I can now use you as a kind of moral basement above which my position is always superior. As long as I have my monsters, I can feel relatively good and worthwhile by comparison, in addition to feeling like a victim.

On pages 216-18 we'll talk about how the remainder of the above conversation went. In later chapters we'll also discuss how we can eliminate victimhood in ourselves and how we can respond to it in others.

The Three Motivations for Responding to Victims

Because of the self-righteous position victims take—and the genuinely sacred place society often confers upon them—we tend to respond to victims with at least three motivations:

- To our credit, in part we really do want to help them. We genuinely care about them and want to relieve their pain and fill their emptiness.
- Regrettably, we are also motivated by a fear of *not* helping them or sympathizing with them. As I suggested above, when someone claims to have been unfairly treated—or to be in pain or have an overwhelming need—who wants to be the *one* person who appears to be unsympathetic? This is a very unhealthy motivation for helping people.
- We want to help them simply to get them to quit complaining.

Victims make use of all the above motivations. In order to appeal to our genuine desire to help them, they give us abundant evidence of their needs—genuine, exaggerated, and imagined. In order to appeal to our fear of *not* helping them, they tell us how unfairly they've been treated, how badly others have neglected them, and so on. Victims have no shame about using other people in any way they can.

Victims never have to be wrong

In Chapter One we discussed that the primary reason we lie is to avoid the unbearably painful position of being exposed to the possibility of having people withdraw their love from us when we make our mistakes. As victims we're already in chronic pain. We certainly can't allow anything to happen that might increase that pain, so we absolutely cannot admit being wrong—about anything. If we were to admit being wrong

- we might lose our treasured positions as victims. We can be victims *only* if we have a perpetrator, a monster, who must by definition be *wrong*—morally, ethically, legally, technically, and astrologically, if need be. If we admitted to being wrong in any way, we'd lose some of our position on the high ground, and that would be very disorienting. If we couldn't be victims, how could we manipulate people?
- we would expose ourselves to criticism, ridicule, and every other kind of attack. We would expose ourselves to feeling even more unloved, to even more pain. That would be unthinkable.

As victims, we never *have* to admit that we're wrong. After all, we've been *wounded*. How could being wounded be wrong? When we have been wounded, it's pretty easy to convince people that any fault must lie with those who perpetrated the wound.

In any given situation we have so many ways to act like victims, shift the blame to other people, and thereby retain the position of untouchable self-righteousness. Let's look at a few such scenarios:

- At work, your department is two days behind schedule in shipping out an important order, and the boss is angry. Many people have been involved in this effort, but you—by way of inattention, procrastination, and some carelessness—are responsible for most of the delay. When the boss demands an explanation, you remember that yesterday the billing department was not only slow in getting some information to you but also rude to you on the phone. By the time you spoke to the people in billing, there was no way the order could have gone out on time, but such facts are irrelevant to a victim. When we feel wronged, we feel justified in heaping as much blame as possible on any perpetrator, and so it is with

you in this situation. You respond, "I'm sorry, but the billing department just didn't get me the data I requested on time." You've blamed the entire delay on people who were responsible for only a small portion of it, if any.
- You had an unpleasant conversation with your husband, during which both of you said some rather unkind things. A friend at work notices that you appear to be upset and asks what is wrong. You blame it entirely on your husband, saying, "He even hung up on me." You see, if he did something especially "bad," you can act hurt and feel justified in blaming him for *all* the animosity of the conversation, even though you were responsible for a considerable part of it.
- "He hit me first." Children love this one. They believe that if a sibling hits them first, any behavior that follows is the fault of the initial perpetrator. Politicians and entire nations are also fond of this particular excuse.

The Downside

Although victims enjoy the self-righteousness of their position, the negative consequences of acting like victims are overwhelming. We'll be discussing these in the next chapter.

VICTIMS MAKE PEOPLE FEEL GUILTY, SO THEY'LL STOP HURTING THEM

One summer day I watched two dogs fighting. It was a rather savage affair, accompanied by snarling, growling, snapping, biting, twisting, and turning on both sides, all for the purpose of intimidating and gaining physical advantage. Both dogs were impressive in their ferocity. For a while, the contest appeared to be evenly matched, but then the slightly larger dog tore into the neck of the smaller dog, who began to bleed.

Within a few seconds, the smaller dog suddenly rolled over onto his back, completely exposed his belly, and transformed from a snarling, frightening beast into a quivering, whimpering puddle of submission. Although the larger dog could easily have killed the smaller one in that moment, the instant the smaller dog surrendered, the other dog stopped attacking him. It was remarkable how quickly and completely the entire tone of the encounter had changed. This is not an uncommon event in contests between dogs and between members of some other species of animals. When they sense that their lives are at risk, they stop attacking their opponent and completely expose themselves, thereby throwing themselves upon the mercy of their attacker. That usually ends the conflict.

Human victims behave in a similar way. When they are being attacked emotionally, they often limit their injuries by rolling over on their backs—metaphorically speaking—where they cry out their surrender and—more importantly—declare to everyone else that only a truly monstrous character would continue to hurt or threaten them. At that point if their attacker continues the assault he does so at the risk of being severely judged morally by everyone else. That risk is often enough to intimidate an attacker and bring a stop to his or her attack of a victim. Victims make us feel too guilty if we continue in our process of injuring them.

On another summer day I was in an amusement park with a heavy crowd of people. There were so many people and so much noise that one could hardly think, but in the midst of all this noise, one child shrieked, "OW! You're hurting me!!" At that moment everyone within earshot stopped what he or she was doing, turned, and looked at the father of that child, who was trying to wrestle his son into a stroller. They speared him with looks of intense accusation, in one voice shouting with their thoughts, "How could you do that to an innocent child? You are such a monster!"

The unspoken accusations and the guilt paralyzed the father, who was instantly transfigured from a condition of aggression and control to an attitude of being tentative and defensive. He stopped wrestling with the child and began mumbling to himself and to the child. I could almost hear him justifying himself under his breath to the entire crowd.

Such is the power of the victim. We have many ways of acting hurt, which often succeed in making people feel guilty and succeed in motivating them to give us what we want. Following are a few examples of victims manipulating people with guilt:

- You've left something at the repair shop, but when you call about picking the item up on the appointed day, you're told that it's not ready. You say, with a slight whine in your voice,

"But you *promised* you'd have this done by four o'clock *today*." With your tone, you're communicating, "You've broken your promise. I was counting on you. You're both hurting my feelings and inconveniencing me." And of course you say this in the hope that the person on the phone will feel guilty enough that he'll then move your item to the top of the list to be repaired, thereby eliminating your inconvenience.

- On pages 57-9 we met Elise, who was hurt that her mother-in-law was critical and inconsiderate. She actually believed—although she couldn't have put it into these words on her own—that if she acted hurt enough, her mother-in-law would feel guilty about her abominable behavior and stop it.
- On pages 59-61 we also met Andy, who had a hope similar to Elise's. He believed his boss was being thoughtless, and he believed that if he acted offended enough, his boss would somehow sense his pain, sympathize with him, and cease his inconsiderate behavior. What a fantasy.
- When our children don't have their chores done before an important event—a school dance, an engagement with their friends, and so on—they say things like, "But I didn't have time." What they're suggesting is that if they "couldn't help it"—a classic victim ploy—then how could we possibly require them to do their work or forbid them from going out with their friends? It would be monstrous of us to restrict them in that manner. They're trying to make us feel too guilty to impose consequences that they have in fact brought upon themselves.

VICTIMS MANIPULATE PEOPLE FOR SYMPATHY AND ATTENTION

Earning the respect of other people often requires considerable time and effort. The same is true of earning power, money, and approval. And even after we've expended a lot of time and energy, the outcome of our efforts can be unpredictable. Despite all your efforts, you can't be absolutely certain of receiving the respect, power, money, or approval you're seeking.

Earning sympathy, however, is usually quite another matter. If you walk into a room with blood dripping from your arm, for example, you're pretty much guaranteed to receive sympathy from almost everyone—instantly, with very little effort, and with much greater predictability than you could expect praise or power for your efforts. As victims we have discovered this reliable source of Imitation Love, and we often use it to our advantage, sometimes many times a day.

One day I was visiting a friend, and one of her children fell and skinned his knee. This mother had been thoroughly trained as a victim herself, so she in turn had trained her children in the same art. When this child fell, he put up a howl worthy of someone being disemboweled. I'm not discounting the child's pain, but after raising seven children myself, and after working in emergency rooms for many years, I do have a sense of what does and does not constitute a significant injury. This child's injury was slight, at worst, but because he knew his mother would pour on the sympathy, he put on quite a show for her.

She certainly fulfilled his expectations and smothered him with attention, sympathy, kisses, everything. She delicately bathed a wound that was barely visible, all the while expressing her concern that it would become infected or worse. Then she dressed it—overdressed it, actually—with bandages, to the point that the child could have passed for a post-operative bone-graft patient. Toward the end of this display, the boy's two-year-old sister appeared and pointed at *her* knee, which had not been traumatized. She had been watching all the attention that the young victim had been receiving, and she wanted some of the same for her "wound" too.

Without meaning to, this mother was teaching her children that victims get the attention they want. It should be no surprise to learn that her children whined and complained at her continually, and, ironically, their behavior utterly baffled her.

Exactly what do victims *do* with sympathy? How does it serve them? With sympathy, victims

- receive ratification of their worth. Sympathy becomes a form of praise. Every time someone sympathizes with them, victims hear that as personal acceptance and agreement with their position. They feel more worthwhile.
- feel connected to the people who sympathize with them. With that connection, victims feel less empty, and since emptiness is a huge source of pain in their lives, sympathy is most welcome.

- simply feel virtuous, no matter what is going on around them. Victims accumulate sympathy like some people accumulate dollars. The more they get, the more they acquire a sense of moral superiority. With that feeling of superiority, they rise above whatever conflict is going on around them, and then they feel like they don't have to get involved.
- feel powerful. When you realize that by acting like a victim you can consistently manipulate people to give you the sympathy you want, that is a powerful feeling. The power to manipulate people to do anything consistently can be quite intoxicating.

We manipulate people for sympathy in a variety of ways:

- We emphasize how we've been hurt. "Look at what he did to me." "Look at all my wounds." "What she did has caused me so much pain."
- We talk about how unfair everyone has been to us.
- We make excuses for our failings: Things are so hard. There isn't time. There aren't enough resources.
- We talk about the oppression of the group to which we belong.

The False Victim

Victims get so much attention that some people actually *pretend* to be victims in order to get in on all the sympathy and attention, much like the two-year-old girl described immediately above.

The 15-year-old Rape Victim

In the 1980's there was a teenage black girl who disappeared for four days. She was finally found alive in a garbage bag near her apartment complex, where it was discovered that she had been smeared in feces, had racial slurs written on her torso in charcoal, and claimed to have been raped. The publicity surrounding the case was overwhelming, with something on every newspaper and news broadcast for weeks. Certain attorneys and celebrities known for using victims as launching pads for their own agendas made impassioned pleas on her behalf to the entire nation.

After seven months of examining police and medical records and listening to the testimony of 180 witnesses, the grand jury determined that the girl's charges were false and that her condition had been self-inflicted. Witnesses testified that she admitted her testimony was false and that they had seen her crawl into the bag herself.

Why did she lie? Some suggest that she had already been grounded on the day she disappeared and had visited her boyfriend in a nearby jail. She knew that if she acted like the victim of a heinous crime, she would get a lot of sympathy and attention and couldn't possibly get in trouble for violating her restriction to stay at home. Acting like a victim is powerful stuff.

If this explanation isn't true, the only other one that makes sense is that she acted like a victim simply for the sympathy and attention she would receive. She was the object of national media attention for some time. Celebrities came from all over the country to indicate their support for her. The family received tens of thousands of dollars. Whichever explanation was true, victimhood was the motivation, and it proved very profitable for her. If you can't be a real victim, you can become a False Victim. The sympathy and attention received are the same.

Repressed Memories and False Memory Syndrome

In the past twenty years or perhaps longer, it has become increasingly common for therapists to help clients uncover "repressed memories," usually of sexual trauma from their childhoods. Regrettably, these memories then often develop into confrontations with the supposed perpetrators—usually family members—and not uncommonly evolve into legal cases.

The accusations associated with these "repressed memories" are enormously problematic for a number of reasons:

- In most cases, there are no witnesses to directly confirm the accusations of the victim, so it comes down to the testimony of one person against the testimony of another.
- These memories tear families apart and often initiate legal proceedings.
- Our society is geared toward victims for reasons we have discussed in this chapter thus far, for reasons we'll discuss

further later in this chapter, and for reasons we'll discuss in Chapter Six. The accused in these cases therefore has a difficult time finding a neutral audience or jury.
- Our society has a special intolerance for those who have sexually mistreated children, and since we have a tendency to leap to the defense of those who even *might* have been sexually mistreated, the accused in these cases have yet another reason to find neutral treatment and fair trials difficult to obtain.
- Lastly, human memory is notoriously unreliable. Just a couple of illustrations here will suffice: First, students at Boston University were shown a series of slides and asked to pay close attention. Between 15 minutes and 48 hours later they were asked to look though another series of photos and decide if they had seen them in the first slide show. Unknown to the students, the first series of slides was of the "causes" of a series of accidents, for example a student carelessly leaning back in his chair or a rip in a grocery bag, while the second series was of the "effects," such as the student falling on the floor and a woman picking up groceries scattered across the floor. So the pictures were actually quite dissimilar, linked only by cause and effect. But when they were shown the second series, 68% of the time students "remembered" seeing the "cause" photo for the second time. They created the memory themselves by filling in the gap between the cause and the effect photos.

Second, in 1992 an El Al cargo flight smashed into an apartment building outside Amsterdam, killing 39 residents and all four crew members in a fiery explosion. Ten months later, Dutch psychologists quizzed colleagues about how well they remembered television footage of the crash. Most remembered it so well that they could describe whether the fuselage was aflame before it hit, where the plane fell after impact, and other details. But there was no such footage: People fabricated their memories of *video* details from what they *read* in newspapers, what they heard in discussions with friends, and from other sources.

Are there cases where people have been sexually abused as children and repressed those memories? Certainly. Most of us have more than enough pain to handle from moment to moment, and we simply cannot handle the additional burden of carrying around extraordinarily painful memories from childhood. On many occasions I have asked adults to tell me some specific experiences they had with their parents, only to hear that they can't recall any. With further gentle questioning over time, these adults can recall many experiences, and they are uniformly quite unpleasant. Nobody represses happy memories.

It only makes sense that some of these repressed memories would be of childhood sexual trauma, but I also firmly believe that these repressed memories of childhood sexual trauma are a *great deal* rarer than is believed by many counselors and therapists who "recover" these memories. I say this for several reasons:

- Thorough legal and psychological research has been done in many of these cases of "repressed memory," and incontrovertible evidence has demonstrated that many of the claims have been simply impossible. The events could not have happened as described.
- I have interviewed a number of these cases, and as a physician I can state that they make claims with great certainty which are medically impossible.
- A number of these therapists who have "uncovered" these "repressed memories" have been found to have histories of childhood sexual trauma in their own lives and therefore have a strong motivation to create a "family" of similar victims with whom they can commiserate.
- As we have already described in this chapter, and as we will continue to describe in the remainder of the book, the rewards of acting like a victim in this society are enormous. Where there is a reward to behave in a certain way, many people *will* behave in that way, solely for the benefits offered. Many people will act like victims even when they haven't actually been victims. If they're not true victims, they will become False Victims.
- I have counseled hundreds of people with repressed memories of various kinds. As they feel unconditionally loved, the repression of their memories simply lifts, and they are able to remember the events from their pasts that they had previously hidden from themselves and others. We hide memories because they are intolerably painful, and as we feel enough Real Love

our pain reduces dramatically, after which we no longer have a *reason* to hide our memories. As I have observed hundreds of people recover their memories, not one of them has recalled repressed childhood sexual trauma.

Again, repressed sexual trauma memories are possible, but most people who recall memories of sexual trauma are "remembering" events that never happened, and they do it for the same reason that the fifteen-year-old girl above created the fantasy of her rape and physical abuse. They do it because they know—as we all do—that victims receive a great deal of attention. In addition, they know that in our society an accusation alone is often enough to make someone guilty.

For more information on this subject, do an Internet search for "false memory syndrome."

Munchausen Syndrome

On page 110 we talked about the young boy who was smothered with attention by his mother for the small scrape on his knee. His two-year-old sister then wanted the same attention for her knee, which was undamaged. If the two-year-old had intentionally fallen and scraped her knee, she would have qualified as a mild case of Munchausen syndrome.

People with this disorder have recognized the sympathy received by sick people, and they want some for themselves, so they actually cause physical problems in themselves in order to receive medical attention and the sympathy of family and friends. They intentionally fall and cause injuries, cut themselves and describe traumatic events that didn't occur, take medications that cause diarrhea and stomach pain, ingest poisons, and so on.

Many of those with Munchausen's have a comprehensive knowledge of medical terms and procedures, so they're able to create plausible explanations for their claims. Their portrayal of symptoms is usually so convincing that medical tests and investigations are necessary to rule out possible underlying medical conditions.

Munchausen Syndrome by Proxy

An individual with Munchausen Syndrome by Proxy makes *another person* sick—usually a child—and in the process achieves the benefits of victimhood. The adult is usually a female with medical experience, and she makes her child sick in the ways described above. She can also simply withhold treatment of common childhood illnesses. He or she receives the benefits of victimhood in two ways:

- Vicariously. When a parent makes a child sick, he or she can vicariously enjoy all the medical and other attention the child receives.
- Directly. When a mother has a sick child, family and friends ask her every day, "How's little Billy?" At that point she gets the sympathy for having a sick child, and then she also has the advantage of being able to go on and on about all she's doing to be a caring mother.

VICTIMS MANIPULATE PEOPLE FOR SUPPORT AND POWER

When we act like victims, we're usually looking for support, and we're trying to influence the behavior of other people, which is a form of power. In a life of emptiness and fear, these can be valuable commodities.

On pages 55-7 we met Sylvia, who complained to me that her husband, Brad, didn't put the toilet seat down for her. She had voiced that complaint—and others like it—to many of her friends on uncounted occasions. Why would she do that? Why do so many of us tell the same stories of woe over and over again? Because each time we describe how we've been victimized, we hope that someone will agree with us and support us.

In the absence of Real Love, that agreement and support is quite valuable. As victims we gather allies like points or votes. As we gather more votes, we experience several benefits:

- We feel more *right*, which gives us a greater sense of confidence and certainty as we proclaim our victimhood. We become more powerful victims.

- We feel less alone. The more allies we have, the bigger the group we become a part of.
- We get a sense of power from actually being the reason for the existence of a group. As I, for example, tell my personal story of injustice, and as I gather my supporters, I *create* the AFTERIOTIDPG, the Association For The Expression of Righteous Indignation Over the Terrible Injustices Done to Poor Greg. I am the Founder, President, and First Member, which gives me a feeling of considerable power.
- When politicians are elected by a large majority, or when the polls indicate that they have a large percentage of support, they feel they have what is called a *mandate*, which is an implied permission or authorization from their constituency to take whatever steps are necessary to carry out their political agendas. Politicians use these votes as a form of currency to get what they want. They use these votes as power. Victims behave in a similar way. As they gather votes, they feel justified in speaking more loudly or even in bullying people to get what they want. As Sylvia gathered more votes in support of her belief that Brad should put the toilet seat down, she sometimes browbeat him with those votes—with her mandate. She would say, "You're the only one who doesn't see that what you're doing is rude. *All my friends* agree with me that you're being inconsiderate." She used the votes she had gathered to intimidate Brad to do what she wanted.

When we act like victims to get power over the people around us, what exactly are we trying to get them to do?

- Make our lives easier. Let's suppose that you haven't been able to get your husband to mow the lawn for a month, so you finally get teary eyed and complain that he never does anything you ask him to do. Feeling guilty, he finally mows the lawn. That's power.
- Spend time with us. "You never do anything with me anymore." This victimy complaint will often persuade a partner to spent time with you in the short term, although in the long term he or she will usually grow to ignore it and even resent it.

- Have sex with us. Many a sexual experience has been motivated by one partner pointing out to the other that "we never have sex anymore."
- Agree with us. As we act like victims we can often get people to agree with our position on an issue.
- Do almost any task. Most of us have acted like victims at various times in order to get people to take out the garbage, take us out to dinner, buy us something we want, and so on.

Victims can absolutely control the people around them, because no one dares to question the validity of their claims. No one dares to ask victims whether their situations might be a natural result of *their* choices or just a natural result of living in a world where mistakes and inconvenience and injustice are unavoidable. Anyone who withholds sympathy or support from a victim risks being labeled as unsympathetic, uncaring, and even unkind or monstrous. That is no small risk. To illustrate the power of a victim, let me tell you the story of a patient, Martha, I once treated during my twenty years as a surgeon.

Martha came to see me for a painful eye condition that could have been permanently blinding if not treated promptly. Patients often come to the office with a family member, but Martha came with an entourage of at least eight, and they attended to her every word, sigh, grunt, and gesture. If she indicated any need whatever, they instantly moved to gratify it.

Fortunately, the treatment for her condition can be very simple. The surgeon sits the patient at a laser machine and eliminates the problem literally in seconds, without anesthesia and with little or no discomfort. It's one of the more dramatic and simple cures in all of medicine. Treatment does involve the surgeon putting a special kind of contact lens on the eye for a few moments, but that usually causes the patient no pain at all. I explained this to Martha and her family, along with an explanation that in the past this condition was treated by taking the patient to the operating room, where we were required to surgically enter the eye with a scalpel.

I tried to put the contact lens on Martha's eye half a dozen times, but on each occasion she shook and thrashed her head so vigorously that the lens placement became impossible. Over the years, I placed that lens on at least twenty thousand eyes, and Martha was the first and only adult where I found placement impossible. On the last attempt, she actually knocked the lens to the floor. I bent over to retrieve it, and as I rose back to a seated position, my eyes briefly locked with hers, and she *winked* at me as she smiled slightly. There was no mistaking her meaning. She was letting me know that she wasn't about to let me treat her problem the easy way. That wouldn't get her nearly enough attention from her family. It was her intention to milk this situation for everything it was worth, and a simple outpatient laser operation just wouldn't traumatize her sufficiently to merit the sympathy and attention she wanted.

I explained that we'd have to go to the operating room and under local anesthesia actually enter the eye and fix the problem. Martha was actually pleased. When we got to the operating room, however, Martha wouldn't even hold still long enough for injection of the local anesthesia, a rather simple affair. Again she fussed like a child, not from the pain but just to make things difficult. We finally had to put her under general anesthesia to do the operation. She milked her condition for every ounce of sympathy she could get, and as I talked to the family afterward it was obvious that she kept them on a short leash all the time. Her demands for sympathy and attention kept them virtually in prison. Victims can be very powerful.

The Vicarious Victim

The rewards of victimhood are so plentiful and so seductive that if we're not being victimized ourselves, many of us will capitalize on the victimhood of *other people*. I once knew a man named Marcus, for example, who had a terrible relationship with his wife, Brenda. He rarely spoke kind words to her, never touched her gently, and gave her virtually no indication that he cared about her in any way. In fact, he criticized almost everything she did, spoke to her in harsh tones, and otherwise ignored her.

In short, he victimized her frequently, both actively and by withdrawing his love, but heaven help anyone else who even thought about being unkind to her. One evening Marcus and Brenda were in a restaurant and someone said something rude to Brenda. "What did you say?" said Marcus, instantly leaping to her defense.

Marcus chose the wrong man to attack. The man who had been rude was in no mood to be confronted, and the conflict quickly escalated into a full-fledged brawl which resulted in both men being handcuffed and taken to jail.

On the surface, it doesn't seem to make sense that Marcus would so vigorously defend Brenda from the slightest offense—to the point that he would go to prison—when he was guilty of far worse offenses himself several times a day, almost every day. But it makes more sense with an understanding of the Vicarious Victim.

A standard victim acts like a victim for his own benefit. A Vicarious Victim acts like a victim for someone else—defending that person or acting hurt for that person. It's a role with attractive features. If I defend *myself* against you, for example, I stand alone in my defense. There's an element of selfishness when I'm defending myself—even if my defense is justified—because it's just my interests against yours. But now let's suppose that you're injuring an innocent child. Now, if I come to the defense of the *child*, my defense doesn't look selfish at all, because I'm defending someone else. I'm also no longer alone in my defense. I come to the conflict armed with

- righteous indignation.
- the sword of justice (in both hands).
- the support of literally anyone whose opinion I might seek.
- the support of the legal system in some cases.

With all that support behind me as I defend the child, I'll feel quite a bit more powerful than I did when I defended only myself. Vicarious Victims feel like white knights, like righteous crusaders in defense of all that is true and right. It's a selfless and powerful feeling, and so it was with Marcus. He got a real rush of power from defending his wife, even though he regularly injured her himself.

Most of us harbor some resentment about past situations where we've been victimized and were unable to adequately defend ourselves or repay our perpetrators in kind. We have an unfilled need for justice, even revenge. When someone else is victimized, therefore, we can use that opportunity to take on the role of Vicarious Victim and lash out at that person's perpetrator with an extra measure of righteous indignation, and in the process we partially fill our own needs for revenge. To illustrate the Vicarious Victim more practically, imagine that you've been hurt in the past by your parents, who have not loved you unconditionally—hardly a rare condition. For a number of reasons you may not be able to hit your father or mother for the times they've hurt you in the past, but you can now derive a certain satisfaction from hitting—physically or emotionally—someone who reminds you of them in the present as they are injuring someone else.

We can be vicarious victims in a variety of ways. For example:

- A woman is irritated at her children all day and says critical things to them on many occasions, but when her husband says something unkind to one of them, she erupts in the child's defense, saying, "I know you had a bad day at work, but don't take it out on him."
- I knew a man who had little affection for people of a particular race and sometimes used racially derogatory language. If *other people* used belittling words to describe people of that race, however, this man didn't hesitate to tell them that their language was inappropriate.
- Some people become very animated in defense of their favorite athletic team. This is often a form of being Vicarious Victims.
- Some people became quite zealous in defense of animal rights while expressing little regard for human rights. Animals are so defenseless that they become wonderful candidates for pure victims that we can then self-righteously defend.
- It is common in this country for people to vigorously defend the human rights of people in other countries—people who are more removed from us and who therefore seem more defenseless—but care little about the genuine happiness of their own spouses and children.
- Vicarious victimhood is the basis of the "yo mama" attack. You can criticize a man's car, his hair, his shoes, or any number of things about him, but don't say something about his mother, because then he becomes the Vicarious Victim and rises in righteous indignation to defend her—even if he isn't very kind to her himself.

VICTIMS COMPLETELY AVOID RESPONSIBILITY

If I choose to be a responsible human being, I'd have to accept two other qualities that go along with being responsible:

- Being wrong. I'd have to admit my flaws and when I made mistakes, which would expose me to the criticism and even rejection of others.
- Accountability. I'd have to account for my mistakes, which means not only admitting them but also cleaning up after my mistakes, where possible.

Being wrong and being accountable are risky and inconvenient, and when we act like victims we believe we can avoid these conditions. Remember that victims are continually proclaiming

- "Look at what *you*—or other people—did to me."
- "Look at what *you*—or other people—should have done for me."
- "It's not *my* fault."

When we are victims, we make other people responsible

- for making us happy.
- for protecting us.
- for the times we're angry.
- for the times we're not happy.
- for our mistakes.

In so doing, we don't ever have to be wrong or accountable. We don't have to work. We don't have to change. We can blame everyone else for everything. We can make everyone else responsible for *almost* everything. The exception? We do like to take responsibility for our *successes*.

In order to achieve the reward of avoiding responsibility we're willing to put up with a lot, as illustrated here by Emily, whose husband, Dean, treats her like a child. He gives her an allowance, and she has to account for every dime. She can't go anywhere without his permission. If he doesn't like the clothes she's wearing, he says so and she changes into something else. He controls virtually every aspect of her life. Emily widely complains about this, and she gets a lot of sympathy for it. "How could he treat you like that," her friends say, and "How in the world do you put up with it?" But a wise woman in Emily's Real Love group knows that we allow ourselves to be victimized for a reason. We get something out of it.

"What do you *like* about your relationship with Dean?" her friend asks.

"Like? Not much," says Emily. "I don't know why I put up with it. I guess I stay with him because I don't think people should get divorced." In so saying, Emily gets to play the victim and the dutiful martyr simultaneously.

"Doesn't Dean completely take care of you financially?"

"Well, yes, but that doesn't give him the right to treat me like he does."

"All right, for thirty seconds we'll talk about Dean. Dean doesn't feel unconditionally loved, and when he controls you, he gets a feeling of importance and power which temporarily makes him feel less empty and alone. That is not a loving way to live and not a loving way to treat you. It's selfish and it's *wrong*, but he has a right to choose to live that way. That's the Law of Choice. Now I'm done talking about Dean. No matter what he does, he doesn't determine your happiness or your relationship. A relationship is the natural result of the choices two people make *independently*. Dean has made the choice to control your life. You can't change that, but you *can* make your own choice, and so far you've chosen to *let* him control you. That's why your relationship is like this. *He* didn't make it that way. The *two of you* did. You can be a victim here only if you *allow* yourself to be."

"I don't understand. *He's* the one who treats me like a servant. What can *I* do about it?"

"You said he tells you what to wear, right?"

"Yes."

"So if you put on something he doesn't like, what does he do?"

"He says he hates it."

"And then . . ."

"I change."

The wise friend smiles. "Does he grab you by the hair, drag you into the bedroom, tear your clothes off, and put new ones on you?"

"No."

"Then you make a *choice* to change clothes, don't you?"

"Sort of. But if I didn't change, he'd get angry."

"You're still making a choice. You make it out of fear, but it's still a choice. He can certainly *tell* you what to do—that's his choice to make—but then you could make the choice to say *no*. You're not a victim or a child. You're a willing participant in this relationship, Emily. Do you see this?"

"I'm afraid of what he'll do if I tell him no."

"Has he ever hit you?"

"No."

"Then what do you really have to fear? You're already unhappy—it doesn't seem like you have much to lose."

Victims get a lot from their behavior. Although Emily complained about her relationship with Dean, the rewards were considerable: She didn't have to work. She made no difficult decisions about insurance, investments, maintenance on the house, or anything else. She played tennis, painted, and worked in her garden. Dean even took her out to eat once or twice a week so she didn't have to cook. The overall experience for her was *positive*, which is why she stayed in the marriage. What she got out of it was more than she suffered from it, but then she chose to complain about the part she didn't like. She was angry that he would inconvenience her while he was completely taking care of her.

As much as victims complain about their suffering, they're rarely in a situation they can't escape. They usually stay where they are because, overall, they relish the combination of sympathy and irresponsibility they earn. They use and abuse the people around them—though usually not intentionally—all the while appearing to be the injured and innocent objects of abuse and neglect. Victims are reluctant to walk away from this productive arrangement.

In Chapter Seven we'll talk about how Emily could change her relationship.

VICTIMS CREATE A PLACE IN THE WORLD WHERE THEY CAN BELONG

When we lack sufficient Real Love, we feel alone, and that is an unbearably painful condition. Almost anything feels better than being alone. When we act like victims, we create a place for ourselves in the world. We feel connected to other people, even though the connection we create is usually unhealthy and marginally satisfying.

When I'm a victim and claiming that you're not doing enough for me—or perhaps are doing something unpleasant *to* me—I gain a sense of connection to both you and other people:

- I feel connected to all the people who feel sorry for me. I value their sympathy and treasure any association with them.
- I feel a deep gratitude for and connection to those who actually help me.
- Odd though it seems, I actually feel a connection to *you*, even though I regard you as a villain. The more demands I make of you, the more connected to you I feel, even if the connection is angry and unhealthy.

Let me introduce you to Tanya, a woman who was a classic victim when I first met her. Like so many of us, she was raised in a family where there was little or no love. Her brother was the first child in the family, and he reacted to the emptiness and pain in his life by becoming an attacker, addicted to praise and power. He was emotionally aggressive and highly successful academically. He became a high-pressure business executive who was respected and even feared by his peers and competitors. The second child in the family, a daughter, was born two years later, and she filled *her* life with Imitation Love in the form of praise, which she earned with her physical appearance and with her singular successes in athletics.

Then, three years later, along came Tanya, who discovered that she couldn't begin to compete with siblings who had already been acquiring—for three and five years for her sister and brother, respectively—an expertise in earning Imitation Love in their respective fields. Her brother and sister had become thoroughly entrenched in the family system as attackers and as practiced buyers of praise and power.

Tanya had to find her own role and her own form of Imitation Love to earn. She couldn't be an attacker, because her siblings could attack much better than she, having had much longer to practice that particular Getting and Protecting Behavior. She couldn't earn praise and power, because her siblings were much better at that than she could ever be. So gradually she learned to act like a victim. That was a role her siblings had little experience with. She learned to earn sympathy, and before long her siblings discovered they couldn't begin to compete with *her* in that arena.

Tanya acted like a victim the rest of her life, continuing the role she learned as a child. As an adult she replaced her parents and siblings with other people who would allow her to take the victim role she had enjoyed as a child. She became rather proficient at her role, but she discovered, as all victims do, that no matter how much Imitation Love she earned, she wasn't happy, a subject we'll discuss much more in the next chapter. As she learned about Real Love and took the first steps toward giving up her victimhood—another subject we'll outline in later chapters—she discovered that she felt quite disoriented.

"I don't know what to do," she said to me.

"In what way?" I asked.

"Before I studied Real Love it never would have occurred to me that I was spending my whole life interacting with people by acting like a victim. As I've learned what I was doing, and now that I'm learning about other choices, I feel kind of lost. I hardly know who I am. If I don't act like a victim, I don't know how to relate to people. I feel confused."

We all need a role to play in the world. Our role gives us a comfortable and predictable way to feel actively involved in the world and connected to other people. In our roles we feel comfortable, useful, and safe. Even though the victim role isn't healthy, it feels better than having no role at all.

Delightfully, we don't have to play out for the rest of our lives the roles we learned as children. We can learn to give up our role as victims, for example, after which we can learn to fill much healthier roles and find a level of happiness that was completely unavailable to us as victims.

Special Victims

Some victims gain their place in the world—along with attention and power—by claiming to have been wounded in a *special* way, so that they will deserve the first and greatest portion of sympathy, attention, power, and so on. Special Victims claim that their wounds are somehow more painful than everyone else's. They are also fond of telling you that you couldn't possibly understand their wounds, which are also far worse than you could imagine.

It's clever reasoning, and for the most part it works. We don't dare question Special Victims, because their unique wounds become, in the world of victims, beyond question or reproach, even holy. There are many people—though not all, it is to be emphasized—within the following groups, to name just a few, who claim this special role:

- African-Americans.
- Gays
- Ethnic groups
- Survivors of incest
- Children of alcoholic parents
- Families of murder victims
- Women
- Religious groups
- Handicapped people
- Addicts
- People suffering from cancer or any other serious illness
- Survivors of cancer or other illness

We enjoy our membership in groups focused on victimhood, because as we associate with people who have been victimized in ways similar to us

- we feel a connection to them.
- we feel less alone.
- our wounds seem more real and valid, because other people have them.
- sometimes we gain an increased sense of power. We feel less helpless as we associate with others who share our wounds.

VICTIMS OF FATE AND SELF

On pages 64-7 we talked about two categories of victims somewhat different from the rest:

- The Victims of Fate, the people who feel victimized not by particular people but by circumstances, time, God, fate, and so on.
- The self-inflicted victims who feel guilty or worthless.

Now let's examine how these two groups benefit from their victimhood, referring to the rewards listed earlier in this section.

Victims of Fate

- are self-righteous and never have to be wrong. If you can blame your unhappiness on your health, for example, or some unseen

forces—even though you may have made quite a number of foolish choices and contributed in a major way to your circumstances—how could anyone possibly find fault with you?
- manipulate people for sympathy and attention with even greater success than "regular" victims. Imagine, for example, that you claim to have been victimized by another person. There is always the possibility that you were wrong in some way, that you had some responsibility for the flawed interaction between you and the perpetrator. If there is a hint that you might have been at fault, the sympathy you would receive would be limited to some degree. But if you have been victimized by a genetic disease, or an act of God—like a tornado, for example—or just bad luck, how could anyone possibly claim that you had any responsibility for your predicament? The outpouring of sympathy you would then receive would be even more unrestrained.
- manipulate people for support and power, in much the same ways as they do for sympathy and attention.
- completely avoid responsibility. As we have discussed, how could you possibly be held responsible for "fate" dealing you a bad hand?
- create a place in the world—pathetic though it is—where they can belong, much as regular victims do.

Self-inflicted victims achieve different rewards than regular victims or Victims of Fate. People riddled with guilt and a sense a worthlessness don't feel self-righteousness, nor to they claim never to be wrong. In fact, they are filled with self-loathing and feel like they're wrong all the time. So what rewards *do* they receive from their feelings and behavior? Self-inflicted victims

- manipulate people for sympathy, attention, and support. As they repeatedly proclaim how wretched their lives are, they rather successfully pluck at the heartstrings of many of the people around them, who feel sorry for them and then try to rally around them to make them feel better.
- create a place for themselves in the world, much as regular victims do.

- avoid responsibility as their main reward. That seems an odd statement, given that people who feel guilty and worthless are usually quick to admit—even loudly proclaim—their flaws. Are they not then taking responsibility for their mistakes? No, actually, rather than focusing on taking genuine responsibility for their mistakes they focus their energy on *their own pain*. They bemoan their mistakes and flaws while continuing to wallow in them, all the while enjoying the sympathy of those around them. When someone truly takes responsibility for his mistakes, he simply tells the truth about them, does his best to avoid repeating them, and does all he can to make amends for them.

☙ Chapter Five ❧

The Negative Consequences of Victimhood

Admittedly, the rewards of victimhood are abundant, but the negative consequences are simply horrific. When we act like victims

- we can't feel loved.
- we can't have intimate relationships.
- we can't grow in our personal lives.
- we can't be responsible, productive human beings.
- we become spoiled.
- we contribute to a society of punishment not learning.
- we are guaranteed to be angry.
- we are guaranteed to lie.
- we can't be free.
- we can't be happy.
- we raise a generation of children who will act like victims.

Now let's discuss each of these negative consequences in greater detail.

WE CAN'T FEEL LOVED

Imagine that I pay you fifty dollars several times a day to tell me that you love me. We could continue in this arrangement for quite some time, but would I ever feel loved? No, no matter how many times you told me you loved me, I'd never feel *genuinely* loved, because Real Love can only be given *freely*, and I could not sense that you were giving me your love freely because of my payments to you. I could only feel that I was *paying* you for your love, which is never a fulfilling sensation.

When I act like a victim, I can get many things from you: sympathy, attention, support, power, money, and sex, to name just a few rewards. But the instant I act like a victim, I've done something to *motivate you* or manipulate you to give me whatever attention, love, and so on you might give me. I've *paid* you for it and therefore cannot feel loved.

Victims can earn sympathy. They can effectively persuade people to do what they want. But victims can't feel genuinely loved, which is what they really need. What a tragic irony it is that the instant someone acts like a victim in order to fill his or her emptiness, he or she makes it impossible for that emptiness to be truly filled.

I once met a woman, Connie, who had been sexually abused by her stepfather, grandfather, brothers, and her brother's friends when she was a child. When I met her, she was a shell of a human being: without friends of either sex, without a job, and as lonely and unhappy as you could imagine. She had been in therapy for many years, during which her therapists had helped her recall memories of many instances of sexual abuse. But she was still miserable and alone.

I recommended that Connie come to a Real Love group, and at her first meeting she began to talk about her abusive past. After she had spoken for a few minutes, I gently suggested that no matter how much she talked about what had been done *to* her, no matter how much she talked about how she had been *victimized*, all she could ever get was sympathy. I emphasized that sympathy was not love—nor would it ever be. No amount of sympathy would ever lead to her feeling more loved. *She* had already proven that herself over many years of experience.

We taught Connie to tell the truth about *herself*, and as she learned to do that, she created opportunities to feel loved for who she really was. She created opportunities to feel Real Love for the first time in her life. In Chapter Eight we'll talk about how she learned to do that.

WE CAN'T HAVE INTIMATE RELATIONSHIPS

Victims are constantly blaming everyone else for whatever goes wrong. Literally *everything* is someone else's fault. Now, imagine that you're trying to establish or maintain an intimate relationship with someone who engages in that kind of wholesale blaming, someone who says things like the following:

- "It's not my fault."
- "Why are you always doing that?"
- "Do you ever do what I ask you?"
- "Can't you ever do that right?"
- "How many times have I told you that?"
- "Excuse me, you're saying this is *my* fault?"
- "What?! What did you just say to me?"

How do you think it would it affect your relationship to hear blaming like that every day? Several times a day? Every time a victim blames other people, they hear the words *I don't love you*. For that reason alone it is virtually impossible to have a loving relationship with someone who acts like a victim.

In addition, victims believe they are the center of the world, so they see everyone and everything in the world in terms of what they might do *to* them (the victims) or *for* them. They see people as *objects*, to be used or to be defended against. Victims don't have *relationships* with people. They take hostages. They negotiate trades. They submit demands and register complaints. But they don't have *relationships*, because you can only have a relationship with a person, and victims can see people only as objects.

Remember that on pages 55-7 I talked to Sylvia, who was angry at her husband, Brad, for not putting the toilet seat down. I suggested to her that she was *requiring* him to be thoughtful, that she was taking from him any *choice* he might have in the matter. Her insistence on that approach was destroying their relationship. Following is a continuation of my discussion with her from page 57.

"So all the details of the toilet seat aside," I said, "do you see now that you've been acting like a victim with Brad about this issue?"

Sylvia paused before she said with some discomfort, "I do now. I sure didn't see all this before."

"And while you're feeling and acting like a victim, you can be thinking *only* about *yourself*, not him. You're being . . . "

"Selfish?"

"Exactly. There's no blaming to this. We're just accurately identifying what's happening so you can make wiser choices if you wish to. And while you're being selfish, do you feel more loving toward Brad?"

"No."

"Happier?"

"No."

"And when you're acting like a victim, Brad can hear you say only four words. What are they?"

"I don't love you?"

"Right, and then how does he feel toward you, do you think? Loved? Closer to you? Is he enjoying an intimate relationship with you?"

"No. I've created a real mess, haven't I?"

"Yes, but you didn't realize what you were doing, so don't feel guilty about it. That would be a real waste. You just need to *understand* what's been happening. Although it seems like a small thing, each time you've made a demand about that toilet seat, it's been like you've put a small rock in the shoe of your relationship. Have you ever been on a long hike?"

"Sure."

"And if you're on a long hike, how big a rock would you like to have in your shoe?"

"I wouldn't want any rock at all. Over a long hike, *any* rock could become a huge problem."

"And marriage is very much like a long hike. Marriage can be difficult under the best of circumstances. You certainly don't want to add anything that could make it even harder. And every time we do something selfish—demand something like a toilet seat being down or act like victims—we add a rock to the shoe of our marriage. Making sense?"

"Completely."

"So in the end there aren't very many *tasks* or *things*—like putting a toilet seat up or down—that are worth tossing rocks in our shoes."

"This would pretty much change the way I see everything in our marriage," Sylvia said.

"Can you think of some other things you do in your marriage that also add rocks to your shoes?"

"Oh yeah, quite a few."

"Now, I'm not saying that Brad is blameless here," I said. "But Brad has to work on himself. You can only work on *you*. Are you willing to do that?"

"Yes, I am," she said, and in that moment Sylvia took the first step toward changing the rest of her life and her marriage.

Victimhood Irritates Other People

On pages 63-4 I briefly discussed one of the consequences of acting like a victim and blaming other people for how we feel. They get tired of being blamed, and then they respond with Protecting Behaviors that tend to be hurtful to us. This pattern certainly makes a loving relationship difficult.

WE CAN'T GROW IN OUR PERSONAL LIVES

In order to grow in our personal lives, we have to make personal choices. We have to learn from these choices. But victims don't make choices. They let other people make choices, and then they attack them, blame them, and second guess them. Let me illustrate this principle by describing an interaction I had with Carl about his wife, Paula.

Carl complained that Paula spent money irresponsibly, whined at him constantly, didn't take care of the house, never had sex with him, and did a lousy job as a mother. I knew one of Paula's friends, and apparently all those things about her were actually true. Carl and I had talked about his situation before.

"I'm sick of this," Carl said. "How can I keep putting up with it?"

"I *wouldn't*. I'd *do* something about it. But so far, you have chosen *not* to."

Carl was surprised at my answer. "What do you mean? What can *I* do? She won't change, and I can't *make* her—you told me that."

"Right," I said. "You can't make *her* change. That's not one of your choices. But you still have the three choices we've talked about from the book *Real Love*, and they don't involve her. You can live with it and like it, live with it and hate it, or leave it. So far, you've made the second choice—live with it and hate it—but that *never* works, does it? It never makes you happy, and it's really a non-choice. There's no real effort involved in that. You're just sitting around complaining and waiting for *Paula* to do something different. It's pretty lazy, really."

Carl's eyes opened wide as he looked wounded. He'd decided to act like a victim—even with me—to get some sympathy.

"Hey," I said, "I'm your friend. Have been for a long time. I care enough about you to tell you something that could make a very positive difference, even if you don't like it at first. If I just tell you what a rotten deal you're getting at home—if I just let you be a victim—what good will that do? Will that make your life any better? No. Do you want to be happy or not?"

"Sure."

"Then *do* something different. Make some positive decisions and act on them. Make the first choice or the third: Live with it and like it, or leave it. Which will it be? Right now, are you ready to divorce your wife and keep being a loser at relationships? Are you willing to bounce your children between two parents? Are you ready to do all that?"

"I don't know. I sure want to sometimes."

"The biggest reason you're unhappy right now is that *you* haven't felt loved all your life, not because of anything *Paula's* doing. If you divorce her, you'll still be unhappy. At this point, you're still learning how to be loving, so in my opinion you'd be crazy to divorce her, because you'd still have almost all the same problems you have now—and then some. So don't even *think* about divorce. First make a decision that you'll finally tell the truth about *yourself* and get the love you've been missing all your life, and then see what happens when you bring to your marriage the one thing—Real Love—that could make it healthy."

"I've been doing that a little."

"How many times in the last two weeks have you talked about yourself to people who could unconditionally love you?"

Carl paused for several moments, so I said, "Exactly. You've been piddling around with this. You haven't taken it seriously. You have a lifetime of feeling unloved, and you can't change that pattern by approaching this casually. If you really want to change your life, it will take a more consistent effort than you've been making. You have to make decisions every day to get what you need. As you do that, your relationship with your wife and children can begin to change. You can begin talking about yourself to Paula, too. Until then, you're just being lazy and hoping that things will magically work out for you. It doesn't work that way."

We find greater happiness only as we make choices, and the more choices we make, the faster we find it. It's true that as we make more choices, we make more mistakes, but we can also learn more and grow faster. With greater risks come greater rewards. It's worth it.

To learn much more about the process of finding Real Love for ourselves, read the two sections at the end of Chapter One (pages 35-9) and all of Chapter Eight.

WE CAN'T BE RESPONSIBLE, PRODUCTIVE HUMAN BEINGS

One day I talked to Tony, a thirty-year-old man who lived with his parents. He didn't have a job—nor was he working at finding one—and he didn't have a car of his own.

"They're just not fair," Tony said.

"Who?" I asked.

"My parents."

"How's that?"

"They're always asking me to do stuff around the house. I'm thirty years old. I'm not a kid anymore."

"What do they ask you to do?"

"Take out the garbage and mow the lawn. They want me to take out *all* the garbage for the whole house, but I hardly *make* any of the garbage. *They* make most of it, and I don't ever *use* the yard, but they want me to mow it. So why should I do either of those jobs?"

"Do you pay rent?"

"No, but they've never asked me too either."

"What else do they ask you to do?"

"Just stuff here and there, but what they ask just isn't fair."

"If you had your own place, wouldn't you have to take out the garbage?"

"Yes, but it wouldn't be the garbage for *three people*, and if I were in an apartment, I wouldn't have to mow the lawn."

"And if you were in an apartment, wouldn't you have to pay for rent? And utilities? Isn't taking out the garbage and mowing the lawn a lot less trouble than paying for an apartment and all the stuff that would go with it?"

"But I don't live in an apartment, and I don't see why I should have to mow a lawn I don't use."

Tony was a complete victim. In his world —the world of the victim—he couldn't even consider the possibility that *he* might be unfair to his parents as he ate their food, lived under their roof (enjoying the benefits of their paying the mortgage, homeowner's insurance, and power, gas, and phone bills), and drove their car. He could only see that *they* were being unfair to require maybe two to four hours of work a week from him. How could he rationalize this enormous inequity? Easily: He was a victim.

As a victim, Tony felt *entitled* to everything his parents had, without paying for anything. He *expected* everything, so everything they gave him counted as nothing. There was no reason for him to feel obligated to them in any way. When they asked *him* to do anything, on the other hand, the inconvenience was intolerably unfair. To a victim this reasoning makes perfect sense. Victims are always entitled and never obligated or responsible.

A week later I spoke to Tony's parents, who wondered what they should do.

"Move him out," I said.

"Oh, we couldn't do that," said his mother.

"Really?" I asked. "Why not?"

"He'd have no place to live."

"Nonsense. The only reason he has no job, no place to live, no car, and acts like a big baby is because you allow it. You *encourage* him to act like a victim. He does it because he gets away with it. In fact, you *reward* him for this behavior. Why should he change? As long as you take care of him like this, what motivation would he ever have to become responsible? You won't be throwing him out of the house as a *punishment*. You'll be doing it because you genuinely *love* him. Real Love means caring about his *happiness*, and he can't be happy while he's irresponsible. If you really care about his happiness, you'll help him become a responsible human being, which means *requiring* that he take independent steps, which he'll take only if you put him out on his own."

After additional discussion, his parents agreed, and they went home to deliver the news. Six months later, I ran into them again, and I asked about their son. He was still living with his parents, because when they told him he had to leave, he had such a fit that they couldn't bear to follow through and make him move out. Victims do that. They incite such emotional reactions with their guilt and anger that they wrap people around their fingers. I suggested that they try again, this time setting a specific date two weeks from that day, at which time he had to be out on his own.

Thirteen days later his father called me and said Tony hadn't made the first move to leave. Tony said he just couldn't find a job or a place to live.

"What should we do?" asked his father.

"Do you really love your son?" I asked.

"Yes."

"Then he needs your help. If you don't help him, he'll be irresponsible and unhappy for the rest of his life. He'll be crippled. Tell him that you'll help him find an apartment. You'll pay the deposit and the first month's rent, but that's all. Then tell him that at five o'clock in the afternoon tomorrow you'll be putting all his stuff out in the driveway and replacing the locks on the house. No kidding. Tell him that the locksmith is arriving at five o'clock. Then you turn around and leave. Don't listen to another word he says, because all the excuses in the world don't really matter."

In the next twenty-four hours Tony found a job and an apartment. As long as we act like victims—especially when people help us to act like victims—we never have to be responsible, so we never are.

Victims are uniformly lazy. They feel entitled, believing that it's the job of everyone around them to take care of them. After all, everything unfortunate in their lives is someone else's fault, so it's also someone else's *responsibility* to fix it. Why should a victim, therefore, ever exert himself or herself to do anything about his or her position in life?

WE BECOME SPOILED

Victims really do believe they're the center of the world, and from that position they *expect* everything they get. On pages 71-4 we talked about the drawbacks of having expectations. If I *expect* something from you

- and I get anything less than what I expected, I'll feel disappointed. Even if you give me a lot, I'll be unhappy because of my expectations—as Tony was on page 138.
- and I get exactly what I expected, I still won't feel happy. I'll feel only *satisfied* that my order was filled, which is a far cry from feeling pleased, excited, or loved.

As you can see, expectations ruin any possibility of our feeling loved, and as victims we have expectations about almost everything. We feel entitled to everything we get. With that attitude, we're grateful for nothing. We enjoy very little. Life becomes an endless series of expectations and disappointments and irritations.

Children who are allowed to act like victims are almost certain to become spoiled. They feel entitled to everything they get. Rather than feeling grateful for what they have, which leads to feelings of happiness, they are demanding and petulant.

WE CONTRIBUTE TO A SOCIETY OF PUNISHMENT, NOT LEARNING

In the process of learning, mistakes are simply unavoidable—our mistakes and the mistakes of those around us. By definition, as we learn, our knowledge grows, so as we move along the road of learning we must at times make choices with imperfect knowledge, and with imperfect knowledge we cannot avoid making mistakes. Success is inevitably preceded by many failures. Frequently, our mistakes will inconvenience other people. As we learn, we all get in each other's way. It could not be otherwise. *To keep from hurting other people, we'd have to make no choices at all, and then there would be no learning, no growth, and no happiness.* In short, as we learn and grow, mistakes and hurting other people are unavoidable. This is not to say that it's all right to hurt people, only that it is an unavoidable part of the process of learning.

In our society, however, we generally don't see mistakes as an integral part of learning, nor do we see Getting and Protecting Behaviors as mistakes. We don't realize that most mistakes are made unintentionally, without any desire to hurt anyone, including us. Most people are simply empty and afraid, and they inconvenience and hurt us only as they make attempts to get love and protect themselves—as was the case with the man drowning in the pool in Chapter One.

Unfortunately, most of us tend to make a big production out of it when people make mistakes that affect *us*. When people make mistakes that affect us in negative ways, we tend to label those mistakes—as well as those who make them—as bad or evil. We want those people to *pay*. We want them to apologize, suffer, be humiliated, be restricted, and never commit a similarly grievous offense again. We choose, in other words, to act like victims.

We also have a tendency to measure the seriousness of mistakes not according to the magnitude of the mistakes themselves but according to how much someone was victimized by those mistakes. That can be quite unfair. If someone makes a huge mistake that affects no one else, we call that a "small" mistake. If the same mistake happens to inconvenience or hurt many people, it suddenly becomes a "big" mistake, because of the Victim Factor.

I once read in our local newspaper, for example, that a man had drunkenly driven into a ditch on a back road, knocking down some garbage cans. The police found him a few hours later and took him home. The same evening, another drunk driver swerved off a similar road, but at the spot his car left the road a child was riding a bicycle, and the child was killed. The second driver was charged with manslaughter and put in jail for a very long time.

Both men did the *exact same thing*. They were both lonely and unhappy. They both inappropriately treated their pain with alcohol and then selfishly and irresponsibly chose to get behind the wheel of a car to drive home. Both became sleepy and disoriented and were unable to stay on the road, but when one man left the road he hit a ditch, while the other man hit a child. The actions of the two men were identical, but we tend to view them quite differently, don't we? The difference? The Victim Factor, and when the Victim Factor is higher we impose higher consequences even if the mistake or the crime was the same.

The death of the child was certainly tragic—there is no minimizing that—but so is our blindness to the pain of people who make awful mistakes as they use Getting and Protecting Behaviors. I am *not* saying we should ignore the behavior of drunk drivers—I feel rather strongly about that crime, actually. I *am* saying that we inappropriately judge people according to the *consequences* of their behavior—according to how victimized *we* are—instead of looking at their *behavior* and seeing it as a sign of their emptiness and fear. We punish people for how their mistakes affect *us* instead of seeing their mistakes as an opportunity to help them.

People do need to be held responsible for their mistakes. They need to experience the natural *consequences* of their unwise choices, so they won't make those unwise choices again. Occasionally they even need to be jailed or otherwise restricted—removing the driver's licenses of people who drink and drive, for example—so they can't make mistakes that endanger the property and health of others. But they don't need to be *punished*. Let's take this opportunity to discuss the difference between punishment and the application of consequences.

Punishment vs. Consequences

The difference between a punishment and the application of a consequence is not a matter of technique or the words that are spoken. The difference is *motivation*. The same action that is a consequence when imposed in a loving way becomes a punishment when it is imposed with disappointment and anger.

Consequences are imposed:

- to teach a principle.
- with genuine concern for the happiness and growth of the person making the mistake.

- with no desire for Imitation Love from the person imposing the consequence.
- with no impatience.
- with no anger whatever.

Punishments are given:

- to make someone "pay" for what he's done.
- to teach someone the "lesson" that he must not inconvenience those administering the punishment.
- for the sake of "justice."
- with impatience.
- to make those administering the punishment feel powerful and "in control."
- with some pleasure that the punished person is uncomfortable.
- with anger.
- with shaming.

In short, the difference between a consequence and a punishment is anger. The instant you're angry, you're not teaching with a consequence; you're punishing the other person, and the only thing he or she will hear from you is, "I don't love you." Any time we feel irritated with another person, we can only punish him and teach him that he's unacceptable to us. He learns that his safety and happiness are far less important to us than our own convenience. He learns that he's an object to be manipulated and controlled, and then he feels empty and afraid, and he responds with his own special recipe of Getting and Protecting Behaviors. In that condition, not only is he miserable, but he also can't learn anything else we're trying to teach him. Punishment might temporarily change someone's behavior, but the overall effect is disastrous.

We also must understand the *purpose* of consequences, which is to make the wrong choices sufficiently *inconvenient* to people that they will want to make the right choices. The correct role of consequences is only to guide people toward long term, genuine happiness. Eventually, people who are sufficiently loved and taught will tend to make right choices simply because they want to—because that behavior makes them happier—and then they no longer need the imposition of consequences.

With punishment—with *I don't love you*—there is no genuine learning, only suffering and pain. The world doesn't need more pain. We don't need more suffering, which only makes us more empty and afraid and *more* likely to use Getting and Protecting Behaviors—more anger, violence, lying, and so on. We only need to learn from our mistakes—sometimes through the imposition of consequences—and to grow, and to become happier.

WE ARE GUARANTEED TO BE ANGRY

When we feel victimized—when we feel like the world is against us, out to do us harm, and intentionally withholding what we need—we can't help but be angry most of the time. But, tragically, anger is a poison that makes us miserable and separates us from everyone else.

Our highest purpose in life is to be happy. By happy I mean genuinely peaceful and filled with real joy, not merely entertained or excited or satisfied with the absence of problems or conflict. That kind of happiness can be attained only as we are feeling Real Love ourselves and—even more importantly—as we are loving others unconditionally. Any behavior or thought or feeling, therefore, that contributes to our feeling loved, loving, and happy would obviously be *right*, since it contributes to our highest purpose in life. Just as obviously, any behavior or thought or feeling that *detracts* from our feeling loved, loving, and happy would therefore be *wrong*.

By *wrong* I do *not* mean to imply those hateful and harmful connotations of evil, bad, wicked, inexcusable, and fatally flawed that many of us have been beaten with all our lives when we have heard the word *wrong*. When I say that anger is wrong, I mean only that anger simply *does not work*. Think about all the times you've been angry at anyone in your life—spouse, lover, sibling, parent, child, boss, co worker—and ask yourself whether on a single one of those occasions you have felt unconditionally loved or loving or profoundly happy. Impossible. Anger is wrong simply because it makes attainment of our highest goal—happiness—utterly impossible.

When I talk about the destructive nature of anger, some people protest, "But anger is a *natural* emotion." Quite right; it *is* natural, but so is snake venom, and both are deadly. Just because something is *natural* doesn't make it *good*.

Others protest, "But I have a *right* to be angry." Indeed you do. You also have a right to stick your head in the toilet, but do you really want to? There are many things we have a *right* to do, but not all of these rights would be wise to exercise.

It is often helpful to both groups of protesters when they hear that I am *not* saying that anyone *shouldn't* be angry. I'm not saying anything of the sort. What I *am* saying is that every day—every moment—we *choose* how we feel. We are not rocks and sticks, which cannot make their own choices and can only be acted upon. We are magnificent beings who can choose what we think, how we feel, what we say, and what we do. We have also demonstrated thoroughly that anger is a uniformly selfish, unloving, and harmful choice, but in the absence of Real Love—when we are empty and afraid—anger is often the only choice *we can see* in response to many people and events. It is one of the great miracles of life that with desire and practice, we can learn to replace anger—as well as all the other Getting and Protecting Behaviors—with Real Love. It's a phenomenally happy way to live. For more about how to find Real Love, read the last two sections of Chapter One and all of Chapter Eight.

WE ARE GUARANTEED TO LIE

Victims have to lie about their responsibility for the choices they make. If they didn't lie, they couldn't remain victims, as we discussed on pages 106-7 . They also have to lie about how other people are perpetrators. These lies have terrible consequences. As we talked about on page 22-3, the instant we lie, we separate ourselves from the possibility of ever feeling loved, in a process we described in the following way:

Truth → Seen → Accepted → Loved

Victims can buy sympathy and attention, but never Real Love, which is the only thing that will make them genuinely happy. They can only feel alone.

WE CAN'T BE FREE

Because victims live in a world dominated by blaming, they can never be truly free. They are constantly chained to the behaviors of other people. When we finally understand the nature of victimhood and Real Love, we can achieve freedom from these bonds.

We Are Not Responsible for the Happiness of Other People

All our lives, we've been taught that we're responsible for the happiness of other people. When we made mistakes, our parents, teachers, and others said things like this to us:

- "I'm disappointed (in you)."
- "You make me so angry."
- "I think you owe me an apology."
- "How could you do this (to me)?"

When we did what other people wanted, however, the feedback was quite different:

- "Oh, I'm so proud of you."
- "It makes me so happy when you do that."
- "You're such a good boy (or girl)."
- "Thank you so much."

These latter messages—although they appear to be quite positive on the surface—were still not healthy in most cases, because we heard them only when we *earned* them with our behavior, and they placed a burden on us to make other people happy. With either the negative or positive messages, we learned that we were *responsible* for the happiness of other people, and we came to believe that.

We simply did not know then that how other people feel is determined not by what *we* do in any given moment but by the overall quantity of Real Love *they* are feeling and sharing in their lives. Using the metaphor from pages 25-6, we can contribute or take or withhold two emotional dollars here and there in people's lives, but whether other people feel happy is dependent on whether or not *they* have twenty million dollars.

Other People are Not Responsible For Our Happiness

It is a small step in our minds from believing that we are responsible for other people's happiness to believing that other people in turn are responsible for *our* happiness. We reasoned—often unconsciously—that if they could tell *us* that they were disappointed and hurt and angry when we failed to behave as they wished, why couldn't we tell *them* the same thing under similar conditions? So we learned to do just that.

The problem with believing that you *make* me mad, however—or sad, or disappointed, or frustrated, or even happy—is that now you *own* me. That's a dangerous position, as I discussed with Sandra, who was complaining about her husband, Charles.

"He makes me so mad," she said.

"He makes you mad a lot, doesn't he?" I asked.

"Yes."

"So what would make you happy?"

"If he quit being selfish and difficult."

"Sounds to me like you could be waiting a very long, long time."

"What do you mean"

"In all the years you've known him, has he shown any signs of becoming unconditionally loving?"

"Not really, no."

"So if you won't be happy until *he* changes, it sounds like you're pretty much doomed for a lifetime. You've put your happiness in *his* hands, waiting until *he* becomes loving, which appears at this point to be very unlikely. If I had to describe that approach in a single word, do you know what word I'd choose?"

"No, what?" she asked.

"Stupid."

"What?"

"You *could* decide to be happy every day of your life, but instead you've *chosen* to tie your happiness to someone who's made it clear that he has no intention of changing. In effect, you've *chosen* to be miserable. That doesn't seem like a very *smart* choice, so what would you call it other than stupid?"

"But *I'm* not choosing to be unhappy. *He* just keeps doing stuff to me."

"Oh, I've no doubt that he's selfish and lazy and all that, but he can't *choose* for *you* to be unhappy. Only *you* can do that." I explained how we can choose to tell the truth about ourselves, find Real Love, and be happy anytime we want, no matter what everyone around us is doing.

We all have that choice, but the instant we act like victims, we're giving up our right to choose our own happiness and our own fate, and we're putting our happiness in the hands of other people. Not a wise choice.

Other people are not responsible for our happiness, nor are we responsible for theirs. We *are* responsible for loving other people. That's always the right thing to do and the best and happiest way to live. It *is* my responsibility to learn how to love you and everyone else around me, and it's your job to learn to love me. But it's not *your* job to judge whether I'm fulfilling that responsibility, and it's not *my* job to judge whether you're fulfilling your responsibility to love me. And if you're not happy, that's not *my* responsibility, nor is my happiness your responsibility. The happiness we both experience depends on the choices we each make: telling the truth, exercising faith, using self-control not to use Getting and Protecting Behaviors, and loving other people.

WE CAN'T BE HAPPY

So far we've established that when we act like victims, we can't feel loved, we can't have loving relationships, we can't grow, we can't be responsible, we can't be free, we become spoiled, we're certain to be angry, we become liars, and we contribute to a society more interested in punishment than learning. In light of all those consequences, how could we possibly expect to be happy as victims?

As I said earlier in this chapter, our highest goal in life is to be happy. It's the reason and end for our existence. Because acting like victims makes that goal impossible, we pay quite a price for that belief and that behavior.

Please notice that at no point am I denying that victims are genuinely hurt or treated unfairly. As I said on pages 25-6, the world is filled with true victims, but *acting like victims* is simply never productive. Let me illustrate this with an experience I once had while working as an emergency room physician.

Years ago I worked in a tiny emergency room in a small town in South Texas. Late one night three large men brought their brother in to get "sewed up." The victim had been in a bar fight, and he'd picked the wrong guy to fight with. His opponent had inserted a large knife in my patient's mouth and then swept it out of his mouth sideways, *through* his cheek. When I saw the patient, his smile extended from the corner of his mouth on the right side to his *ear* on the left side. The laceration of his left cheek was long and severe. In addition, it was no great surprise to learn that he had drunk the usual quantity of alcohol for those who have been in bar brawls: "two beers."

I tried to sew the young man up, but he wouldn't hold still. Instead he chose to thrash about and scream obscenities about the man who had cut him, all the while describing how he was going to get his revenge on "that @#%& fool." I asked his brothers to help me hold him, but even three large men can't hold another man still enough to allow meticulous surgical repair. So I told his brothers to just take him home.

Half an hour later, the young victim returned, this time with his mother dragging him by his ear. She delivered him to me and said, "He'll hold still for you now." Indeed he did. He didn't move a muscle while I repaired his cheek.

This young man nicely represented most of us when we act like victims. We might genuinely be in pain. We might genuinely have been treated unfairly. But as the young man in the emergency room demonstrated, we can choose either to complain about our wounds—which benefits no one—or we can quit acting like victims and make more productive choices that lead to actual healing.

WE RAISE A GENERATION OF CHILDREN WHO WILL ACT LIKE VICTIMS

When we act like victims, our children are virtually certain to pick up that set of beliefs and that mode of behavior. Then they manipulate us and others for whatever attention they get. Anything they subsequently receive, therefore, cannot feel like Real Love. While they act like victims, they can feel only empty and alone.

If we do nothing while our children act like victims, we guarantee that they will be unhappy. We cripple them when we respond to their victim behaviors with sympathy, rescuing, spoiling, anger, or any of the other Getting and Protecting Behaviors.

In order to learn a great deal about responding to children who act like victims, and how to prevent children from acting like victims, read the book *Real Love in Parenting*.

❧ Chapter Six ❦

Conditions Caused or Worsened by Victimhood

Because victimhood is a response to emptiness and fear, we can expect to find victimhood anywhere we find emptiness and fear, which is pretty much *everywhere*. Because victimhood has such a devastating effect wherever it is found, it is therefore important that we examine how victimhood affects

- our personal lives.
- our marriages.
- our families.
- our relationships with co-workers.
- our relationships with friends and others.
- our society as a whole.
- international relations.
- the events of history.

In this chapter, as we study how victimhood affects all these relationships and conditions, we'll gain a deeper understanding of what victimhood is and how we can best respond to it.

MARRIAGE CONDITIONS CAUSED BY VICTIMHOOD

The single ingredient most necessary for a healthy marriage is Real Love, and because Real Love becomes impossible when we act like victims—as we discussed in Chapter Five—victimhood is deadly to marriages. I have counseled with thousands of couples, and almost without exception when marriages are in trouble, one or both partners are loudly complaining about what their partner isn't doing *for them*, or they're complaining about what they partner is doing *to them*. This is classic victim language and drives Real Love from the marriage as surely as June follows May.

Let me illustrate the effects of victimhood in marriage by describing two classic syndromes—among many—commonly found in marriage:

- The Sex-Starved Husband
- The Abandoned Wife

The Sex-Starved Husband

One day in my office I spoke to a married couple, Bob and Melanie. It was obvious that Bob was irritated about something, so I asked him if he'd like to speak first.

"We never have sex anymore," he said. "I'd just as well not be married as married to her."

"And all you ever want is sex," Melanie said. "It's like you think that's all I'm good for."

"Bob," I said, "it sounds like you believe Melanie is withholding sex from you."

"She *is*," he said.

"And Melanie, you feel like Bob is just *using* you for sex. Is that right?"

"Yes."

"It's important," I said, "that both of you pay attention to what you're doing here. Bob, when you say that Melanie is withholding sex *from you*, you're making it all about *you*. You're the center of the universe, and you don't care that Melanie might be acting out of motivations to protect *herself* or to fill *her* needs. You're not thinking of *her*, only *yourself*. You're feeling *victimized* by her."

"And Melanie," I continued, "when you say that he's *using you*, again you're thinking only of *yourself*, not him. You're feeling and acting like a victim. With both of you thinking about yourselves, you set up a kind of battle where no one can ever win. Bob, when you're demanding and angry, with your behavior you're clearly saying, *I don't love you*. And then, Melanie, you respond with behavior that says *I don't love you either*. How could that exchange of *I don't love you*'s possibly work out well for either of you or for your marriage?"

For the first time in their marriage, they both began to see how selfish they had been with each other, and then it became possible for them to begin working on a solution, which we'll discuss in Chapter Eight.

Although I characterized the husband in the above example as the partner desiring more sex, in 30% or more of marriages it is actually the wife who is the partner pushing for more sexual activity.

The Abandoned Wife

Carla came to see me about her husband, Glenn.

"He never does anything with me anymore," she said. "He comes home, watches television, and goes to bed. We don't talk, nothing."

"Have you talked to him about it?" I asked.

"Sure, but it doesn't make any difference."

"When you talk to him, are you irritated, as you are right now?"

"Maybe a little."

"When you're angry at him—which is probably much more than you realize—what message does he hear?"

She and I had spoken before, so she knew the answer to this question. She frowned and said, "I don't love you."

"Do you really believe that?"

"I guess, but what am I supposed to do? I feel like I'm not married."

"When you're angry, you make it clear that your primary concern is for yourself. I'm not saying that Glenn is *right* here. I'm not denying that he's neglecting you. I'm only trying to help you understand how you got where you are in your marriage and how you can find any possibility of moving forward toward what you really want in your marriage. When you talk to Glenn about his never spending time with you, how does he react?"

"He gets angry."
"And then he spends even *less* time with you."
"How did you know that?"
"When you come to him demanding more time, you're acting like a victim. You're telling him that what *you* want is more important than *his* needs. You're not even asking yourself what motivates *him* to do what he does. You're only caring about *yourself.* He *feels* that, and then how do you suppose he would react? Then when you get angry at him, he hears *I don't love you.* You don't mean to do it, but you're telling him all the time that you don't care about him, and then you wonder why he doesn't want to spend time with you. Why would he? Why would he want to spend time with somebody who doesn't care about him?"

The moment we begin to act like victims, our relationships worsen with *everyone.* By acting like victims, we're attempting to get more attention, more affection, and more sympathy, but, ironically, all we really get is more empty and alone.

DATING CONDITIONS CAUSED BY VICTIMHOOD

Most people who are dating are looking for a real partner, somebody who can be a genuinely loving companion in a healthy and unconditionally loving relationship. Unfortunately, the instant we behave like victims, we make such a relationship impossible, as illustrated in three common scenarios in dating:

- Women who resent men who won't commit
- Men who complain about women who won't have sex
- Women who resent being treated like sexual objects

Women Who Resent Men Who Won't Commit

After a seminar, a woman, Andrea, approached me and said, "I have a pretty good relationship with my boyfriend, Eric, but after being together for six months he just won't make a commitment to our relationship, and I don't understand why. It's frustrating."

"So it feels like he's withholding commitment from you?"

"Yes. I don't know what more I could do, but he'll hardly talk about it."

"There's only one reason I can think of that in a relationship you call 'pretty good' he would refuse to discuss any subject with you."

"What is it?"

"Eric feels pressured by you. You obviously want commitment more than he does, and you're *pushing* him toward it. So think about it: How do *you* react when people push you to do something—anything—you don't want to do? Do you feel good, or do you feel bad? If they keep pushing you, do you feel like they care about *you*, or does their pushing feel like evidence that they care about *themselves*?"

"I guess I never thought about it like that."

"You believe Eric is withholding commitment *from you*, but that's a selfish way to look at it. That's how a victim would see it. What he's doing isn't about *you*. It's about *him*. As you push him, you're making it clear that you're not really thinking about *his* needs, and understandably that makes him uncomfortable about having a long term relationship with you. It makes sense that if you're pushing him about this issue now, he'd be concerned about all the things you'll be pushing him to do in the future. In addition, he has some of the same concerns about commitment that most people do."

I then described to Andrea why people avoid commitment generally, a discussion found in the following sub-section.

Why do men (and women) avoid commitment?

Why are so many people reluctant to make the commitment to get married? In this case, I'll describe a man as the one reluctant to make a commitment to marriage—or a long-term relationship—but I do so with the recognition that in many cases it is the woman who is reluctant. Let's suppose that you've expressed your love to a man over a period of time, and he just won't make a commitment to you. What's the problem?

When a man has had little experience with Real Love, he has a hard time imagining anything but Imitation Love. So when you say, "I love you," what he really hears you say is this: "I love how I feel when I'm around you, and I need you to keep making me feel like that. In fact, from now on I'll be giving you the responsibility for making me feel good. And now that I've put myself out on a limb and shared my intimate feelings, I need you to do the same. I need you to love me too. In fact, I expect it."

In response to this perceived message, his thoughts—mostly under the surface, mostly feelings without actual words—run amok, including a combination of the following:

- "The people in my life have always wanted something in exchange for whatever they gave me, and I have no reason to suppose that you would be any different. In fact, I can see it in your eyes right now, that you expect me to tell you that I love you too."
- "Sure, you love me, but what will *I* have to do—what will I have to *pay*—so you'll *keep* loving me?"
- "Do I really want to take on the responsibility of doing everything it will take so you'll keep loving me?"
- "Yeah, you say you love me, but how long will this last?"
- "You love me? So what? Lots of people have told me that, and I didn't end up any happier because of it. In fact, it's always turned out badly—from my parents on down. It's always been one disappointment after another."
- "You say you love me now, but how long will it be before you hurt me like everyone else who's claimed to love me?"
- "*I love you?* I hate those words, because now I'm just obligated to tell you I love *you*, or you'll be hurt and angry."
- "Oh sure, it's nice to hear that you love me, but I don't know if I'm capable of *returning* your love in the way you want, and if I fail, there will be hell to pay."

We're afraid of making a commitment only because we are overwhelmed by the following fears:

- Somehow we sense that the thrills of Imitation Love we enjoy in the beginning of a relationship will not last. We've all seen the fleeting effects of Imitation Love all our lives, and even though we're pretty excited about the praise, power, pleasure, and safety we enjoy while we're in love, we have serious, well-founded doubts that these feelings will continue. We've seen "love" fail too many times.
- We're afraid that we just don't have what it takes to love our partners in the ways they need. Falling in love is fun, but we realize that it can't be a one-way street. We can't just *receive* love from our partners. We also have a responsibility to love *them*, and we're not sure we can do that.

Is it any wonder, then, that many people are reluctant to make a lifelong commitment to keep struggling with all the doubts, fears, and obligations outlined in the two lists above? With all those fears—almost all unconscious—it's a miracle that anyone ever overcomes them long enough to make a commitment to marriage or any long term relationship.

Men Who Complain about Women Who Won't Have Sex

After a Real Love group meeting, Adam asked me about his latest girlfriend, Diane.

"Diane seems resistant about having sex," Adam said, "and I must admit I'm getting impatient."

"How long have you two been seeing each other?" I asked.

"Two weeks."

"Wow, that long?" I said, with an obvious hint of gentle sarcasm. "You in a rush?"

"I'm just wondering why she's avoiding intimacy."

"Is it *intimacy* she's avoiding? Or is it *sex* with you? I'm guessing that if you're impatient as you're talking to *me* about having sex with her, you're almost certainly communicating your impatience when you're talking to *her*—probably even more to her—and what she's feeling is that you're more concerned about *yourself* than about *her*. You're just not getting *your way*. You're behaving like a victim, looking for what she can do for *you*. And that attitude makes a truly loving relationship impossible. Isn't that what you really want? Don't you want a genuinely loving relationship even more than you want sex?"

"I guess I'm not quite getting the point yet."

"Because you're focused on having sex with Diane, you're making it quite clear—to me and to her—that you want to *use* her, and surprise! she doesn't like feeling used. Imagine that." Again, I spoke the last sentence with a smile and a touch of gentle sarcasm.

"But I'm not trying to *use* her. I just think sex is a natural part of a close relationship."

"Let me make this a little clearer by sharing a story with you. For two years I lived in the islands of the South Pacific, where they have some rather odd customs, at least by our standards. One of them is that when the host of the family—especially if he's a tribal chief—offers you something at a meal, it's considered rude to refuse it. On several occasions, because of that custom, I had the opportunity to eat some rather disgusting foods: live worms, fish eyes, sea cucumber guts, and the like."

"Now imagine," I continued, "that I decided to take this custom back home with me, and I invited you to go with me to a sushi bar. I ordered some dishes that you wouldn't put on the end of a fishhook, much less in your mouth. Like uni, the raw eggs of the sea urchin—which is something of an acquired taste and texture—as well as raw eel and octopus. You decline my offer, but I tell you that if you're a real friend, you'll eat this stuff. You continue to refuse, but I push you harder and harder. How do you feel? Do you feel like my primary concern is for you? Or do you feel like I have some agenda of my own?"

"I'd feel like you were pushing me, and I wouldn't like it. I think I'm starting to get the point now."

"That's how Diane feels. In an unconditionally loving relationship where there is a long-term commitment, sex can be a wonderful part of the relationship, but if you begin using sex too early, it can become a *huge* distraction, for reasons you will find in the books *Real Love* or *Real Love in Dating*. But the real point right now is that the instant you push her to do *anything* she doesn't want to do, you are *not* caring about her happiness. You're not loving her, and she feels that. It's little wonder that she would resist you at that point."

Women Who Resent Being Treated like Sexual Objects

Many women are annoyed at being treated as sexual objects, and understandably so. A large proportion of men are rather noted for seeing women only as objects to gratify them with various forms of Imitation Love: praise, power, and pleasure. Because sex is an abundant source of all these forms of Imitation Love—not just pleasure—it's natural that men would seek sex as eagerly as they do.

Considering the following evidence, it's hard to deny that men see women as sexual objects:

- Advertising is absolutely driven by sex. In newspapers and magazines, and on television, we see an endless parade of women who dress, move, smile, pose, and otherwise portray themselves in sexually attractive ways. Such women are used

to sell everything: cigarettes, trucks, wrenches, beer, and so on. The unspoken implication is that if you buy this truck, for example, you will be more likely to "get"—with all the connotations of that word—women who look like this.
- Movies are saturated with references to sex and with gratuitous sex scenes that provide no meaningful addition to the plot or content of the movie whatever. Sex is used to sell movies.
- Whereas television used to be a "safe" place to go for entertainment without a concern about being assaulted by sex, it is now almost as rife with sex as movies.
- There is no single product sold with greater frequency on the Internet than pornography.
- Men joke about sex, talk about sex, brag about sex, dream about sex, fantasize about sex, hope for sex, and make plans for sex.

The fact that men often see women as sexual objects, however, does *not* make women victims, as many women claim. Let me illustrate this with a conversation I had with a woman named Sharon immediately after a Real Love seminar.

"I just hate it," Sharon said, "that men see women as sexual objects."

"No, actually, you don't," I said.

Sharon was surprised at my response. "What do you mean?"

"Look at how you're dressed right now."

"I don't understand."

"Sure you do. Remember, I'm not here to criticize you. I'm using the truth to clear up your confusion about why men treat you as they do. When you talk about how men treat *women* as sexual objects, you're really talking about how they treat *you* as one. So I'm trying only to help you see why that would be. Right now, with no effort on my part, I can see a considerable portion of your breasts, which to most men would be sexually provocative. You simply can't tell me that you're not aware of men's interests in that regard. And you're dressing like this at a seminar, so I can only imagine how you dress when you're out on a date, for example."

"But I—" she sputtered.

"This is a simple question: Can I see your breasts or not?"

"Well, yes, a little, but—"

"Do the vast majority of men find that sexually provocative, or at the very least sexually distracting?"

"I guess so, but—"

"Sharon, my dear, you *guess* so? What would happen if you stripped down to your waist in the middle of this room? Would men notice you more?"

"Okay, I get the point, but most women dress like this."

"That may be, but you wondered why men treat you like a sexual object, and I'm telling you why. You *dress* like a sexual object. Now, let's keep going. I've watched you talk with men, and I can tell you with absolute certainty that you flirt with them in sexual ways."

"What do you mean?"

I laughed. "You know, I actually believe that you don't realize what you're doing as you flirt with men. But let me put it this way. When you talk with *women*, do you talk to them the same as you talk with *men*? Be very honest here."

Sharon paused before she spoke. "No, you're right, I don't, but that's not the same. Women are quite different from men."

"Okay," I said, "do you talk to *me* the same way that you did earlier tonight to that man over there (pointing to a man across the ballroom)?"

Now she was really thinking. "I'd never thought that deeply about this," she said. "You're right, I did talk to that man differently than I'm speaking to you now."

"Why?"

"This is painful for me to say," she said, "but it's because I know that you have no sexual interest in me. I've watched you over the weekend, and you don't ever look at other women in a sexual way. Ever. So there's no reason to flirt with you."

"Outstanding honesty. Now keep going, and keep being honest. On *average*, after how many dates with a guy do you have sex with him?"

"Well, probably one or two, but that's what a lot of women do."

"And again, I don't dispute what you say, but are you beginning to see why you are treated as a sexual object? It's because you *act like one*. Simple. If you *act* like one, men will *treat* you like one. I know many other women who do *not* act like sexual objects—and they're physically gorgeous women—and men do not treat them like sexual objects."

When it comes to sex, women are *rarely* victimized without their cooperation. Genuine rape and sexual abuse certainly does occur—I have counseled with many women who can testify to that firsthand—but the phenomenon of being sexually used involuntarily is a great deal less common than most women believe. In our quest for Imitation Love, we all tend to use whatever assets *work* for us— whatever will get us the greatest amount of Imitation Love we can find—and most women discover at an early age that sex and sexual desirability are valuable forms of currency in the trading of Imitation Love. When a young girl begins to mature sexually, she suddenly finds herself the object of more attention than she's ever known, and in the absence of Real Love it's only natural that she would want that attention to continue, even if what she's receiving is Imitation Love. In their defense, young girls are encouraged by magazines, movies, boys, other girls, and even their own parents to accentuate their sexual desirability, because in our society that is a highly prized trait.

There is no blaming or fault-finding in this, only a description of what is natural in the absence of sufficient Real Love. This trading of Imitation Love is often unconscious on the part of women and men, which leads to unfortunate beliefs like Sharon's, that she is a victim. We must realize the truth about our behavior, however, so we can then begin to make wiser decisions.

In exchange for the sex that Sharon offered, she received

- praise. In our society there are few compliments more coveted than being found sexually desirable. That's why the cosmetics, fashion, hair, and plastic surgery industries thrive as they do.
- power. Sharon learned as a young girl that with the promise of sex men would eagerly do things for her that she would otherwise never get.
- pleasure. Sex was not an entirely unpleasant experience physically for her either. She loved it.
- safety. When she was with a man, she enjoyed the feeling of being protected by him.

As Sharon realized that she was not a sexual victim, but instead was making a choice to participate in a trade, she gained the power to change her choice. There is much power in knowledge, especially self awareness. When I saw her many months later, she was dressed quite differently from when I first saw her, and she said to me, "I'm amazed at the difference that our one conversation has had on me. I realized what I was doing, and I decided I didn't want to do that anymore. I'd been lying to myself. I'd been acting like a victim when I wasn't a victim at all. Now that I'm making different choices—dressing differently, behaving differently—I'm attracting an entirely different kind of man than before. I had begun to wonder if nice men were out there anywhere. It turns out that they're all over, but because of who I was, I wasn't attracting them."

For a great deal more about how to date productively and easily, read *Real Love in Dating*, which you can find at www.RealLove.com.

ANGRY AND REBELLIOUS CHILDREN

What children need most is to feel loved unconditionally. When they don't get that, they simply can't help feeling victimized, because they *are* true victims of the worst possible wound, which is to be deprived of the Real Love they need to feel happy and to have fulfilling relationships for the rest of their lives.

As parents we are often mystified by the anger and rebellion of our children. We're frustrated by it and angry because of it, when it turns out that their behavior is caused by *us*.

In order to learn a great deal more about parenting, read *Real Love in Parenting*. It will change forever the way you see parenting and children.

ADDICTION CAUSED BY OR WORSENED BY VICTIMHOOD

Most people associate the word *addiction* with alcohol or drugs, but that association severely and inappropriately limits the extent of addiction in our society. A new definition of addiction is needed, one that will give us a better grasp of the nature of addiction and will enable us to approach its treatment in a far more productive way:

> Addiction is the compulsive use of any substance, person, feeling, or behavior with a relative disregard of the potentially negative social, psychological, and physical consequences.

This definition creates a much broader—and more accurate—picture of addiction, which I will demonstrate in much greater detail throughout the remainder of this section. Before we can meaningfully continue our discussion of addiction, however, we must first consider its causes in a new way.

Despite all the research done on this subject, there is no consensus on the cause of addiction. Some theories have been repeatedly proposed, however:

- Genetic: We are born with a genetic predisposition to addiction.
- Bio-chemical: There is a chemical imbalance in the nervous system that makes us more susceptible to addiction.
- Mental illness: Addicts have a kind of mental illness.

Regardless of the specific cause espoused, most experts regard addiction as a *disease*, and many believe it's inherited. They believe that people inherit the *tendency* to addiction, even if they never actually become addicted to a specific substance.

A New and Powerful Explanation for Addiction

I have now worked intimately with thousands of addicts, and I propose a cause for addiction that is radically different from those generally discussed. This proposal explains the overall data of addiction much better than other theories do, and this proposed cause has allowed the development of a treatment plan that has proven to be very effective with thousands of addicts.

Addiction is not a disease. Addiction is a *response to pain*.

After proposing this cause for addiction in extensive interviews with addicts, less than one percent of them fail to respond enthusiastically to it, whereas most of them have had serious problems with the usual definitions and explanations.

In order to understand the cause of addiction, we must first understand what is required for human beings to be *happy*, a subject sorely neglected in mental health research and literature. In the study of mental illness and mental health, we tend to focus our attention to an inappropriate degree—almost exclusively, in fact—on illness and on the treatment of *disease*. We all understand that *physical* health requires more than simply the elimination of disease. In order to be physically healthy, we must also attend to *positive* qualities and behaviors—nutrition, exercise, shelter, and so on. In a similar way, *mental* health requires that we attend to the acquisition and maintenance of positive required elements, not just the elimination of negative factors or disease.

As we discussed in Chapter One, the most important requirement for our emotional health and happiness is to feel loved. Our souls *require* Real Love in just as real a way as our bodies require air and food.

Addiction: What We Do in the Absence of Real Love

Without sufficient Real Love in our lives, the pain and emptiness are intolerable, and in order to eliminate or reduce these feelings, we're willing to do almost anything. *This desire to eliminate pain is the key to understanding addiction.* When we find something that temporarily reduces the emptiness and pain of not having enough of that one element essential to our emotional health (Real Love), we pursue that temporary source of relief—that substance, person, feeling, or behavior—with great zeal, even desperation, and when that desperation leads us to regularly disregard the potentially negative social, psychological, and physical consequences of our pursuit, we have satisfied the definition of addiction.

And what do we use to reduce the pain of insufficient Real Love in our lives? We use Imitation Love: praise, power, pleasure, and safety. We use the Getting and Protecting Behaviors, as outlined in Chapter One, including acting like victims. And the more we act like victims, as we discussed in Chapter Three, the more likely we are to use the other Getting and Protecting Behaviors.

In short, the more empty and afraid we are, the more addictive behaviors we engage in. In addition, the more we feel and act like victims—the more we use that one Getting and Protecting Behavior in particular—the more addictively we tend to behave, as I'll explain in the next sub-section.

Victimhood: How It Leads to More Addiction

I have yet to meet an addict who wasn't in pain, and addicts overwhelmingly agree that they use their addictions to diminish their pain. In addition, those who feel victimized are in greater pain than those who do not feel victimized. Let me illustrate this concept with a metaphor.

Imagine that you're in New York City. After leaving a subway car, you begin walking through a crowded subway station filled with people you don't know. In the process of making your way through the press of humanity, you are jostled repeatedly by people walking by. At one point, you stumble over a man's feet and almost fall to the ground. A passing elbow knocks a book from your arms, which you stop to pick up. It's all a bit trying, but under the circumstances you think little of it. Upon climbing the stairs and reaching the street, you see the friend you had anticipated meeting, and she asks you, "How was your trip here?" You reply that it was nothing of consequence, and the two of you go off to spend the day together.

Now, let's do the same scene again, but this time before you leave the subway car, a man wearing sunglasses and a trench coat approaches you and tells you that there is an entire team of people waiting for you in the subway station. These people believe that you're a foreign agent, and they'll be doing everything they can to take your wallet and your belongings to check for information about your mission of espionage in New York. They may even try to stop you from leaving the station.

Now, as you walk through the crowded station, you encounter exactly the same people and the same circumstances. People are everywhere. They naturally jostle you, elbow you, and get in your way, but this time how do you feel about it? You'll feel *far more* inconvenienced, far more threatened, perhaps even paranoid, as you make your way through the station.

Why the difference? In both scenarios the people around you behaved identically. In the first scenario they inconvenienced you the same as in the second, but you were minimally bothered the first time and considerably threatened in the second scene. Why is that? Because in the second scenario you were certain you were being victimized, and that made all the difference. As soon as we believe and act like victims, we actually *feel more pain,* and then it becomes much more likely that we will addictively seek relief for that pain, which is exactly what addicts do.

VICTIMHOOD IN THE WORKPLACE

500 successful corporations were studied to find a correlation between their success and a particular business or leadership plan. There was *no* correlation. Success in business is not determined by programs or plans, nor is it determined solely by information or technology. We cannot expect our businesses to succeed until we understand what leaders, employees, suppliers, and customers all need more than anything else, and so far most of us simply are not capable of addressing that essential need.

As we discussed in Chapter One, what everyone needs most—employees, customers, supervisors—is sufficient Real Love in their lives. If they don't have that, they carry their emptiness and fear—and their Getting and Protecting Behaviors and addictions to Imitation Love—with them everywhere they go: at home, on the road, at play, and . . . in the workplace. People can't be one thing in the workplace and something else at home and elsewhere.

When people don't feel loved, they bring their unhappiness with them to work. They bring their emptiness and fear, and then they are compelled to respond with anger, criticism, withdrawal, gossip, passive aggression, silence, a reluctance to take risks, and a feeling that they are victims—all of which have enormously destructive effects on productivity in the workplace. Until we understand this, and until we address it, we cannot meaningfully improve our businesses.

In order to get an idea about how victimhood plays a role in the workplace, let's examine just three common phenomena seen in that environment:

- The Angry Customer
- The Unappreciated Employee
- The Critical Boss

The Angry Customer

As you participate in the following mental exercise, you'll get a better idea of one area in the workplace that can be strongly affected by victimhood.

Imagine that you're at the Customer Service counter at work when a customer storms up to you, slams a set of stereo headphones down on the counter and says, "I bought these from you, and now they don't work."

"Did you buy them from our store, sir?" you ask.

"What difference does that make?" he says with disgust. "But no, I bought them in California," which is 2500 miles from your store.

"Do you have your receipt?" you inquire.

"Do you keep all *your* receipts?" he snaps.

"How long ago did you purchase these?"

"How the hell should I know? Maybe five years ago."

"The warranty for this item is only twelve months."

"They're supposed to *work*, aren't they?"

The headphones he purchased were obviously intended for gentle indoor use, but it appears that a tree has fallen across them and that they were then left out in the rain for a month. Clearly this product has encountered circumstances for which it was not designed. So you ask, "How did these break?"

"So you're saying this is *my* fault?"

This man could go on forever venting his anger at you, and until you understand his *real* problem, you will not be able to help him. He's feeling victimized, and his anger is a way of protecting himself. It's likely that many other things in his life aren't going well either, and he probably feels victimized much of the time. In most situations, however, there's not much he can do. If he snaps at his wife, for example, she bites his head right off, or she withholds sex for a month, so he's learned not to press too hard on that particular battlefront. He can't yell at his boss, and he feels helpless in almost every other situation. But because he paid his hard-earned money to buy this item from *your* company, he feels like he's purchased a permit to abuse *you*.

In Chapter Nine we'll talk more about what to do in cases like this, but for now it's important to understand that if you don't recognize the victimhood in this man, you won't be able to help him.

The Unappreciated Employee
The Critical Boss

I had a conversation one day with Geoff, who was unhappy with his job. "No matter what I do," Geoff said, "my boss is critical and angry. He doesn't recognize a single good thing I do for him or for the company."

"So no matter how hard you work, he withholds praise and approval from you?"

"Yes."

"The way you see him is a huge part of the problem. You feel like this is something he is doing *to you*, something he is withholding *from you*. That's how a victim sees things. And because of how you see this, you have negative feelings toward your boss. Without realizing it most of the time, your feelings come out as you interact with him. When you see your boss at work, for example, are you *happy* to see him?"

"No.

"And do you think there is any way in the world that he *misses* that signal from you? You obviously don't like him, and without intending to, you *broadcast* that fact every time you see him. Every time you see him or talk to him, you are communicating with your behavior—your facial expressions, your choice of words, your posture, many things—the message *I don't love you*. He feels attacked by you, *victimized* by you, and without even realizing it, he then responds to you by protecting himself. He protects himself by avoiding you (running), being critical and angry (attacking), and outright acting like a victim. When he's doing all that, there's *no way* he's ever going to express appreciation toward you. Do you see that? Without meaning to, you've actually helped *create* this problem you hate."

Geoff was silent for a moment before he said, "I hardly know what to say. I just never would have seen all this."

"And then when he treats you like he does, you respond by protecting *yourself*. Who knows where it started, but the two of you make it worse every time you interact. Victimhood causes more victimhood."

Again, we'll talk more in later chapters about how to handle these situations—specifically this one with Geoff in Chapter Seven—but for now it's critical to understand that victimhood causes devastating effects in the workplace that we can eliminate if we can learn to recognize them.

HANDICAPPED PEOPLE

This is a group of people—like all those we have discussed thus far—who actually have been victimized: physically, emotionally, and psychologically. They are true victims, as we discussed on page 26. Most of them have not been responsible in any way for causing their handicaps. They were born with them, or their handicaps were inflicted upon them through no fault of their own. And, here again, within this group of people are those who choose to act like victims and those who do not.

People with handicaps are some of the most remarkable human beings I've ever known. At the age of thirteen I spent a summer volunteering at a camp of young men and women with Down's Syndrome. They were all mentally and physically challenged to various degrees, and I enjoyed every minute of it. Some of them had the sweetest dispositions I've ever encountered. Since that time I've had an affinity for spending time with such folks.

Among the handicapped are people of extraordinary courage. We've all read some of their stories:

- Erik Weihenmayer, the blind man who climbed Mt. Everest
- Christopher Reeve
- Stephen Hawking
- The paralympic athletes
- Brooke Ellison, the quadriplegic who graduated summa cum laude from Harvard

These are just some of the notables. Most of their stories escape the notice of the press. When I was in college, I met a young man with severe cerebral palsy who nonetheless completed his college degree. It took him longer to type a sentence than for me to type a page, but he never gave up. One day I literally strapped him to my back, and we got on my motorcycle together to attempt to reach the top of a nearby peak in the Wasatch Mountains. The trail was perilous, and we very nearly went off a cliff to our deaths three thousand feet below. I was terrified, but he thought it was great fun. I've always admired his superior courage and persistence.

During my years of surgical practice, I came to know many disabled people quite well. I'll never forget one young man who was moderately to severely retarded. He could easily have milked his disability in such a way that other people would have taken care of him all his life. He could have chosen to act like a victim, but instead he got a job wiping tables at a Pizza Hut—a task that was right at the limit of his intellectual abilities. He asked a friend to help him with his finances, and he took care of his own apartment. To me he was, and always will be, a hero.

And yet, among all these stories of courage, we find—as we do in *any* group—those who use their disabilities to justify their acting like victims:

- "I have ADD, so I just didn't try hard in school."
- "I was deaf in one ear, so of course I couldn't get a good job."
- "I was sick for two years in elementary school, so that put me behind, and I never could recover."

I am *not* saying that having such physical or other obstacles doesn't make life more difficult. Of course it does. But these disabilities do not of themselves determine our attitude toward them. As we stated in Chapter One, the fact that we *are* victims doesn't not mean that we must *act* like victims.

THERAPY AND SELF HELP

I do not exaggerate when I say that in the United States, perhaps more than in other nations of the modern world, we have virtually become captive to the notion of victimhood. Victimhood has become something of an institution, even a religion. The world of the victim rules. We see victimhood justified and even exalted in news reports, in our laws, in our conversations, in our behavior, and elsewhere, but for a moment we'll discuss how we see the effect of victimhood in therapy and in self help literature and teachings. The mental health field has gradually come to adopt an almost worshipful attitude toward the wounds we suffer:

- In therapy, there is endless talk about how we have been victimized by parents who were alcoholics or addicts or who were emotionally, physically, or sexually abusive.
- It's popular to talk about nourishing our "inner child," who, of course, has been victimized.

- We're all "survivors" of something: sexual abuse, physical abuse, emotional abuse, alcoholic parents, co-dependence, and so on.
- We talk about alcoholism, drug addiction, and other addictions as diseases that *happen* to us, rather than understanding what they really are, as defined on page 163 of this chapter.
- In therapy, it's very common that clients and patients are encouraged to "vent" their anger at the monsters in their lives who have victimized them.

As I have discussed in several of the Real Love books, I got to a point in my own life where all the Imitation Love and all the Getting and Protecting Behaviors became less and less rewarding. Eventually, my life became hollow and frustrating, and I reacted by turning to drugs and nearly to suicide. After leaving drug treatment I was sober but still miserable, a common condition among the newly sober, and I began exploring quite a number of other modalities in hope that I could find the happiness I sorely desired.

I made use of individual therapy, group therapy, support groups, men's groups, Native American rituals, Eastern philosophies, and so on, but still I didn't find what I was looking for. I did notice that in therapy and in the self help community victimhood was enormously popular. For some time I became quite involved in a national group where men gathered to discuss their problems and potential directions for growth. One approach these men commonly used was to share the truth about their feelings, which on the surface sounded like a great idea.

The first time I saw a man stand before other men and fully express his anger, I was energized. It was an emotional, exciting experience to see someone be that honest about his feelings, and the rest of the men present were very supportive of the man who had spoken. What I began to notice after many months of attending such meetings, however, was that the same men were expressing the same anger, over and over again, as though they were draining the same wound again and again. Despite repeated and absolutely uninhibited expressions of anger at those who had victimized them, they were not one bit happier. This puzzled me, and it wasn't until I left that group that I began to realize why simply expressing feelings—no matter how openly—wasn't effective.

The problem was that the men in that organization were—and still are—acting like victims, and it is not possible for a victim to feel what he needs most: Real Love. Although they were telling *some* of the truth about their feelings—to their credit—the truths they were telling were far from complete. In Chapter Eight we'll talk about a far more effective approach to healing our wounds, and we'll continue our discussion of expressing anger.

INFAMOUS HISTORICAL CHARACTERS AS VICTIMS: ADOLF HITLER AND SADDAM HUSSEIN

History has long wondered what conjunction of events, what concatenation of circumstances and perhaps astrology or fate, was required to produce such remarkably infamous characters as Hitler, Saddam Hussein, Pol Pot, and so on. Considering that emptiness and fear are virtually omnipresent in our world, and that victimhood is a very common reaction to emptiness and fear, it's not difficult to imagine that victimhood has played an enormous part in the creation of many of these characters. Because of the length with which I will treat my support of this proposal—especially with regard to Hitler—I will not take the time here to continue a discussion of this subject. Instead I refer you to pages 314-48. You can stop and read those pages now or continue to read through the remainder of this chapter and treat Chapter Ten as a kind of addendum.

CIVIL AND INTERNATIONAL CONDITIONS

We carry who we are as individuals everywhere we go, to all our interactions. If you're the leader of a country, for example, you'll carry your emptiness and fear into the international arena, and your victimhood will influence international relations or the relations among factions within a country. Let's look at a couple of situations where individuals and leaders have had profound impacts on the relations within their country and with other countries:

Rwanda

In 1994, in the small country of Rwanda in Africa, during a period of only 100 days, one *million* people were killed in a civil war. They were killed not with high explosives or battalions of tanks but with knives, clubs, and machetes wielded by neighbors, face to face. The world was horrified. How could such a thing have happened? There were many factors involved, but at the root of it all was a sense of victimhood that fueled the fires that nearly consumed the country.

For hundreds of years Rwanda was ruled by the Tutsi tribe (11% of the population), while the Hutu tribe (88%) was relegated to a position of lesser significance politically, socially, and economically. During that time, many of the Tutsis treated the Hutus as their inferiors, and some of the Tutsi kings even used Hutus as slave labor. This social hierarchy was reinforced by the Germans in the late 1800's and again by the Belgians beginning in 1921.

In 1959 the last Tutsi king died, and in retribution for the many ways they had been victimized over hundreds of years, the Hutus massacred at least ten thousand Tutsis, causing at least one hundred thousand others to flee the country. Hutu political parties won the elections of 1960, and in 1963 the Rwandan army carried out the first widespread Tutsi massacres.

Despite the bloodletting and subsequent release of centuries of tension, resentment between the two tribes continued to build, and in April 1994 the Hutus again lashed out at the Tutsis, this time in a killing spree possibly unmatched in human history for its intensity. For one hundred days an average of 10,000 people died per day, the enormity of which becomes especially apparent when compared with the United States Civil War—considered in this country an exceptionally bloody affair—where six hundred thousand people died over a period of four years (an average of 400 people per day). In addition, in Rwanda 2.5 million people fled the country to filthy refugee camps, where further mass deaths occurred. The infrastructure of the country was also essentially destroyed: utilities, roads, and hospitals. 3.5 million people were killed or displaced in a country whose population is now only 8.3 million.

All this happened because one group of people—and the individuals in that group—felt that they had been victimized by another group. In the book *Machete Season*, Jean Hatzfeld describes her interviews with a handful of Hutus who were convicted of slaughtering Tutsis during the 1994 massacre. We can learn a lot about victimhood by listening to them, and in the remainder of my discussion of the massacre I shall mostly be quoting from her book or paraphrasing it. (Excerpts from MACHETE SEASON by Jean Hatzfeld, translated by Linda Coverdale. Translation copyright © 2005 by Farrar, Straus and Giroux, LLC. Reprinted by permission of Farrar, Straus and Giroux, LLC.)

The Hutu killers weren't shoving faceless people into gas chambers, where their deaths were unwitnessed. Nor were these killers experienced military men, practiced in the dispensation of violence. No, on the whole these killers were simple farmers who hunted down the people who had lived next to them all their lives. They caught them in their homes, in their churches, in their fields, and in the nearby marshes, where they cut them to pieces with machetes or clubbed them to death with pieces of wood. They stood next to their neighbors as their blood flowed onto the ground until they died.

Such a thing could not have happened without enormous justification, and victims can always come up with plenty of that. Victims don't need to be offended personally. They can use any kind of offense, real or imagined. None of the killers interviewed by Ms. Hatzfeld had ever quarreled with his Tutsi neighbors over land, crops, or women, for example, but during the course of many interviews, the killers mentioned many characteristics of the Tutsi in general which at some time or other had offended them, caused them to feel inferior, or otherwise been a source of irritation:

- Past offenses of the Tutsi minority as a whole. Parents told their children stories about the old Tutsi kings and their commanders, how they used to make the Hutus do unpaid forced labor and humiliate them. Children were told that these old oppressors might come back, just as we might now threaten a child with the "boogeyman."
- The simple injustices of the old system, where the aristocracy was mostly Tutsi. The Tutsis founded a monarchy that lasted eight centuries in Rwanda, where they wielded absolute power. History lessons and radio programs incessantly hammered the unfairness of this system into the students and the general population, and one Hutu said, "These programs had a big impact on me even though I never personally had a problem with Tutsis. I wanted the power they had."
- Not enough land. More than eight million people lived in a country that would have measured only 100 miles on a side

if it were square. It was the most densely populated country in Africa. People complained that there needed to be more land—which was obviously not possible—or fewer people, and if someone had to go, it should be the Tutsi minority.
- Cattle trampling crops. Hutus were predominantly farmers, with some fishermen, while Tutsis raised cattle, which often trampled the land and the crops of the Hutus. This provoked considerable resentment from the Hutus.
- Because Hutus didn't spend time around cattle, they were simply ill at ease around cows. They regarded them as large and potentially dangerous animals, and when they encountered them by the water or in the bush, they became uncomfortable. They blamed the Tutsis for their discomfort.
- On the whole, Tutsis were wealthier, partly because of their overall superior political position and because of their ownership of cattle.
- Protection from imminent threats and revenge for recent offenses. In 1990 and 1991 Tutsis who had previously fled the country began to return as an organized militia, and they captured parts of Rwanda. When that happened, according to some Hutus, "we were angry and frightened, and then we felt justified in taking it out on other Tutsis. The politicians wanted revenge, and we went along with them." One leader of the Hutu massacre said, "The more the inkotanyi (Tutsi militia) pushed into the country, the more we would massacre their Tutsi brothers on their farms, to deter them and halt the advance."
- Whether founded on truth or not, the Tutsis were widely believed to possess characteristics that did not endear them to their neighbors: cowardice, slyness, treachery, greed, and arrogance.
- Pride. Because of their longstanding positions of political superiority, Tutsis were resented for looking down on their Hutu neighbors. Sometimes this was called "noble bearing" or being "high and mighty."
- Physical features. Although intermarriage made it increasingly harder to distinguish Hutus and Tutsis by physical characteristics alone, Hutus made frequent references to the differences. They referred to the Tutsis'

- greater height. Most Tutsis were taller than Hutus, and Hutus believed that Tutsis thought this made them superior to the Hutus.
- delicate features. Tutsis generally had more delicate, refined facial features, which were considered by both Tutsis and Hutus to be more attractive.
- longer, straighter noses.
- longer necks.
- dainty fingers.
- slender figures.
- high foreheads.

Hutus and Tutsis spoke the same language, shared the same religion, and were both dark-skinned, and yet it seemed that the Hutus were *looking* for ways to separate themselves from the Tutsis and to feel wounded by them. After you have found enough ways to point out that someone has treated you badly, it's easy to justify doing anything you want to that person in the name of either protecting yourself or seeking revenge for the pain that has been inflicted upon you by those monsters.

After we find enough excuses for blaming someone for our unhappiness, in fact, we can just generalize and blame them for everything. As one killer said, "We knew our Tutsi neighbors were guilty of no misdoing, but we thought all Tutsis at fault for our constant troubles. We no longer looked at them . . . as colleagues. They had become a threat . . . That's how we reasoned and how we killed at the time."

Blaming someone else—or a group of people—becomes especially easy if we're *taught* from an early age by our parents to do that. "We were taught to blame things on the Tutsi," said one killer, "to feel jealous. Our parents taught us. Even as children we glared at Tutsis who just happened to be passing by."

In the end, said one Hutu leader, "It's all about grudges," which is exactly the language any victim uses.

If you haven't received sufficient Real Love in your life, identifying people as monsters worthy of your revenge becomes very easy. It's Real Love that we all need most. When I receive enough Real Love from you, a connection forms between us, and I no longer feel alone. I feel included in your life, and—as an interesting bonus—that bond extends to the rest of mankind, of which you are a part. When we feel loved unconditionally, we feel connected to everyone.

When I do not receive sufficient Real Love, on the other hand, that healthy and indispensable bond between myself and other human beings is not likely to form. If it doesn't, I will feel alone and disconnected. And that is what happened with the Hutu killers. They had no bond of love with other people, so when they perceived that they had been injured, they didn't see other people as fellow human beings at all. Following are some of the comments the killers made about their activities during the massacre:

- "I killed my first victim all in a hurry, not thinking anything of it, even though he was a close neighbor on my hill. In truth, it came to me only afterward: I had taken the life of a neighbor. At the fatal instant I did not see in him what he had been before . . . My thinking had grown clouded."
- "They had become people to throw away, so to speak."
- "When we found a Tutsi in the swamps, we no longer saw a human being."

Once a victim has begun to rationalize what he's doing to those who have injured him, his abilities to rationalize become amazing. Following are some rationalizations used by the Hutu killers:

- Depersonalization. If you're hurting or killing something sub-human, it can't really be morally wrong. The two large radio stations in the capital city began to call the Tutsis "cockroaches" years before the massacre. They used humorous sketches and songs to call openly for the destruction of the Tutsis. They were so clever and funny, and repeated so often, that even the Tutsis laughed at the jokes.
- The tacit permission of others. In the early stages of the massacre, the foreigners all left the country, and the Hutus rationalized, If the whites all left and showed their lack of concern for the Tutsis, why should we care? When we feel victimized and want to get revenge, any excuse at all will do.
- Descriptive words. The killers never used the words *massacre* or *genocide*, which they knew were wrong behaviors. Instead they made their efforts noble by referring to their efforts as *work* and as *battle*, thereby turning something ugly into something acceptable.

- Use of pronouns. When the killers described the killings, they used the word *we*, carefully avoiding use of the word *I* to describe anything they did.
- The behavior of others. Many killers expressed a personal reluctance to engage in their dreaded work but felt compelled by the numbers of their friends and neighbors who were killing the Tutsis. Said one killer: "I never thought about killing Tutsis (before). Even pushing or trading harsh words didn't seem right. But when everyone began getting out their machetes at the same time, I did so too, without delay. I did what my colleagues did."

Once a victim has tasted enough of revenge, he loses sight of the original offenses that prompted the revenge, and power alone becomes enough of a motivation to keep him going. One killer said, "Man can get used to killing, if he kills on and on. He can even become a beast without noticing it." This same man said that when some Hutu killers ran out of Tutsis to kill, they began to threaten each other with their machetes. "In their faces, you could see the need to kill," he said. Another killer said, "It just made us feel powerful."

The Nature of Victims

The writer of *Machete Season* makes an incisive observation about victims when she says this: "If I had to pick out the most impressive facet of (the killer's) personalities on display, it would be not their calm detachment but their egocentrism . . . at times just unbelievable . . . they focus only on themselves in the story, then and now." One of them actually referred to the fact that some killers had "amused themselves by torturing the Tutsis who had made them sweat day after day." The killers actually felt victimized at their having to work in the hot sun day after day, killing their neighbors. Most of the killers had no nightmares. When they did it was about how *they* had been treated badly in the prison. This kind of self-centeredness isn't at all unusual for victims.

Since the massacre, victimhood has continued to define social life in Rwanda. Reprisals from Hutus and Tutsis have continued to break out, and even the way people gather in villages has been re-defined. People used to live primarily in single-family dwellings, with each family living close to their own plot of land. Since the genocide, large numbers of box-like dwellings have been densely clustered together, housing 30-3000 people. These dwellings, called mudugudus, exist to give the inhabitants a greater sense of security. As one person living in a mudugudu said, "Ever since the genocide, I always feel hunted, night and day." Regrettably, this new mode of gathering people together has resulted in people living farther and farther from their homes. Even the bars are segregated according to those who are survivors of the massacre and those who fall into other categories. Victimhood has come to define these people.

Israel and Palestine

I have read many articles and books about the origins of the Israeli-Palestinian conflict, which has been going on for generations. The disputations about the causes of that conflict are legion, but I suspected that there was a simpler thread running through all the complexity. And then I watched an interview with Ariel Sharon, who served as Prime Minister of Israel and who probably had more political and military interaction with the Palestinians than any other person. He said that the conflict wasn't about religion or land or beliefs. It was a conflict between two people who could no longer talk with each other because of the wounds they had inflicted upon each other over the years.

The conflict between these two peoples is about victimhood. It's about "Look what you have done to me." It's about "Look what you should have done for me." It's about "It's not my fault. It's your fault." Until someone understands this—until many people understand this—the conflict will continue.

❧ Chapter Seven ☙

Eliminating Victimhood with Understanding

Now that we've discussed at length the origins of victimhood and how it manifests itself in many aspects of our individual lives and in our relationships, it's time to talk about what we can do to diminish and even eliminate the uniformly destructive effects of victimhood. In this chapter we'll talk about how to eliminate the victimhood in our own lives simply with an increased understanding of principles, while in Chapter Eight we'll discuss how we can eliminate our victimhood with the power of Real Love. In Chapter Nine, we'll talk about how to respond to *other people* when they act like victims.

In order to highlight the importance of this chapter, let us consider three facts:

- As we established in the first six chapters of this book, acting like victims has devastating effects on *each of us*: on our personal happiness and on the health of our relationships with our spouses, our children, our parents, our other family members, our lovers, our friends, our co-workers, our bosses, our customers, and with other families, other tribes, and even other nations. Victimhood makes us blind, selfish, angry, isolated, irrational, unloving, unkind, and, most importantly, unhappy.

- The *incidence* of victimhood is staggering, both in breadth and depth. On a given day, nearly 100% of us act like victims, and we do so on many occasions. Further, on each of these occasions our victim-associated behaviors—anger, lying, complaining, blaming, withdrawing, and so on—affect many of the people around us. We in turn are affected by the victim behaviors of large numbers of other people as they act like victims around us.
- Assuming that it were possible to perform such gruesome arithmetic, let us then multiply the two factors above—the frequency of our victim behaviors and the severity of the effects of each of those behaviors—and then we'd have a glimpse of the overall damage done by victimhood among the family of mankind. Its effects on our emotional, spiritual, and physical health are worse than those of AIDS, tobacco, hypertension, heart disease, malnutrition, and illiteracy combined.

If there are any principles, therefore, which can help us diminish the effects of victimhood, we would be well advised to study these principles with all diligence. A simple *awareness* of victimhood and its manifestations can be a powerful tool in our efforts to limit the effects of victimhood. In previous chapters we have seen examples of the power of this awareness. In addition to this general awareness of victimhood, however, in this chapter we will be studying the following principles and actions regarding their benefit in eliminating our own victimhood:

- The Law of Choice
- The Law of Responsibility
- The Law of Expectations
- Telling the truth about ourselves

THE LAW OF CHOICE

On pages 68-70 we discussed at length the Law of Choice, which states:

Everyone has the right to choose what he or she says and does.

This is easily the most important principle of human relationships, because without it there could be no learning, no growth, no individuality, and, most importantly, no love or happiness.

As victims, we routinely violate the Law of Choice—or at least we indicate a strong desire to do so. When we act like victims, we demonstrate with our words and our behavior that we believe the Law of Choice should certainly apply to *us*, but we also believe that when *other people* make choices that inconvenience us, the Law of Choice should be repealed, and we should be allowed to control their choices so they can't hurt us or refuse to give us what we want. The different ways in which we violate the Law of Choice with our victimhood are described in detail on pages 67-70.

The effects of violating the Law of Choice are horrifying—both to ourselves and to others. When we act like victims and violate the Law of Choice,

- we're saying that the rights of other people do not matter. We couldn't be more insulting to others than to say this.
- we're saying that we do not love other people but instead that we care only about ourselves and our own needs. With that attitude, how could we ever have loving relationships?
- we become self-centered, isolated, and eventually completely alone, which guarantees our misery.
- we are certain to be angry at people all the time, because imperfect people—a description that applies to everyone—*will* make decisions on a regular basis that will inconvenience us.

Any time we are tempted to feel like victims, it is essential, even life saving, that we remind ourselves of the Law of Choice and of the selfishness—the astonishing arrogance, actually—of violating it. Other people *really* do get to make their own choices—including the unwise choices that affect us in negative ways—and that's just the price we pay for living in a world where *we* get to make *our* choices, the choices that are essential to our learning and growing in the process of becoming happy. Let me briefly add here that just because other people are allowed to make their own choices does not mean that we have to allow them to use us or hurt us, nor do we always have to give them what they want. Loving people unconditionally does not make us doormats. We'll discuss this subject more in Chapter Nine.

On pages 32-4 I shared with you the metaphor of the drowning man, and you experienced what it was like to have your feelings change immediately upon learning that he was drowning, instead of laboring under your old assumption that he was trying to inconvenience or harm you personally. Now let's learn something further from that metaphor. Let's suppose that *each of us* is the person drowning in the water. Understandably, the temptation is strong to believe that we have been victimized. After all, we're about to lose our lives. Our need is great—at the very limits of imagination, in fact—and surely under these circumstances we have a right to demand that the people around us come to our aid.

But no, we still do not have that right. Why not? Because

- if we assume the right to demand the help of other people when we're *drowning*, where would it end? Once we had *that* right safely under our belts, we'd never be satisfied. Next we'd move on to insisting on the right to demand help from others when we're in *pain*, and then when we stumble and fall, and then when we don't feel good, and then when we just plain feel like it. No, the Law of Choice must be operational all the time, without exceptions. We simply can't be trusted to self-limit our desires to control other people.
- we really don't have the wisdom to know whether another person is *capable* of helping us out of the water in any given moment. We may *think* we can make that judgment, but the fact is that most people around us are also drowning, even when they *look* like they're not. Many people are quite good at pretending to be functional—they hide their drowning condition from us quite well—but they simply are not capable of helping us or anyone else. In addition, when we're drowning, our judgment of *everything* is seriously impaired.
- before we demand that other people help us from the water, we have an obligation to make the most of our own efforts to get out of the water. We could—emotionally speaking—look for floating debris for support, we could possibly sink to the bottom and push off toward the shore, and in some cases we could ask for instruction about how to swim. It is always our responsibility to do what we can to get to the shore, not the responsibility of someone else to save us.

The Ultimate Choice in Victimhood

As human beings—and as victims—we have far more than a *right* to make our own decisions (the Law of Choice). Making decisions is also a grand *opportunity* available to us every moment of every day, an opportunity for us to learn and find a greater measure of happiness. One of the more important decisions we will make concerns the position we will take regarding our own victimhood: From what perspective will we view the people and things we encounter every moment we're alive?

During our lifetimes we will unavoidably experience quite a variety of unpleasant, unkind, painful, unfair, unjust, inconvenient, and even intentionally vicious and vindictive people, events, and circumstances. In a world where people make their own choices, it could be no other way. No matter how careful we are, these people and events simply cannot be entirely avoided, so we must give up the illusion that controlling them is one of our reasonable options. The only choice left is how we will *feel about* and *respond to* these people, events, and circumstances. Our reasonable choices really boil down to two:

> First, we could choose to feel as though we have been personally singled out for abuse by unpleasant people, events, circumstances, and essentially the whole universe for the rest of our lives;
>
> OR
>
> Second, we could choose to realize that inconvenience, pain, and injustice are
>
> - unavoidable. We will always be around other people who are trying to fill their own needs, and as they do that, it is certain that on occasion they will affect our ability to get what *we* want. As other people satisfy their own needs, they will sometimes take the parking space you wanted, make you wait in line, receive the promotion you expected, and so on.
> - not the end of the world. Inconvenience and pain are simply *some* of the threads in the grand tapestry of our lives, and sometimes it is from these most difficult threads that we learn the most, grow the most, and derive the most genuine happiness.

- not to be shunned, avoided, and campaigned against as though they were the worst possible elements of life. Our highest goal in life is not ease and comfort but to learn to be loving, and sometimes it is from the most inconvenient and painful experiences that we learn the most profound degrees of loving.
- rarely done *to us* but mostly happen as a result of the natural and unavoidable mistakes that people make when they are empty and afraid, and also result from events and circumstances quite beyond anyone's control.

When we make the first of these two choices—to take all inconvenience and pain personally—we are absolutely guaranteed to feel victimized and to act like victims. We are guaranteed to feel angry and miserable and alone. We are *choosing* to be unhappy, which would seem to qualify as the single dumbest choice we could make.

When we make the second choice, however, we open the doors to learning, growth, and joy forever. Difficulties and even tragedies no longer destroy us; rather they give us opportunities to learn and grow. This is not a fairy tale. I know many people who live this way, and they possess the genuine peace and joy that most people can scarcely imagine. This second and higher way of living can be *learned*—we are not randomly assigned to live as victims or not—as illustrated in a conversation I once had with one of my daughters, Janette.

Janette was working hard at school: taking a full academic load, working part time, juggling a social calendar, doing her student teaching rotation, and so on. In our family, we don't just pay our children's way through college, because we believe they learn more by earning their own way, and she was in the thick of that learning process. She described to me two difficult interactions she'd had, one with a roommate and another with a co-worker, and finally she said, "Sometimes, life just seems too hard. Why does it have to be that way? Why couldn't it be easier?"

She had been on an athletic team before, so I knew she'd understand what I said next. "Let's suppose," I said, "that I'm training you for an athletic event. The training is exhausting, so one day in the middle of a session I announce, 'Janette, I just can't bear to see you get all uncomfortable and sweaty, and I don't want to see you injured either, so here's what we're going to do: From now on when you come in to do your training, I'll do it for you. You relax on the couch, take the load off your feet, and either I'll do the exercises for you, or we'll just cancel them for the day.'"

She was smiling, so I continued, "That would be pretty nice for a while, wouldn't it? No pain, no sweating, no straining."

"Yes," she said, "but you'd be a pretty lousy trainer."

"How's that?"

"You'd be making me comfortable, but you'd also be making me weak. By taking the load off me, I wouldn't get any stronger. And that's the point you're making about my life, isn't it?"

"Sure. It's very tempting to look for the easy way, and to resent the hard way, but all the experiences in our lives are just training opportunities. We can spend our entire lives feeling victimized by our difficult experiences, or we can be grateful that we have these opportunities to grow. I mean it. With every single experience of our lives, we *choose* whether we'll be resentful or grateful, and that choice determines the outcome of our entire lives. Once we decide that we can learn from everything that happens to us, we never feel victimized again. That's a monumental decision."

How Knowledge of the Law of Choice Can Influence Victimhood

Let me further illustrate how a knowledge of the Law of Choice can strongly influence our feeling and acting like victims as we look in on a conversation I'm having with Melinda, who is raising a four-year-old son, Cody, by herself. Her boyfriend abandoned her during the pregnancy, and now she's working full-time while going to school. She's been attending Real Love group meetings on and off for months and is always complaining about how difficult her life is: Nobody ever helps her enough, people are always treating her unfairly, and nothing is ever her fault. I'm attending a meeting where she is repeating some of these complaints.

"My mother's always telling me how to raise my son," Melinda says. "She thinks I spoil him. And then she disciplines him right when I'm in the room—can you believe that? Things aren't easy at school either. The other day I was only one day late with an assignment—because Cody was sick, for heaven's sake—and the teacher took ten points off my grade. I couldn't believe it! Nobody seems to understands how hard it is to go to school, work full-time, and try to raise a child."

I can't do Melinda's schoolwork for her, or go to work for her, or raise her son. I can't solve her immediate technical problems, but I *can* offer her the tools that can help her find genuine happiness. I can help her avoid the terrible life of a victim, and that is *far* more valuable than any physical thing I could ever do for her. If I can help her take a step toward Real Love—instead of victimhood—I may help empower her for the rest of her life.

"Are you spending time every day," I ask, "with people who can give you the love you need?" (We'll be talking more about the subject of finding Real Love in Chapter Eight, by the way.)

"I don't have time for that," she says. "Like I said, I'm already too busy to do everything I'm supposed to do. How would I have time to call people and share myself with them?"

Victims characteristically present long lists of problems that need to be fixed, but when a solution is offered that involves *their* doing something different, they invariably respond with reasons why the solution won't work. They're looking for an answer where *other people* will save them. They're not malicious about this, just lazy and irresponsible. They've learned from past experience that they can get other people to give them sympathy and support, so they continue to act like victims instead of telling the truth about their irresponsible choices and learning to make better ones.

When talking to victims—and when acting like victims ourselves—it's especially useful to remember the Laws of Choice and Responsibility (pages 68 and 71). Victims need to be reminded that they always have a choice and are then responsible for the choices they make.

"How long does it take," I ask, "to pick up a phone and call people who can see and accept you?"

"I just don't have time to do *everything*."

"There's no doubt that your life is difficult. There's also no doubt that in everything you do, you're making a *choice*, and so far you're making a choice *not* to feel loved. You're choosing to act like a victim instead of changing the way you live."

"I don't understand."

"You're acting like all these problems were dumped on you, but that's not true. You *chose* to go to school. You *chose* to have your job. You *chose* to have your son, and you *chose* to have your mother take care of him. As you choose to make no contact with people who could love you, you're also choosing to stay unhappy. And now you're complaining about the natural consequences of your choices. It doesn't make much sense."

"Are you saying I *chose* to be a single mother? I'm not the one that ran away. My *boyfriend* did that."

"Did you have sex with the father of your son or not?"

"Well, yes, but *he* left me to raise Cody by myself."

"That *was* his choice, and I don't deny that it was irresponsible of him, but I'm trying to help you see how many choices *you* had in this. *You* chose to have sex with this man, and you chose to do that while you were single. I'm not judging the morality of what you did, only pointing out that *you* created the possibility that you would become a single mother. Were the two of you absolutely in agreement about raising a child together for the child's entire life?"

"Well, not exactly."

"So he *didn't* agree to raise a child with you, and you weren't married. Knowing that, having a child was very risky indeed. In light of that, did you do everything possible to keep from getting pregnant?"

"Well, no, I—"

"If you two hadn't agreed completely that you were going to raise a child together, and you weren't doing what it took to keep from getting pregnant, didn't you virtually guarantee that you'd be a single mother? In effect you made a *choice* to raise this baby alone."

Melinda is eager to change the subject and says, "So what about my mother? Are you saying that's my fault, too?"

"No, you're not responsible for her behavior, but you *did* choose to be around it, and now you're complaining about the choice *you're* making."

"I don't get it."

"You know exactly what kind of woman your mother is, don't you? Haven't you been around her all your life?"

"Well . . ."

"Hasn't she *always* given you advice—about everything—and tried to control you?"

"Yes."

"Then when you decided to leave your son with her to get the free babysitting, you *knew* she would give you advice and try to control you, didn't you? You knew that would be part of the package. You *chose* that."

"But what else can I do? I don't have the money for anybody else to take care of him."

"So be grateful that she helps you out when you can't afford anything else, and quit expecting her to suddenly become a different person for your convenience."

"Well, I still don't have time to make those phone calls."

"There's no doubt you have a lot of demands on your time, but you're ignoring the most important thing you need. You need to feel loved, and if you don't get that, everything else you do won't really matter. Is your son important to you?"

"Of course."

"You've often said that when you get busy with so many things, you get tired and grouchy. When you're like that, are you kind and loving toward him?"

Melinda pauses before she says, "I try to be, but no, I get impatient with him—and I hate that."

"Do you hate it enough to want to change? There's nothing in your life right now more important than being happy and raising your son to be happy. If you had to drop out of school for a semester to learn how to do that, it would be well worth it. That may not be necessary—I'm just making the point that you need to do whatever it takes to get what you really need. No amount of school or money will mean anything if you're unloving and miserable. What could be more important in your life right now than being happy and raising your son to be happy?"

"I see what you mean."

"Melinda, if I didn't care about you, I wouldn't say anything when you say you don't have time to make phone calls and do what it takes to change your life—but I really do care about you. If you want to change your life, you can. It's a choice. You are not helpless. You are not a victim."

Melinda begins to take the time to make the calls to members of her Real Love group, and slowly she begins to see how she's always acted like a victim. She also begins to feel accepted by the members of the group. She's still a single mother and has to work to support herself and her son, but she's finding the happiness she's always wanted. She's also much more loving to her son.

Helping victims see the truth about themselves can sometimes seem harsh—especially when read on the printed page—but there's no other way to help them change their destructive course. We can help victims see that almost all their problems are a result of the choices they've made, and that there's always a way they can find happiness, regardless of what their problems are.

Teaching Our Children About the Law of Choice and Victimhood

We give our children a great gift—a key to happiness—when we teach them that they never have to be victims. We have many opportunities to do that. Every time a child is disappointed or angry, he's acting like a victim. His disappointment is a direct result of his belief that other people have an obligation to please him. We must teach children that other people have a right to make their own choices and mistakes, even the ones that inconvenience us.

Even more important than our teaching our children with *words* that they're not victims is our giving them enough Real Love so they *feel* loved. Without emptiness and fear, they won't *feel victimized* when people treat them badly, and in those potentially difficult interactions they can then choose to be loving and happy instead of afraid, demanding, selfish, and angry. Such children enjoy profound peace all their lives, regardless of the choices made by others.

Imagine how the world will change when we raise the upcoming generation without the feelings and behaviors of the victim. To learn more about how we can make this happen read the book *Real Love in Parenting*.

With the Law of Choice Comes the Absence of Guilt

When we act like victims, one characteristic we commonly demonstrate is a tendency to make everyone around us feel guilty when they won't do exactly what we want. It's only natural that we then demand apologies from those people, and the apologies we demand are often endless. When we understand that other people really do have a right to make their own choices, including the ones that inconvenience us, we usually see two results: First, we no longer feel like victims, nor do we require guilt and apologies from others.

Second, we no longer feel unnecessary guilt for the mistakes *we* have made that have caused inconvenience and even pain for other people. I am not suggesting that we should be cavalier about our mistakes, nor that we should dismiss the pain of others, only that we should not indulge in suffering *unnecessarily* for our mistakes.

If an apology will help another person feel more loved, offering one might be appropriate, but you should not apologize because you feel motivated to do so by guilt. You are not responsible for the unhappiness in the lives of other people, only for the mistakes you make. Remember that other people felt unhappy and unloved long before you "offended" them, so you do not have a responsibility to remove their anger or make them happy, despite their vigorous and repeated claims to the contrary.

When I suggest that you take responsibility for your mistakes, that might mean that if you took money that wasn't yours, you would admit that and return it. If you broke a window, you'd fix it. If you were unkind, you'd admit your mistake and apologize. But unloved, victimized, and unhappy people often demand that the emptiness of their whole lives be filled with the apologies and suffering of those they believe have offended them—and that is not possible.

THE LAW OF RESPONSIBILITY

Connected irrevocably to the Law of Choice is the Law of Responsibility: I'm always responsible for the choices I make, which we introduced on page 71. Without responsibility, the freedom to make our own choices becomes nothing more than an excuse to be selfish, as one father teaches his son, Gary, below.

Gary's father spoke to him at a family meeting. "Gary," said his father, "last night you ate dinner in the living room while you watched television. Do you remember what happened to your food and plate after that?"

"No," said Gary.

"You left your plate in the living room, you spilled food on the floor, and you didn't clean it up. With your behavior, what were you telling everyone else?"

Gary shrugged his shoulders, so his father helped him see that with his behavior he was saying "I expect other people to be responsible for the choices I make."

"*You* chose to take your plate into the living room," said the father. "All the consequences of making that choice then became *your* responsibility. Can you see how it wouldn't make sense for anyone else to be responsible for your choices?"

"I didn't think of it like that."

Gary assumed someone else would choose to take care of his mess. When we're lazy and irresponsible, we hope—and often demand—that other people will choose to serve us. When our children are lazy, it's unproductive to make them feel ashamed. With that approach they learn only to be afraid and angry. Instead we just need to consistently point out their lazy behavior and unconditionally love them while we teach them. When we do that, they can feel safe enough to tell the truth about themselves—as Gary did—and can learn to be more responsible and happy.

Children need to be given many opportunities to account for their behavior. They need frequent evaluation and guidance. We need to point out when they do well and when they do poorly. That's how they learn.

Now for an Adult Version of Accountability

Now that we've discussed how we can talk to a child about responsibility and accountability, let's examine how this might be done with an adult. We'll observe an interaction at work between one man, Joseph, and his supervisor, Nathan. As you consider Joseph's behavior, I encourage you not to identify *his* victimhood but to realize how on many occasions *you* have acted like a victim in similar ways. If you do this, you'll learn much about how you can eliminate victimhood in your own life, which is a far more productive goal than to learn how Joseph did it in his.

Joseph had long established a habit of being late. He was famous for it. Work started at 8:00 a.m., and Joseph routinely arrived at 8:05,

8:12, sometimes as late as 8:20. Most of the time, it wasn't a big problem, but sometimes it was obviously disruptive in a number of ways:

- He came into meetings late and required an update about what had happened, which wasted everyone else's time.
- When he came in late, sometimes he occupied the time of many people as he chatted them up on the way to his desk.
- Apparently encouraged by Joseph's example, a few other employees began to arrive late with increasing frequency.

Nathan had talked to Joseph about his lack of punctuality on a number of occasions, and he *always* had great excuses:

- The traffic was bad.
- The traffic was really bad (this was a favorite).
- His car wouldn't start.
- He forgot a file for work and had to go back and get it.
- He forgot about the change in Daylight Savings Time.
- His alarm clock didn't work.
- His dog was sick.

In short, it was never Joseph's fault that he was late. He was a perfect victim, and employers—or anyone else, for that matter—have a difficult time dealing with victims, for the reasons we discussed in Chapter Four: Victims make us feel guilty; they manipulate us and others for sympathy, attention, support, and power; and they somehow manage to hold a position of self-righteousness while they do it all. Nathan had tried pushing Joseph harder, but Joseph just came up with more victimy excuses, and then he went back into the office and complained about what an insensitive and terrible boss Nathan was.

Nathan was at his wits' end, until he read an early manuscript for *Real Love and Freedom of the Soul,* at which point he realized that he simply needed to quit playing on the Field of Death—which we discussed on page 45—with Joseph. Nathan realized that as a victim Joseph was a master on the Field of Death, and if Nathan played any part of Joseph's game, he would lose, because *everyone* on the Field of Death dies. The only way Nathan could win—or help the company or Joseph win—was to get completely off the Field of Death and on to the Field of Life, where everything is run by the truth, by true principles, and by Real Love. Getting and Protecting Behaviors and Imitation Love have no place on the Field of Life.

Nathan called Joseph in to his office, and immediately Joseph said, "Look, I was only a few minutes late, and I couldn't help it. You see, I—"

Already Joseph had leaped on to the Field of Death to do battle, and Nathan made a conscious decision: He refused to have any part of it. "Oh, I don't care about your being late today, Joseph."

Immediately, Joseph's excuses were over. He was disoriented. He didn't know what to say next. He was comfortable only when he was speaking on the Field of Death. "So what do you want?" he asked.

"I'm never going to bother you again about being late," Nathan said. "That will be entirely your decision to make."

Joseph was becoming increasingly puzzled. There was simply no opportunity here for him to act like a victim, or to get angry, or to use any of the Getting and Protecting Behaviors, so how could he participate in this discussion? He couldn't use any of his usual tools. "I don't get it," he said. "You don't care if I'm late?"

"Nope," said Nathan. "Your choice. You can be late all you want, but you can't do it here. If you choose to be late, you'll also be making the choice to do that at another place of employment."

Ah, thought Joseph, *here's the attack. How could they possibly disregard my contributions here over such a small thing as being late? Now I have an opportunity to act like a victim.* "So if I'm late, you'll fire me?" he asked with some indignation.

"I just realized recently," said Nathan, "that *I've* been doing this all wrong. Not *your* fault at all. What's been happening is that *you've* been making the choice to be late, and then *I've* been taking responsibility for *your* choice and suffering the consequences. It's entirely my fault that I've been doing that. I've just finally decided that I won't be doing it anymore."

"So what we'll be doing," Nathan continued, "is simply adhering to the company policy manual that has already been written. It clearly specifies exactly how many times a month and how many times a year—and by how many minutes—you can be late before you receive a written warning. If you then violate that code one more time, *you* will be declaring your belief that being late is more important than working here. You have a right to be late, by the way, but not at this place of employment. So you don't have to come up with anymore reasons why you're late. You don't have to feel like I'm watching you. You need only be aware that every time you make a choice to be late, you're also choosing to leave your job here. Simple as that. All *your* choice."

It took time, but Joseph slowly realized that he was not a victim at work, and he further realized that he had been acting like a victim in many areas of his life. When people don't jump on the Field of Death with us, it's easier for us to see our victim behaviors and then to make different choices.

THE LAW OF EXPECTATIONS

In Chapter Two we discussed the Law of Expectations, which states:

We never have the right to expect anyone to do anything for us.

This law naturally follows from the Law of Choice, because if you have the right to make your own choices, how could I possibly expect you to change your choices to meet my expectations? And yet when we act like victims, we routinely disregard the Law of Expectations. In fact, our victimhood is actually *founded* on a disregard for that law, because as victims we expect almost everyone to do what we want and never to do anything that inconveniences or hurts us.

Perhaps the most important corollary of the Law of Expectations states:

Never expect any one person or group of people to love you.

Let's look at how an understanding of the Law of Expectations can help us overcome our feelings of victimhood. On page 167-8 we looked at a conversation I had with Geoff, who complained that no matter what he did, his boss was critical and angry. Let me suggest that you review that conversation. To summarize, I suggested to Geoff that by acting like a victim, he was loudly communicating with his behavior that he didn't like his boss, and his boss was *feeling* that message. Geoff's boss felt attacked by Geoff, and he responded by protecting himself, in part by attacking Geoff. Both Geoff and his boss were making the behavior of the other person much worse.

Following is a continuation of that conversation between Geoff and myself:

"So you understand that your anger at your boss threatens him," I said, "and he reacts by getting angrier at you. That in turn threatens *you*, and you get more angry at *him*. And so on. It's a cycle. Now comes an important question: What *starts* the cycle? *Why* do you get angry at your boss in the first place? When he is short with you or critical or angry or whatever, *why* does that bother you?"

"Wouldn't it bother *everybody*?"

"No, actually," I said. "I know quite a number of people who would not be bothered. In a minute I'll tell you why they wouldn't. You are bothered only because you *expect* him to treat you differently. You expect him to treat you with a little respect and a little appreciation, don't you?"

"Well, yes."

"Respect and appreciation are just forms of praise, forms of Imitation Love. What you really expect of him, strange as it sounds, is that he'll *love* you in some small way, because you've gotten very little of that in your life."

"I don't know about the *love* part, but yes, I do expect some appreciation, just a little."

"When you go to work, do they pay you?"

"Yes."

"Do they always pay you what they promise you?"

"Sure."

"You have a *contract* with the business that employs you. You agree to do certain work for them, and they agree to pay you. When you were hired, did they agree to give you *anything* other than the check they give you every two weeks, along with whatever medical or other benefits they give you?"

"Well, no, I guess not."

"Then the fact is that you have *no right*—none—to expect anything at all from him, other than what is in your business contract. We've talked about the Laws of Choice and Expectations before, so you understand *why* you have no right to make demands of your boss or anyone else. This is important, because you keep having feelings of irritation only because you feel that you *do* have a right to your expectations. When you can let go of those, and accept your boss as he makes his own choices—even the unkind ones as he learns to be a more loving person—you won't have any anger toward him."

On page 225 we discuss another approach to resolving a conflict with an unappreciative boss. It's a continuation of the story of Andy on page 59.

An Exception to the Law of Expectations

When I say that we never have the right to expect anything from anyone, it should be obvious that there are exceptions, as in the case above with Geoff. When he was hired at his place of business, he entered into a formal contract with the owners and supervisors there. He made a promise to do certain work, and they promised to pay him and give him certain other benefits. A contract is an exchange of promises, and in the case of a promise, we *do* have a right to expectations. When Geoff's boss promised to pay him, Geoff had a right to expect a check twice a month. He had no right, however, to expect anything that was not promised.

In some cases, however, a promise between people can be far less formal than a business contract, as in the following situation described to me by a woman named Abby.

"Men are such liars," Abby said with obvious anger.

"I have no doubt of it," I said, "but you seem to be talking about something specific. What is it?"

"When I go out with guys, sometimes at the end of the date they'll say, 'I'll call you.' Half the time I don't know if they really mean it, or if they're just saying what I want to hear. The ones that are saying it just to get rid of me—the ones that never call—really irritate me. Why don't they just tell me the truth?"

"Oh, that's an easy question."

"Really?"

"Sure. Now, do a little mental exercise with me: Suppose somebody asks you a question, and you *know* that if you tell them the truth they'll get angry, but if you kind of sugarcoat the answer—tell them what they want to hear—they probably won't be angry. Which answer do you think you'd be likely to give?"

"I suppose I'd probably sugarcoat it a little."

"Right. Nobody likes confrontations, and most of us learned that little trick at our parents' knees. We learned to tell people what they wanted to hear so they wouldn't be disappointed or irritated at us. Right now as you're talking about how guys behave, you're angry, and when things happen that you don't like, you have a general tendency to get irritated. *That* is why some guys promise to call you when they don't really plan to. They *know* you won't like the straight answer, and in order to avoid feeling your disappointment or irritation, they lie to you. I'm not saying that what they're doing is justified or right. I'm just *explaining* why they do it."

"But they *say* they'll call."

"You're quite right. They're *lying*. They're breaking a promise. You do have a right to expect that they'll *keep* their promises, but they don't. But you need to appreciate the difference between *having* a right to an expectation and *insisting* that your expectation be fulfilled. Let me illustrate. Suppose you pull up to a four-way stop sign at exactly the same time I do, and I'm on your left. Who has the *right* to pull into the intersection first?"

"I do, because I'm on the right."

"Correct, but now let's suppose that as you pull into the intersection, I drive forward also, at the same rate you do. Do you still have the right to continue driving?"

"Yes, I have the right of way."

"Yes, you do, and if you *insist* on that right, you may be *dead right*. With the men in your life, you're taking the same risk. Normally, you don't have a right to expect that they'll do anything for you, but when they make promises you do have the right. But then you take that *right* as a justification for *pushing them* or becoming angry at them, and it simply *doesn't work* when you do that. Insisting that people keep their promises makes you unhappy, and the guys you date will resent you when they feel your insistence."

The guiding principle here is that even in the case of a promise made, never, never expect another person or group of people to give you *love* in any form. The instant you expect love, it will never be fulfilling. Consider the discussion of the roses on page 73.

TELL THE TRUTH ABOUT YOURSELF

Thus far in this chapter we have discussed some *principles* that can be very helpful in eliminating victimhood in our lives. Now let's talk about the first *active step* we can take toward eliminating victimhood, which is to tell the truth about ourselves. When you're complaining about some terrible injustice—about how something just wasn't "fair," or how someone should have done something for you—you are actively throwing fuel on the fires of victimhood. If you will stop and simply tell the truth about how *you* are acting like a victim, you'll remove the fuel from the flames, and the fire will go out. Let me illustrate how this might look with an example. In Chapter Four we met Julie, who was complaining in a group meeting about her husband. Please review that brief conversation on pages 103-4, where I also promised to continue it here.

In Chapter Four I last said to Julie, "You've proven with *your* experience—over a period of many years—that your efforts to change *him* are doomed. So let's try something different instead. Let's talk about *you*. What do *you* do in your relationship that makes your marriage unloving? How are *you* unloving?"

"*Me?!*" she said. "*I'm* not the problem here. *He* is."

"Oh, I have no doubt that he is selfish, inconsiderate, thoughtless, a poor listener, demanding, angry, defensive, and withdrawn. Did I miss anything important?"

Julie looked surprised. She thought I hadn't been listening. "Not really."

"In fact," I said, "couldn't we pretty well summarize your husband's behavior by saying that he's doing a lousy job of loving you unconditionally?"

"Well . . . yes, I guess so. That's certainly true."

"So every negative thing you might say about him after this would only be a confirmation or a restatement of what we already know, that he's unloving, right?"

"I suppose so."

"And no matter how many times you've described how he's unloving, no matter how many details you've provided to prove it, has he ever changed?"

"Not really."

"So despite a lot of effort in all these years, your approach to changing your relationship hasn't worked very well, wouldn't you say?"

Julie was speaking pretty slowly by now. "Not very well, no."

"So why not try something else? You couldn't do much worse. Even better, what I'm going to suggest here isn't just 'something else.' It's not some random shot at doing relationships another way. I'm suggesting that you learn a new and simple way of *understanding* things differently and a way of *living* that have proven effective so consistently and so many times that I can virtually *guarantee* it will work if you'll really try it. Would you be willing?"

"I suppose." Julie's response was less than fully enthusiastic.

"Let's start now. Talking about your husband has never worked, so let's try talking about *you*. Like I said, I believe you when you say that he's been unloving, but you've proven you can't change that. Let's see if we can help *you* change. How do *you* behave toward your husband?"

"Better than he behaves toward me."

Smiling, I said, "Oh, that's comforting. So if you hit me, and then I hit you, but not quite as hard as you hit me, does that make me loving? Will we have a great relationship?"

"Probably not."

"Exactly. Back to you. Do you get irritated at him?"

"Sometimes."

"Let's try that again. When you're here in the group, at least during the times I've heard you speak, you're angry at him constantly, and that's without him here doing anything to you. So I'm guessing that at home, with all his unloving influence in your face, you might be irritated at him more than *sometimes*. Would that be fair to say?"

"Yeah, probably so."

"And you're angry because you believe he's doing unkind things *to you* and withholding kindness and love *from you*, right?"

"Yes."

"We've talked about this before. The belief that his behavior is all about *you* is called what?"

Julie hesitated before she said, "Acting like a victim?"

"Yes, and *that* is a beautiful example of telling the truth about *yourself*. How did it feel?"

"Not as bad as I thought it would be. You kind of led me there."

"Most of us have been lying about our own faults and pointing out the mistakes of everybody else for so long that we've become accustomed to it. We're not even aware we do it—really. So in the beginning, telling the truth about ourselves can seem quite strange, like learning a foreign language. It doesn't come naturally, so let me try to make this a little easier for you. I'll try to describe your behavior toward your husband in more straightforward and truthful terms, and if I say anything that's *not* true, I want you to stop me. Will you do that?"

"Sure."

"For years," I said, "you've expressed anger at your husband quite often." I paused. "You've acted like a victim with him. You've withdrawn from him emotionally, physically, and sexually. You've criticized him. You've been demanding. Overall, you haven't been supportive and kind. How am I doing?"

"It's not fun to hear, but what you're saying is true."

"So now let's sum up the whole picture: Your husband has been unloving toward you, and you have responded by being unloving toward him. So in your relationship we have *unloving* (which I said while holding out one hand, representing one of them) and *unloving* (which I said while holding out the other hand, representing the other person). Which of the two of you is more of the problem here?"

"He *started* it," she said.

"You *might* be right, but would it really matter? Let's say he *did* start it, and you're only *paying him back*. As Gandhi said, 'An eye for an eye makes the whole world blind.' Do you want to pay him back forever—and destroy your happiness and relationship—or do you want a loving and happy relationship?"

"This is hard to do," Julie said.

"Harder than what you're doing now?" I asked. "How is that possible? How could anything be harder than all the effort you two put into protecting yourselves and hurting each other?"

Gradually, Julie began to tell the truth about *herself*, and she discovered the miracle that we can't tell the truth about ourselves and act like victims simultaneously. The subsequent changes in her marriage were gradual, but also dramatic and permanent.

Telling the Truth about What We Get from Acting like Victims

In Chapter Four we met Emily, who complained that her husband controlled her in many ways. I suggested that she wasn't a victim at all but instead was a willing participant in a relationship where *she* was getting as much as *he* was getting from this controlling situation. Victims feel trapped, and if someone will lovingly help them see that they do have choices, they will sometimes begin to make those choices, one of which is to choose the freedom of telling the truth about themselves. Emily did that. She began to see that in her marriage, the rewards were many:

- She didn't have to earn a living.
- She didn't have to manage the finances.
- She had all day to play tennis, paint, work in the garden, or whatever else she chose.
- She didn't have to make any difficult decisions.
- She could wait until her husband made the hard decisions and then criticize them.
- She felt safe and taken care of.
- Even though her husband controlled her, at least he spent time with her. While he was controlling her, she felt some sense of connection to him.

As Emily told the truth about the rewards of her relationship—the rewards of acting like a victim—she found it much harder to continue her complaining.

One day I asked her, "Do you want your relationship to change?"

"I do," she said

"If you start making some of your own choices—about clothes, money, or whatever—you'll see changes in your relationship with Dean. It *has* to change, because *you* will be different. Sometimes people in relationships who have been controlled or victimized believe that the solution to their situation is to 'stand up for themselves' and respond with anger or an attitude of resistance, but that's just replacing one Getting and Protecting Behavior with another, and that's all on the Field of Death."

"You don't need to be demanding or angry with him," I continued. "That won't help your relationship, and you won't be happy. Simply state what you want to do, and offer gladly what you are willing to do. Similarly, when you *don't* want to do what he asks, you lovingly respond with *no*. On some occasions you may *want* to do things his way, just because you care about him, but then it becomes a loving choice—an unconditional gift—rather than something you do as a victim."

"If I start doing this—if I start making my own decisions—I know he'll get angry. What do I do then?"

"Then you call people who you know are capable of accepting and loving you, and you talk to them—not to complain, but to tell the truth about *you*, about how you are afraid or angry or acting like a victim. If you feel sufficiently loved by other people, it won't bother you as much when Dean gets angry at you. When you feel more loved, you'll find it much easier to talk to Dean when he's angry—about money, about how you feel, about your mistakes, about everything. If he cares about you at all, he'll work this out with you. Don't give up. A worthwhile relationship takes time to develop."

For a great deal more about how a healthy relationship looks, read *Real Love in Marriage*.

Helping Children Tell the Truth about Their Victimhood

Children often claim to be victims. Why? Because we *taught* them this behavior with our own examples, and because it *works*. One of their common refrains is, "I couldn't help it." They want to shift responsibility for their behavior to anyone or anything but themselves. Now they need our help to see that they are not victims and always have choices. Children often need to be loved and taught many times before they learn this desired lesson. To demonstrate how we could teach children about victimhood, let's observe one mother, Janet, as she talks to her daughter, Holly.

Holly had the responsibility of cleaning the kitchen before she went to school each morning, and she was less than completely reliable about completing that task. One evening Janet spoke to her about it.

"You didn't clean the kitchen before school this morning," said Janet.

"I couldn't help it," said Holly in classic victim style. "I started to clean it, but I didn't have time to finish before we had to leave for school."

"What time did you get up this morning?"

"Seven."

"Who *made* you get up at that time?"

"Nobody."
"So you *chose* to get up at seven, is that right?"
"Yes."
"Then you *could* have chosen to get up *earlier*—at six-thirty, for example—and then you *would* have had time to clean the kitchen."
"But I was up late last night!"
"And who *made* you do that?"
"Okay, I get the point."

Janet explained to Holly that when she chose to get up at seven o'clock, she *knew* she would not have time to clean the kitchen. As Holly chose her time to get up, therefore, she also effectively *chose not to do her assigned job*. She could have chosen to get up at six-thirty and fulfill her responsibility, but she didn't. Because her mother explained this without accusation or irritation, Holly saw that she had not been a victim of "time." She realized instead that her negligence was a choice, not something she "couldn't help."

THE POWER OF UNDERSTANDING IN THE ELIMINATION OF VICTIMHOOD

Victimhood is such a trap. Once we consistently claim to be victimized by others, we are truly stuck in a painful cycle of blaming and misery. In the presence of knowledge and Real Love, however, it is possible to shake off the chains of victimhood entirely.

Let's look at a single practical example of how this can happen in a given moment. Your spouse is nagging you about your clothes being all over the bathroom floor—again. You *could* make excuses (lying) like a victim, or you could tell her you're sick of her nagging (attacking, acting like a victim), but have you *ever* seen a happy result from either of these approaches or from a combination of them?

So this time, you tell the truth about *yourself* and say to her, "I was just too lazy to put them where they belong. No excuse. I'll go pick them up. Sorry I've been such a pain about this in the past." Can you imagine your spouse's reaction to this approach? Can you imagine how much more pleasant this interaction would become for *you*? Telling the truth is infinitely superior in every way to acting like a victim or any of the other Getting and Protecting Behaviors.

Mr. Fine and Mr. Whine

To illustrate further the power of eliminating victimhood, let's look at three examples of how ordinary events are viewed by a victim and a non-victim. Mr. Fine understands the principles we have discussed thus far in the book, and Mr. Whine does not.

Waiting

Mr. Fine and Mr. Whine both wait in line for an hour to register their cars at the Department of Motor Vehicles. When they get home, their wives each ask them about the experience.

> Mr. Fine says, "It wasn't bad. I had to wait in line for an hour, but I read a magazine I'd brought with me. There was a problem with the registration, too, but it's all done now."

> Mr. Whine says, "Those stupid people made me wait in line forever. Nobody down there knows what they're doing—as usual. Idiots—all idiots." He rants like that for several minutes.

Work

After lunch on Friday, Mr. Whine and Mr. Fine are each given difficult assignments at work that must be accomplished before the end of the day. When they get home late that evening, they talk to their wives.

> "Long day," says Mr. Fine. "Sorry I'm late, but I had to finish that project. At least now I won't have any work to do over the weekend."

> When Mr. Whine gets home, he's in a terrible temper: "They're always doing this to me. They never plan ahead, and then they dump stuff on *me* at the last minute. And did anybody offer to help me out on a Friday afternoon? Oh no, of course not. There I was in the office all by myself doing *their* work. Do you think they appreciate it? Hah!" Mr. Whine complains about his experience until he goes to bed—and for much of the next day.

Punctuality

Mr. Whine and Mr. Fine each arrive a few minutes late at their first business meeting of the day.

"I'm sorry I made you wait," says Mr. Fine. "I knew I should have left the house earlier, but I didn't. Poor planning."

Mr. Whine says, "The traffic was terrible. When are they finally going to do something about those roads?"

❧ Chapter Eight ☙

Eliminating Victimhood with Real Love

To this point in the book, we have discussed the origins and manifestations of victimhood, as well as how an understanding of true principles can help us eliminate our own feelings of victimhood. Now let's turn our attention to what can happen when we add the actual power of Real Love to the mix.

As I first said in Chapter One, we act like victims only because we're empty and afraid, which feelings in turn exist only because we lack sufficient Real Love in our lives. In short, victimhood exists only because we don't have enough Real Love. The way to eliminate victimhood should therefore be obvious: We need more Real Love.

On page 22 we began a discussion about how to find Real Love, and we used a simple linear diagram to illustrate the process:

Truth → Seen → Accepted → Loved

Regrettably—and by way of stark contradiction to this process—most of us have spent our entire lifetimes *earning* or *buying* the Imitation Love of others as we have carefully presented to the people around us what they have wanted to see or hear. In order to earn this "love"—which comes in the form of praise, power, pleasure, and safety—we have lied, used anger, acted like victims, clung, and run.

Until we tell the truth about ourselves, however, without manipulating other people in any way for what they give us—with what we say, with what we do, or with how we look—we cannot know what Real Love is.

As I tell you who I really am—with my mistakes, flaws, fears, foolishness, and all—I create opportunities for you to accept and love me for who I really am. That is Real Love, and this is what makes us whole and happy.

TELLING THE TRUTH ABOUT OURSELVES

In the two sections at the end of Chapter One I outline some educational materials that would enable you to optimize your search for Real Love. I heartily recommend that you obtain and review these materials. In the meantime, however, allow me to summarize how we can find the Real Love that will fill our lives and eliminate our victimhood—emphasizing at the same time that this summary will not replace a more thorough study of the Real Love materials described in Chapter One.

In Chapter One I suggest that we tell the truth

- about ourselves, not everyone else.
- gradually.
- to people capable of accepting and loving us.
- eventually as often as possible.
- about our mistakes.
- about our lies.
- about the selfishness of our anger.
- about the times when we act like victims.
- about the occasions when we run and cling.
- about our fears.

Now let's study some of these recommendations individually.

Tell the Truth about Yourself, Not Everyone Else

I have spoken to many people who have prided themselves on their honesty, but it turns out that most of these people are really primarily honest about *other people* and their flaws. Most of us, in fact, just *love* to tell the truth about other people's mistakes, but the problem with that approach is that no matter how much I tell you the truth about everyone else's flaws, *I* will never feel more unconditionally loved by you. *That*—our belief that we can find some measure of genuine satisfaction and even happiness in exposing the flaws of others—is perhaps one of the greatest deceptions that has kept us empty, alone, and miserable.

I can feel unconditionally loved by you only as I share with you who *I* really am, and talking about other people can be only a terrible distraction in that process. In order to help all of us remember this principle I suggest here a small pearl that has the potential for bringing great peace into our lives: *Other people's mistakes are none of my business.*

Tell the Truth Gradually
Tell the Truth to People Capable of Accepting and Loving Us

The idea of telling the truth about ourselves is frightening to many of us, in great part because we imagine telling everyone all the secrets of our lives. Such a course of action, however, would be foolish. It's too frightening for us, and it's just too much information for others. Do *not* begin the process of truth telling by sharing the truth about yourself with a lot of people, and don't begin by sharing truths that are especially frightening.

Start with little truths, and share them with people you have observed to be fairly calm when dealing with the mistakes of others. Look for people who exhibit a minimum of Getting and Protecting Behaviors. Later in this section, we'll look at more examples of truth telling, but for now let's look at just one.

Suppose you're talking to a friend about an interaction you had the day before with your husband. In the past, you would have blamed your husband for your irritation, but today you remember what you've learned about Real Love and victimhood. So you say, "Yesterday my husband didn't pick something up from the post office like I asked him to, and I was really irritated and critical toward him. Instead of paying attention to what he needed from me—instead of loving him—I was selfish and only thought of myself and what I wanted."

Your friend responds, "I think you have every right to be irritated. My husband does that kind of stuff to me all the time. He says he'll pick something up, or he'll do something for me, and then it's like he never thinks of it again. Men are just rude and inconsiderate, and if we don't say something, they'll ignore us forever. They're all alike."

This small interaction is very instructive. You told a small, non-threatening truth about yourself. No deep, dark secrets from the past. No sexual fantasies. Nothing you'd be embarrassed to have repeated anywhere. And what did you learn? You learned that this particular friend is not capable of seeing you clearly, nor can she unconditionally accept and love you. Your friend would rather act like a victim herself. But what did you lose by attempting to tell her the truth about yourself? Not a thing. Now you can easily change the subject back to shopping or the weather or whatever else you'd like.

Now what? Now you share the same truth with another friend you believe might be able to see and accept you. And this time your friend says, "Wow, that's amazing. I don't think I've ever heard anyone take responsibility for being selfish in a conversation before. Where did you learn to do that?"

This small interaction is also very instructive. Again you shared a small truth, but this time you experienced a moment of unconditional acceptance from a friend. These moments of Real Love—as in this case—are often quite undramatic. There need not be hugs, kisses, or verbal expressions of *I love you*. In this case, you described one of your flawed behaviors, and your friend simply accepted you. She even expressed delight at your honesty and sense of responsibility. *That* is a moment of Real Love, and as we string more and more of these moments together, we'll find our lives changed forever.

Once we have tasted enough Real Love, we can never see the world quite the same again. In addition, each experience we have with Real Love moves us closer to our goal of accumulating the twenty million dollars we talked about on page 25. At that point, when we have enough Real Love, we lose our emptiness and fear, and then we lose all our reasons to use those unproductive Getting and Protecting Behaviors. It's a powerful experience.

In Chapter One I said, "When we find people who are capable of seeing, accepting, and unconditionally loving us as we tell the truth about ourselves, I call those people wise men and women, a term that comes from 'The Story of the Wart King and the Wise Man' in the book *Real Love*." As we tell the truth about ourselves, two miracles become possible simultaneously:

- First, we create the opportunities to feel accepted and loved by those around us, as you did with your friend in the hypothetical situation we described above. In other words, as we tell the truth about ourselves, we *find* wise men and women.
- Second, we give the people around us an opportunity to practice loving us. In many cases they learn *for themselves* that they are capable of loving us—often for the first time. In the interaction with your second friend above, she may *not have been aware* that she was capable of unconditionally accepting you until you told her the truth about yourself. In other words, as we tell the truth about ourselves, we actually make a contribution toward the *creation* of wise men and women.

Eventually Tell the Truth as Often as Possible

As we find wise men and women, we need to tell the truth about ourselves more frequently and more directly. After a lifetime of insufficient Real Love, we need more than an occasional experience with love before we can find the happiness we're looking for. If we don't feed our *bodies* every day, we become weak and can even die. There is no less urgency about feeding our *souls*. As soon as we feel comfortable with telling the truth about ourselves, we need to make contact with a wise man every day. Get in the habit of making regular phone calls and, even better, meet with wise men and women in person. That personal contact is far better than talking to a faceless voice on the phone. In our society we tend to depersonalize our interactions as much as possible, using the phone and the Internet.

Tell the Truth about Your Mistakes

In the beginning of the process of truth telling, I tend to emphasize our need to share the truth about *mistakes* primarily because if we share our successes we'll have a natural tendency to be buying Imitation Love in the form of praise.

As I share with you the truth about the mistakes I have made, three delightful benefits occur rather consistently:

- Any conflict we might be having tends to be over immediately. Most conflicts are fueled by a contest over who is *right*, and if I admit how I am wrong, the conflict usually dies from a lack of fuel. Some people are afraid to admit they're wrong because then their partner will believe he or she is *right*. In the first place, if I'm wrong, that doesn't make you right. We can both be wrong. Second, it wouldn't matter if you were right or wrong, because, as I said earlier in this chapter, your mistakes are none of my business. I need to focus on correcting my own mistakes—that will keep me plenty occupied—and leave you alone to take care of yours.

- I create an opportunity to feel loved unconditionally by you. It is only while I am telling the truth about my mistakes and flaws that I can be certain that your love for me is unconditional. If you love me while I'm flawless, that's not worth much.
- I create an atmosphere of safety for you. If I tell you about my mistakes and mention nothing of yours, you will almost certainly feel much safer than if I attacked you for your mistakes, and in that atmosphere of safety, it's much more likely that you would discuss the truth about your own mistakes. And if we're both telling the truth about our mistakes, is there anything we can't work out between us?

We make so many mistakes in any average day that it should be easy to find something to tell the truth about. Mistakes include our Getting and Protecting Behaviors, so telling the truth about our mistakes could include some of the following examples:

- "This morning my boss asked several of us if we knew who had made a mistake that made us look foolish to a client. I had a significant part in that mistake, but I didn't say anything. I was more interested in protecting myself than I was in admitting my mistake."
- "Last night my husband was driving us to a dinner date with some friends, and he got lost. Instead of just supporting and loving him, I sat in my seat fuming and muttering under my breath about being lost again, which infuriated him and ruined our evening."
- "Yesterday my six-year-old was late getting ready for school, and she was frantic to find a particular shirt she wanted to wear. I could have stopped for just a moment to love her and make her feel a lot better, but instead I yelled at her and told

her to hurry up, which only made her feel unloved and made things a lot worse."
- "I get so irritated with my mother for intruding herself into our lives. She butts into everything. But the truth is, she has never felt loved in her life, and she reacts by trying to control everyone and everything around her. It gives her a feeling of power. I'm not strong enough to love her when she acts like that, so I choose to feel like a victim instead."
- "Last night I drank more than I should have, and then I said some unkind things to my wife that I normally wouldn't have. Sometimes I drink to numb out in the evening, and I need to look at that behavior. It's not helping my marriage."

Tell the Truth about the Selfishness of Your Anger

On pages 144-5 we discussed how anger is uniformly selfish and destructive. As we tell the truth about the selfishness of our anger—to ourselves and to others—we break the inflammatory cycle of anger. Let me illustrate this effect by sharing the following interaction between Claire and her supervisor at work, Helen.

For some time Claire had been pushing for some changes in office policy, and in great part because of Claire's pushy attitude, Helen had been resisting or ignoring her. In one conversation, both women were becoming increasingly aggressive, but Helen remembered what she had read on the website www.RealLove.com.

Helen stopped in mid-sentence, in fact, and said, "Claire, I'm getting irritated here, and—"

Claire immediately interrupted to defend herself. "Look, I was only—"

"Claire, let me finish saying this. I'm getting irritated, and it's *not* your fault. What I want you to know is that if I'm irritated, I'm paying attention to what *I* want instead of listening to what *you're* trying to tell me, and that's selfish. It's wrong of me. When I'm irritated, I don't listen well, and that serves both of us poorly, so let's do this: Give me a day to think about what you've been trying to tell me, and we'll meet again tomorrow. By then—I hope—I'll be able to listen to you much better. You deserve that. Would that be all right?"

Claire was blown away by Helen's honesty. All the defensiveness left her immediately.

Helen and Claire met the next day, and for the first time they had a productive conversation about potential changes in office policy. When Helen admitted the selfishness of her anger—when she admitted that she was wrong—she instantly defused the conflict, and she also created a safer environment for a productive conversation with Claire. Note that when Helen admitted she was wrong, she was not admitting that she was wrong about any particular office policy—or that Claire was right—only that she was wrong to be *angry*. It made a huge difference.

Tell the Truth about the Times When You Act like a Victim

We discussed this in great detail in Chapter Seven. As we tell the truth about the occasions when we act like victims, we have a natural tendency to see other choices—much more productive choices—that are available to us.

Faith

If the benefits of telling the truth about ourselves are so enormous—if we feel like we have twenty million dollars all the time as we acquire enough Real Love—why don't we do it more often? Why do we continue acting like victims and using Getting and Protecting Behaviors when we know they can result only in unhappiness? Partly, we just don't know any better—we use these behaviors because it's what we've always done, and what we've seen everyone around us do—but even after learning about truth-telling, we tend to avoid it like we would a colonoscopy. We've had countless past experiences where people have not accepted us when they've learned the truth about us, so we're understandably terrified that we'll experience that same painful lack of acceptance each time we're truthful about who we are. Instead of telling the truth, therefore, we keep using those Getting and Protecting Behaviors that have caused us so much pain.

Telling the truth about yourself requires faith—a *decision* to try something different even when you don't know what the results will be. If you really want to feel the power of Real Love, you simply have to share who you are and take the risk of people not liking you. It's really not such a big risk, however. If you already don't feel unconditionally loved, that's the worst possible feeling. If you share yourself with other people, and they don't accept you, you'll only experience a *continuation* of the emptiness you already feel. That price seems small when you consider that telling the truth creates the possibility that you will find the Real Love you've always wanted, which is priceless.

We don't share who we really are because we're afraid people won't like us, and then we'll feel unloved and alone. But as soon as we hide who we are, we *guarantee* that we'll feel unloved and alone. You really have nothing to lose by taking the tiny risk of telling the truth. Finding wise men can sometimes be difficult. It may take patience, but it's well worth the search. You're creating the opportunities to feel loved and change your life.

THE HEALING POWER OF REAL LOVE

On pages 170-2 I talked about the tendency of therapy and self help techniques to cater to the culture of the victim, and I mentioned that I had once belonged to a group where men were encouraged to openly express their feelings, especially their anger. They learned to completely throw themselves into these expressions emotionally and physically, to the point that they could be described as semi-controlled explosions of anger, and for brief periods these men enjoyed enormous emotional rushes and releases from these experiences. When they were angry, they achieved a sense of power and a relief from the feelings of weakness, helplessness, and loneliness that otherwise dominated their lives. These men began to look forward with considerable eagerness to these opportunities to vent their anger, and, in fact, many of them became anger junkies.

These men were certainly telling the truth about the *existence* of their anger—and other men congratulated them for their honesty in sharing their feelings—but I realized that something had to be missing from all this "honesty," because it wasn't effecting real change. The same men were expressing the same anger—about the same issues—over and over again. They were no happier as a result of "venting" all that anger. As I said in Chapter Six, part of the reason for their lack of growth was their belief that they were victims. In addition, however, they were telling only *part of the truth* about their anger, the part about its *existence*.

It's not nearly enough for us simply to say that we *are* angry, because there is so much more to say about our anger. These men I have been speaking of, for example, were *not* telling the truth about

- the *cause* of their anger.
- their personal *responsibility* for their anger.
- the *effect* of their anger on other people.
- the *solution* for their anger.

In their defense, they didn't *know* the truth of these additional elements of their anger. Like almost all of us, they were taught to blame others for their anger, and that's exactly what they did. Blind to the truth, they were feeling and acting like victims. They were mired in blaming and attacking other people, which never leads to anyone feeling happier. Let me illustrate how we can tell the truth about our anger quite differently as I relate my experience with a group of people who were relatively new to the principles of Real Love.

In their meeting, as they shared a bit about themselves, one man, Brian, talked about how angry he was at his wife, Emma, because of something she had been doing for a long time. One of the other men, Daniel, spoke up and said, "Brian, I've always had a hard time being open about my anger, as you just were. I want to thank you for your honesty."

Brian thanked Daniel for his comment, and they both briefly bathed in the glow of a moment of emotional intimacy until I said, "Daniel, what did you find about Brian's comment that was honest?"

"Well," said Daniel, "most men I know just simmer and seethe with their anger. It's under the surface, ready to explode, but they don't come out and express it as openly as Brian just did. I think what he said was really honest and healthy."

"I certain agree," I said, "that Brian was honest about *being* angry, as opposed to claiming that he was *happy* when he was really *angry*. But was he honest *about* his anger? Notice that he said he was angry *because* of what his wife did. He *blamed* her for his anger. He was claiming to be *victimized* by her. Is all that true?"

The room was very quiet. I shared with the group the drowning metaphor on pages 32-4 and explained how other people never *make* us angry.

"I believe," I continued to the group, "that Brian was as honest as he *knew how* to be, but he was really *inappropriately* blaming his wife for his own anger—which is *not* telling the truth—and look at the result of that. You have all known him for some time now. In all the times he has blamed his anger on other people—no matter how *open* he has been about *having* his anger—has he ever become genuinely *happier*? That's the final test of whether a behavior works or not: whether it leads to greater happiness."

Brian spoke up. "I can answer that question. No, I'm not happier. For a long time I really I thought I was accomplishing something by talking about my anger, by venting it. But I'm still as angry as ever, if not more, and lately I've been wondering why. What you just said rang true in my head like a bell. It's true. I really would like to do something more productive."

"Great," I said. "I would never *tell* you that you had to do anything, but if you *want* to do something that works better than acting like a victim, there really is a better way."

"I'm dying to hear it," Brian said.

"So, Brian," I said, "in light of what we've learned here tonight about Real Love, what's the real reason you get angry at your wife?"

"From the time I was a child, I've never really felt unconditionally loved, so I've felt empty and alone all my life. That means that I'm in pain almost all the time." Brian had to pause here to keep from crying. Men have been taught that crying is weak, so they tend to stifle that behavior.

After a few moments he was able to continue. "So because *I'm* in pain all the time, the slightest inconvenience—like when my wife doesn't do something I want, or she does something I don't like—seems like more pain than I can stand, and then I fall apart. I feel even weaker. I get angry at her because then I feel a little less helpless. With anger I can take my frustrations out on her. When I blame her, I get kind of a rush out of it too."

"So let's summarize: You get angry at your wife, you act like a victim, you withdraw from her—which is running—and overall you're not very loving toward her. Is that pretty much the picture?"

"That's not very pretty, but yep, that would pretty much describe it."

Turning to the remainder of the group, I said, "Now *that* is telling the truth about yourself. That was amazing, actually." Turning back to Brian, I asked, "Having said that about yourself, how do you feel?"

"Well, at first it was hard to hear that I'd been *lying* and *acting like a victim*—and that I haven't been loving all these years—but you're not making any of this up. It's just true. I thought I would feel embarrassed to admit this. I thought I'd want to defend myself, but everyone here has been very accepting of me. I can feel that. It's like I can see things differently now. It's kind of like getting out of prison. I feel free."

Although Brian would have found it difficult to use the word on this first occasion of his telling the truth, what he was really feeling was a measure of Real Love, and it made quite an impact on him. In the next group meeting, a week later, he spoke again.

"The day after our last group meeting, my wife said something snippy to me that would have thrown me into a fit just months ago, but I was blown away by what happened next: I didn't feel angry. No kidding. That was so unusual for me that for a second there, I thought maybe I was having some kind of out-of-body experience. I couldn't believe I didn't get mad at her. I can't remember the last time I felt calm when she spoke to me like that. Maybe never. And then I remembered that just the night before I had been in this group. Now, can you all remember what happened in group? In group I told the truth about myself—about how I've been afraid and how I've lied and attacked people and acted like a victim my whole life—and all of you just accepted me. And I felt accepted and calm during the group. So I figure that the day *after* the group, when my wife said something snotty to me, I was still carrying with me some of that peacefulness from the group, so that my wife's comment didn't really bother me. It was pretty great."

"Of course," he continued, "after another couple of days the peacefulness and the love kind of wore off, and I was back to getting angry at her again, but at least this time when I was angry I knew—at least in my head—that it wasn't her fault."

"So now imagine," I said, "what it will feel like as you keep coming here—week after week—and keep getting accepted and loved by these men. The more loved you feel, the more Real Love you'll have to take home and everywhere else you go. Instead of keeping that peaceful feeling for two days, you'll be able to keep it for three days, then four, then more. Eventually, it will become the standard pattern in your marriage—in your whole life, for that matter—and what would that be like?"

"Hard to imagine," he said, "but I wouldn't mind it. Anything would beat what I have now."

As long as Brian acted like a victim, all he got was more pain and more victimhood. By simply telling the truth about the existence of his anger, he got no better. But when he told the truth about *his choices*—about his *decision* to act like a victim and his *decisions* to use other Getting and Protecting Behaviors—he created an opportunity to feel unconditionally loved by others. The more of that Real Love he felt, the less empty and afraid he became. As his emptiness and fear disappeared, he simply lost his *need* to feel or act like a victim. There is just no power in the world that eliminates victimhood as effectively as Real Love.

Real Love: A Power Like No Other

On page 132 I introduced you to a woman, Connie, who had been sexually abused as a young girl by many men in and out of her family. Despite years of therapy and recollections of the individual occasions of her abuse—which recollections her therapists considered "successes"—she remained alone and miserable. In a Real Love group she again began to tell stories of her abuse, but after a few minutes I interrupted.

"As we tell the truth about ourselves," I said, "we create opportunities to feel genuinely loved, and Real Love has the power to change our entire lives. So far, though, you're not telling the truth about *you*. I am not criticizing you in any way. I'm sure you have been taught to do this. What you're doing is telling the truth about what was done *to you* by other people. You're describing how you were victimized."

With a tear in her eye, she said, "But I'm sharing how *I* feel. These are *my* feelings."

Such is the power of the victim. All her life no one had ever had the courage or knowledge to offer Connie anything but sympathy when she expressed such heartfelt pain, and understandably so. When someone is in such pain, who would dare question her about the role *she* has played in it? But all the sympathy she had received had accomplished absolutely *nothing* good. Sympathy never does. Think about the experiences of your own life. When has sympathy ever made you feel genuinely loved and happy?

"They *are* your feelings, Connie," I said, "and *nobody*—certainly not I—could ever know the pain you've experienced. I couldn't begin to know. And in many ways *you* have also underestimated your pain, because you have thought your pain was only about being sexually abused. But it's about much more than that. Your pain isn't about being sexually abused. It's about *not feeling loved.* All your life people have told you in a variety of ways that they didn't care about your happiness, and these people who used you sexually simply expressed their *I don't love you* and their willingness to actually hurt you in an unusually dramatic way and in a way that left no doubt whatever about their message. You've been told that people didn't care about you so many times now that you're like a walking wound—an open sore."

Connie wept. She knew that I was offering something much more than shallow sympathy, that I was really seeing the extent of her wounds and offering her some genuine compassion. But that was still not enough.

"I have learned, though, Connie," I continued, "that it's not nearly enough to be loved for our wounds or our pain. We need to feel loved for the choices *we* have made, because it is our *choices* that most accurately reflect who we are, not what has been done *to us*. When you can talk about *your* mistakes and *your* Getting and Protecting Behaviors, you'll begin to create those critical opportunities to feel unconditionally loved."

With a touch of hysteria in her voice, Connie said, "Are you saying it was *my fault* that I was sexually abused?" She had always been so certain that her victimhood was utterly untouchable, and she had to defend any perceived threat against it.

"Oh, heavens no," I said. "You were a child. How could it be your fault that adults took advantage of you and robbed you of your childhood? That's not the issue at all. We're not talking about your childhood here. We're talking about the rest of your life. As a result of what happened to you, you have felt victimized all your life haven't you?"

"Yes!" she said. "Wouldn't you?" Again she was trying to draw me onto the Field of Death, where victims *believe* they will win but where, in reality, everyone dies.

"I have no idea what I would do. That's not the issue. The point is that *you* have been angry about being victimized, haven't you?"

"Yes!"

"And in many cases, you have taken your anger out on people who had nothing whatever to do with your admittedly terrible childhood experiences. You have often expressed anger and resentment and a feeling of victimhood toward men in general, haven't you? Don't you distrust almost all men?"

She paused, for the first time unsure of herself, because I was not on the Field of Death with her. I wasn't attacking her or defending myself or sympathizing with her. This approach was new to her. "Yes, I guess I have distrusted men."

"And if you have distrusted them, I can tell you for a fact that you have hurt the feelings of some of those men here and there. With your anger and distrust, you have communicated to them the message *I don't love you* in much the *same way as that message was communicated to you.*"

Connie looked as though I had slapped her across the face. Not once in her life had it ever occurred to her that she might have hurt someone else as she herself had been injured. "I didn't mean to hurt anyone," she said.

"And, darlin', those men who used you didn't *mean* to hurt *you* either. I'm not kidding. They were just empty and miserable, and they had gotten to the point in their pathetic, lonely lives where they were willing to use a child to get a moment of pleasure and power for themselves. If that caused you pain in the process, frankly they were in enough pain that they didn't care. They simply didn't *think* about you, just as you didn't think about the people you have hurt when you've been in pain."

Connie wept again, but this time with greater intensity then before. She was beginning to see the light. She was beginning to see a way off the Field of Death, and that is a huge moment for anyone.

Several of us helped Connie see how she had been angry all her life and how she had used her anger to achieve moments of power. She had acted like a victim in order to self-righteously win the attention and sympathy of the people around her. She had withdrawn from people for safety, avoiding relationships and hurting people in the process. As she realized what she had done, and as she shared the truth about these feelings and behaviors with others, she created life-giving opportunities for people to love *her*—not her wounds—unconditionally.

The effect was dramatic, even though it took place over a period of months. Gradually, she quit blaming the men who had hurt her. She quit talking about them altogether and eventually got to the point where she genuinely forgave them. What does real forgiveness look like? When I say that Connie genuinely forgave them, I mean that she

- understood that these men had injured her because they had been empty, lost, confused, and afraid. This does not mean that she excused their behavior—which was obviously terribly wrong—but she *understood* the reasons for it.
- lost her anger at the men who had hurt her.
- felt compassion for the pain *they* must have felt in order to do such terrible things to her. They behaved badly, after all, only in response to their own pain.
- quit thinking about her injuries as the central event of her life.

Moreover, Connie learned to establish healthy relationships with both men and women. It was a touching and powerful transformation to witness.

I am not saying that victims don't need to talk about their pain, or that they don't need compassion surrounding their pain. They do. But victims need to avoid making their wounds the focus of their lives. Their wounds are a *part* of who they are, but only *one* part, not the *definition* of who they are. They also need to talk about their mistakes and flaws, just like everyone else does. They need to talk about their Getting and Protecting Behaviors. They need to see how they sometimes manipulate people by acting like victims. They need to talk about how they use their anger to get people to do what they want. They need to talk about how they run from relationships because that's an easier way to live than telling the truth about their own mistakes.

People who have been abused need to feel Real Love and then to look outside themselves and love other people, because that's where they'll find true happiness. It's often not an easy process, but the healing is beautiful.

WHAT CAN REAL LOVE LOOK LIKE?

On pages 59-61 I introduced you to Andy, who was quite unhappy with the way his boss treated him. You might benefit from reviewing that interaction now. After Andy and I had a discussion about the principles of Real Love and justice, he gained a new understanding of his boss. Instead of seeing his boss only as a monster, Andy began to see him as a man who was unloved, empty, and afraid. He realized that his boss had been lashing out only to achieve a temporary sense of satisfaction that he needed in the absence of sufficient Real Love. Andy also realized that the way *he* behaved only made his boss feel *more* empty and afraid, and then he treated Andy *worse*.

Allow me to share how our conversation continued from page 61.

"So tell me," I said, "how you see your boss now, in light of all you've learned about Real Love."

"Well, I used to think the problems I had with him were all *his* fault. I thought he was just being thoughtless and intentionally unkind to me. Simply put, I thought he was a butthead. But now I see there's more to it than that. He's just empty and alone, and he gets angry because it makes him feel less helpless."

"You learn quickly," I said.

"So, what can I do now?"

"About what?" I asked.

"About my boss. I *understand* him better now, but what can I *do* about how we interact with each other?"

"At least a couple of things come to mind. In the first place, now that you see him as lost and afraid, how does that change your feelings toward him? Or does it?"

"Actually, it does. I feel less irritated at him already. It's harder for me to be angry at somebody who's just empty and afraid—somebody who's drowning—than it was for me to be angry at somebody I saw as a monster. So yes, just understanding him makes a difference, but I wonder if there's something more I can do."

"Sure there is. Like you said, why does your boss behave like he does?"

"He doesn't feel loved."

"So what does he need most from you?"

Andy's face contorted as though he were sucking on a lemon before he said, "Love?"

"Yes."

"At work? You've gotta be kidding."

"No, I'm not kidding at all. It's odd to think of loving your *boss* isn't it? Or anybody at work, for that matter. The problem is that almost everyone is quite confused about what the word *love* even means. We tend to believe that *love* means hugs, kisses, and romance, but I don't think your boss needs or wants a kiss from you. Remember the definition of Real Love: caring about the happiness of another person. Without Real Love your boss is drowning, and if you care about his happiness, what would you give him? A drowning person doesn't need a hug, or a kiss, or a romantic poem. What does he need?"

"A helping hand?"

"Yes. That's all. It's not complicated. So what could you do to offer your boss your hand? At work what would it look like to offer a drowning man your hand?"

"I suppose I could apologize for how I've been behaving toward him."

"You *could* do that, but on the whole apologies don't mean much. Look at how often we apologize and then we go right back to doing what we apologized for. And he probably wouldn't understand what you were even apologizing *for*. He wouldn't understand any explanation about Real Love or emptiness or your being a victim or any of what we've been talking about. So you *could* apologize, but I wouldn't make that my first recommendation."

"So what *would* you recommend?"

"Remember, he's drowning, so you could literally reach your hand out to him. You already know the projects and things around the office that bug him the most, don't you?"

"Sure."

"So walk up to him tomorrow and say, 'Hey, is there some way I can help you with ____ (name the project or thing you know is bugging him)? It looks like it's a real burden, and I'd like to help if I can.'"

"Wow, that's pretty simple. He'd probably fall over if I did this."

"How do you think he'd feel about an offer like that?"

"I get the point. I think he'd love it."

"He will. He'll feel like you care about *him*, and *that* is Real Love. It's the Real Love he's missing in his life."

Andy did exactly what we discussed. The next day he simply offered to help the boss with an unpleasant task that everybody had been avoiding, and the boss was stunned. Andy finished the project and asked if he could help with another. I talked to him a couple of months later.

"How's it going with your boss?" I asked.

"It's embarrassing," Andy said.

"What's embarrassing?"

"It's embarrassing how long I hated him and hated my job, when all I had to do was be nice to him."

"You mean *love* him."

"Yes, *love* him. I never thought I'd use that word and the word *boss* or *work* in the same sentence, but I really have learned to. All I had to do was care about him—love him. Now it's like we're best friends at work. I feel stupid for not doing this earlier."

"You couldn't have," I said. "You didn't understand what was going on between you. You didn't understand him. You didn't understand yourself. There's an amazing power that comes from first *understanding* what you're doing and then from making a decision that you'll be loving instead of acting like a victim."

Notice that in the stories of Brian and Connie earlier in this chapter, they gave up their victimhood as they *felt loved*. The story of Andy is somewhat different in that he lost his victimhood as he chose to *be loving* toward someone else. Real Love is a powerful force in our lives whether we're receiving it or giving it.

The Cost of Victimhood in the Workplace

I have been asked this question many times: "Do the principles of Real Love apply in the workplace?" I chuckle every time as I answer, "Are there human beings in the workplace?" Every customer, employee, supervisor, vendor, vice-president, owner, and so on take with them into the workplace all the emptiness and fears of their lives, and each time these people interact with each other they tend to confuse their communications with an endless stream of Getting and Protecting Behaviors. These all have a terribly negative—and often measurable—effect on productivity, service, employee morale, and customer satisfaction, to name just a few of the activities of the business world.

Let's look much more closely at the cost of victimhood in the example of Andy and his boss. Andy was the supervisor of a department of fifteen employees who provided support to corporate customers who had purchased the expensive computer software produced by Andy's company. Andy had a number of ideas about how his department could increase its effectiveness, but when his initial efforts didn't receive sufficient appreciation from the boss Andy felt like a victim—for reasons we discussed in this chapter and in Chapter Two—and responded in the following ways:

- Andy withheld any further creative ideas that would have contributed to the growth and well-being of the company.
- The ideas Andy had about significantly improving customer service were never implemented.
- He was slow to implement policies suggested by his boss. That meant that fifteen employees responded slowly to company policies and were also slow to pass on the latest information to customers.
- His entire department was also slow and inefficient in transmitting information in the other direction: getting valuable feedback from customers about the product to the engineers, salesmen, and others that could have made use of this information.
- Morale in the whole department was poor, leading to a rate of personnel turnover considerably higher than the industry average.

In a corporate environment already dominated by emptiness and fear—and by Getting and Protecting Behaviors—the above responses weren't even noticed, so nothing was done about them and invaluable opportunities to improve company performance were lost. In most companies, Getting and Protecting Behaviors—and the losses that accompany them—are simply the norm.

We have mentioned elsewhere that victims—with their constant complaining, blaming, attacking, whining, and so on—can be incredibly irritating. In a corporate environment, they can also be quite costly in a purely financial sense. Victims

- resist direction. They find fault with everyone who attempts to tell them what to do, so working with them is very difficult.

Because they blame and find fault with little things incessantly, they slow up the implementation of every task and program they're involved with. The expense of this attitude alone in the corporate world is staggering. It can actually be measured, but because it's not recognized, it rarely is measured.
- spread discontent. Victims are never satisfied with keeping their negative observations about people and situations to themselves. They love to share how they have been treated badly—or simply how others are fools—with everyone, and this can poison a company, quite literally.
- steal. When a victim believes he has been treated unfairly, he feels justified in almost any behavior directed against the person or people he believes have wronged him. Stealing then becomes entirely justifiable. The theft of a pen is hardly noticeable, but when many employees are routinely taking what doesn't belong to them, or when employees are stealing information and company time, for example, the effects can be crippling.
- complain. Victims can find something to complain about in any act or proposal, and in so doing they can make the work environment miserable for everyone. It's difficult to put a price on this, but ask the people who work around a victim what they'd pay to make the complaining stop.
- make mistakes. Victims are so concerned with what should be done for them, or what should not be done to them, that they couldn't possibly devote all their attention to any task that is solely for the benefit of others, including the company. They are therefore quite prone to make mistakes, and when they make them, they never admit to their responsibility for them. These mistakes can often be quite expensive.

In many cases, we appreciate what negative behaviors cost us only when they're fully corrected, and that proved to be the case here with Andy and his boss. After Andy learned to see himself, his boss, and their relationship differently, the subsequent changes in his behavior had a widespread ripple effect:

- Because Andy no longer viewed the boss in a negative way, he put a much higher value on information from the boss and began to facilitate the flow of information from the top down in as rapid a fashion as possible. Because of Andy's change in

attitude, employees were immediately informed about changes in company policies, programs, and offerings to customers, and customers were immediately informed as well.
- Because Andy no longer behaved like a victim, the boss found it easy to listen to him and no longer resisted his ideas. In this newly receptive environment, Andy was able to introduce departmental innovations that resulted in a 40% increase in the customer support offered by his department without an increase in the number of employees.
- The improved relationship between Andy and his boss immediately translated to improved morale within the department, further aided by Andy's no longer acting like a victim with the people in his own department.
- With the improvement in department attitude, and with the better communication between employees and customers, the company began to see an entirely unanticipated source of sales. The people in Andy's department, in addition to providing better service, also began to sell new units of the company's software.
- Employee turnover disappeared in Andy's department, which eliminated the need for the training of new employees.

The simple change in attitude of one man—Andy—toward his boss resulted in changes that led to

- new sales (more than a hundred thousand dollars per month initially).
- markedly improved morale (beyond price in its own right, but also leading to a measurable decrease in waste and theft).
- an increased flow of ideas in both directions within the corporate hierarchy, which resulted in an improvement of existing products, creation of new products, and streamlining of production, all producing increased revenues.
- increased employee retention (saving tens of thousands of dollars in training).

All of these benefits added up to hundreds of thousands of dollars saved and produced in profits in a single department, not to mention the many intangible rewards that had great value but no measurable price tag.

The bottom line? Real Love can dramatically affect the bottom line in the corporate world. Victims are very expensive, and Real Love can eliminate victimhood.

Other Faces of Real Love

Because Real Love can eliminate victimhood, we must learn to recognize the many faces of Real Love. In this way, we can best make use of Real Love's many manifestations, and when it appears in an unanticipated form, we won't fail to benefit from it. I re-emphasize that the picture of love painted by society as a whole has become quite distorted. We see love as

- hugs.
- kisses.
- sex.
- more sex.
- romantic poetry.
- candlelight dinners.
- flowers.
- gifts.
- *expensive* gifts.
- elaborate and sentimental expressions of "I can't live without you."

Sometimes love *does* involve the elements we just listed, but just as often love has nothing to do with these expressions. Real Love means caring about another person's genuine happiness, *not*

- doing something for others so we'll get something for ourselves.
- doing what is expected of us.
- avoiding the disapproval of another person.
- trying to keep someone from being mad.
- buying the approval of others.
- exchanging Imitation Love.

Caring about someone's happiness is a highly individual concern. Each person who is literally drowning in water requires a different kind of assistance. One person might need you to extend your hand, while another would fare better with your throwing a rope, while yet another would benefit best by your sending a rowboat to help him or her. Similarly, how we can best help people who are drowning or struggling emotionally depends on the person and the situation involved. Some of the ways we could love people might include the following:

Situation	Expression of Love
Your child has fallen and skinned a knee.	You say, "That looks like it hurt. Do you want me to look at your knee and see if it needs anything?" No sympathy, no encouragement of victimhood, just a genuine expression of concern for her welfare.
Your wife looks sad or distant for reasons unknown.	You sit next to her and lightly put your hand on her knee or shoulder. Then you say, "You look distracted or concerned about something. You don't have to tell me what it is—no pressure at all—but if you want to, I'd love to hear about it."
Your husband is angry because you left the car in the driveway—*again*—instead of putting it in the garage. What he doesn't know is that when you came home, *his* lawnmower was right where your car was supposed to go, and you couldn't put the car in the garage without putting his mower away.	You have a perfect opportunity here to defend yourself and make this all his fault, but you *don't*. You realize that he needs love, not your defending yourself, so you walk right up to him, cup his face in your hands, and say, "You are so right. I haven't paid nearly enough attention to that. I'm going to write *Park the car* right now on an index card and tape it to the dash. Maybe that will help."
An employee seems confused and frustrated.	You say, "You look a little overwhelmed. How can I help you?"

When we are genuinely interested in what another person wants, we can think of many loving things to do.

On pages 152-3 I introduced you to Bob and Melanie, who were arguing about sex in their marriage. Bob believed that Melanie was withholding sex, and Melanie resented feeling used by Bob for sex. I helped them both see that they were feeling and acting like victims, which could only lead to more selfishness and unhappiness in their marriage. We'll continue that discussion here.

"So what are we supposed to do?" asked Melanie.

I described the process of finding Real Love,

$$\text{Truth} \rightarrow \text{Seen} \rightarrow \text{Accepted} \rightarrow \text{Loved}$$

and I suggested that they engage in that process as fully as possible. I offered them the same tools available to all of us:

- Practice telling the truth about yourself—about your mistakes, flaws, fears, and so on. Learn a great deal more about how to do this in the books *Real Love* and *The Essentials of Real Love Workbook*, both described at www.RealLove.com
- Tell the truth about yourself gradually, at first just about the little mistakes you make every day.
- Participate in a Real Love group, where you'll have the opportunity to tell the truth about yourself in person, which creates life-giving opportunities for feeling loved unconditionally.
- Become a member of www.RealLove.com, where you'll find a wealth of education about Real Love for a lifetime.
- Read the book *Real Love*, found in all major bookstores.
- Read the book *Real Love in Marriage* together and use the exercises to assist you in telling the truth about yourself.
- Read the book *Real Love in Parenting* with your children.
- Watch the six-DVD recording of *The Essentials of Real Love*, found on www.RealLove.com
- Read, listen to, and watch the great variety of other Real Love educational materials that can be found at www.RealLove.com

"The more loved you two feel—by *anyone*—the more you'll be able to love each other," I said. "Right now you're each trying to force from the other person what he or she simply doesn't have. If you spend time with other people who can love you, that will help a lot."

"You mean we can't do this with each other?" asked Bob.

"Look at how you've done so far trying to do it with each other," I suggested. "But now that you understand better what you've been doing, I *do* think you'll be able to take some of these steps together. In the book *Real Love in Marriage*, for example, you'll find pages and pages of suggestions about little loving things you can do for each other. As you offer these loving acts freely—instead of demanding something from your partner or protecting yourself—it will build the love in your marriage."

"The initial subject you discussed," I continued, "was sex, but that's not the real issue. The real issue is that neither of you feels sufficiently loved—not by each other and not by anyone else either. So let's deal with the real issue first—Real Love—and the sex will follow. I do want you to know, however, that I heard what you said about sex. In the short term, the most loving thing *you* could do about sex, Bob, is *never* to push Melanie about it. None. As you do that, what you'll be telling her is that you care about *her*, and that you would never gratify your own desires at her expense. That will come across as a big *I love you*."

As I was saying this, Melanie was vigorously nodding her head, and I pointed that out to Bob. "Bob," I said, "she just wants to feel loved before she can get all excited about sharing herself in a sexual experience with you. That's all there is to it. It's not complicated. And the most loving thing *you* could do right now, Melanie, is to *offer* sex to Bob whenever you feel you can do it in a loving way. Instead of seeing yourself as a victim, look at sex as a way of *expressing your affection* to him. You've made sex some special area of your life where you feel especially victimized, and it doesn't have to be like that. You feel *violated*, which is kind of crazy. Sex should be an opportunity to express unconditional affection, not something you give or withhold as he *deserves* it. Only victims see sex in that way. You both have a lot to learn about it. But first, let's learn about love."

Over the following couple of weeks, Melanie and Bob practiced being loving toward each other:

- Whenever she spoke to him, he consciously chose to put down his newspaper or turn off the television and look her in the eyes while he listened to her.

- Every time Bob came home, Melanie stopped what she was doing, found him, sat down with him, and touched him while she listened to him talk about what he did that day.
- At least once every day Bob stopped what he was doing, for no reason at all found Melanie wherever she was in the house, and touched her gently while he asked what she was doing.
- Instead of complaining when Bob watched football on Sunday, Melanie asked him if there was anything he'd like to eat or drink.
- He sent her loving emails from work.
- Each night before they went to sleep, she reached over and stroked his shoulders for several moments.
- He asked her if she wanted to just go on a walk around the neighborhood.
- She asked him if there were any particular foods he'd prefer for dinner more or less often in the future.

At the end of two weeks, Bob called me. "Okay," he said, "now how do I get her to stay *away* from me. I don't know if I can keep having sex at this pace. I'm not as young as I used to be, you know."

I laughed. This is not uncommon at all among people who are finally learning to love each other.

A couple of days later Melanie called and said, "I had begun to wonder if I'd ever want to have sex again. This is way better than sex *ever* was before. It's not just more fulfilling emotionally. This is better *physically* than anything I've ever known. I once heard you say that it's all about Real Love, and I thought, 'Yeah, sure.' But you were right. It really is. Now that I feel loved by Bob, I want to be with him all the time. I like this."

It really is all about Real Love. When people feel loved, and when they are being loving, victimhood—as well as the other Getting and Protecting Behaviors—simply vanishes. It has no function.

GETTING REAL LOVE WHEN YOU NEED IT

Real Love in any relationship or situation is so important that I suggest people never proceed in any given conversation or circumstance if they don't feel loved or loving. If we speak or act without love, we *will* make things worse. Let's look at an example of a man, Edward, who reached out for the love he needed while he was in the middle of a tense situation with his girlfriend, Amanda.

After a shower, Edward left the bathroom a mess, and Amanda was angry about it. As she nagged him, his first impulse was to attack her by describing all the times *she'd* made messes around the house. And then he thought about just leaving the room and refusing to talk to her (running). He'd had considerable experience using both victim approaches. But this time he remembered a conversation he'd had with a wise friend, Ian, during which he'd admitted that acting like a victim and defending himself had never made him happy.

Edward knew he couldn't speak to Amanda at that moment without saying something unkind, so he decided to keep quiet and simply said, "Excuse me, I have to go and make a phone call. But I'll be right back to finish this discussion with you."

Edward then called his friend Ian so he could talk to someone who wouldn't play the victim game and jump on the Field of Death with him. You might wonder if Edward's leaving the room wasn't *running*, a Protecting Behavior he had used many times before when conversations became difficult. No, he was not running, because this time when he left the room his motivation was to get love and guidance, not to withdraw from pain.

"Amanda is yelling at me," Edward said, "and I don't know what to do. Instead of blowing up at her and getting into a big fight, I stopped what I was doing to call you."

"You're getting pretty smart," said Ian. "You already know you can't demand that *she* change in any way. That never works. But there is something *you* can do that involves only you. You can tell the truth about yourself."

"About what? That I'm feeling unappreciated and angry?"

"Yes. Let's start with *angry*. It's important that you feel accepted *while* you're angry. But as you know, expressing your anger to Amanda wouldn't work out very well. I don't think she'd be ready to accept you while you're expressing your anger right now."

"That's why I called you."

"Very wise. How are you feeling at this moment compared to when you were talking to Amanda?"

"Well, I do feel less angry than when Amanda was yelling at me."

"Excellent. Now let's talk about something a little harder. You said you were feeling 'unappreciated.' When Amanda attacked you, you became afraid, and after that you immediately began to protect yourself, at least in your head. It's easy to see that anger is one of the Protecting Behaviors: it's attacking. But it may not be as easy to see what Protecting Behavior you were using when you mentioned the word *unappreciated*. Do you see it?"

Edward frowned. "Actually, I think I do see it, but I don't like it much. I was being a victim, wasn't I?"

"Of course you were. Don't feel ashamed about it. Just see the truth of it. Now, don't stop there. If you were attacking with anger and also acting like a victim—even though it was just silently this time—what is the likelihood that you were feeling loving toward Amanda?"

"Zero?"

"Exactly. You were being angry and unloving, which is as selfish and ugly as it gets. And yet here you are being absolutely honest about it, something very few people on the planet can do. I think you're amazing. How do you feel now?"

"I'd rather spend the rest of the day talking to you than go back and talk to Amanda."

"Take all the time you need. When you feel loved enough, you can go back and tell the truth about yourself to Amanda instead of getting into another useless argument. You won't believe what a relief it is just to say you were wrong."

"But all I did was leave a little mess in the bathroom. Does that justify her yelling at me?"

Ian laughed. "No, it doesn't, but we're not here to talk about her, just you. Do you want to blame her and have an argument, or do you want to learn how to be loving and happy? It seems to me that you already know how to blame and argue. Why not learn something new?"

"Good point."

"Was it thoughtless of you to leave a mess in the bathroom?"

"Well, yes, but—"

Ian interrupted. "There is no *but*. It's just a fact that in that moment you were thoughtless and selfish. That doesn't make you a bad person, but you can't become happy or have a loving relationship until you accept what you did. You only resist it because the people in your life have always loved you less when you made mistakes like this. But I won't love you less. So face this one small truth: If you really cared about Amanda, you wouldn't have left that mess in the bathroom—true?"

"I guess so."

"Now if you feel loved enough, go and tell the truth to Amanda."

"Actually, I think I can do that. It's helped a lot that I could talk to you and feel accepted before I talked to her."

"Oh, I know. I had to do this with friends a million times before I stopped arguing with my wife. But now we hardly argue about anything anymore. And I can tell you, it's a lot more fun this way."

Edward told Amanda he'd been thoughtless and wrong. She was dumbfounded and responded by apologizing for having been so unkind toward him. It was a turning point in their relationship.

THE "POWER" OF VICTIMHOOD

I have had the opportunity of becoming intimately acquainted with a great number of human beings. I have seen them suffer, stumble, learn, grow, and experience a wide variety of situations. I have seen what happens when individuals and groups are affected by

- disease.
- the deaths of family members.
- war.
- injustice.
- disability.
- aging.
- prejudice.
- anger.
- poverty.
- imprisonment.
- addiction.
- abuse.
- unwanted sexual encounters (rape and the like).

After all these observations, I have concluded that the effects of victimhood are worse than the effects of all the negative experiences listed above. Victimhood becomes an addiction that distorts everything we see and do. It isolates us and makes us miserable. As victims once we believe that other people owe us something, that can be a very difficult belief to unlearn.

Victimhood *can* be overcome, however, with sufficient knowledge and unconditional acceptance. Victimhood is a kind of profound darkness that renders us blind to all that is true. It is fortunate, however, that darkness is not actually a reality. Darkness is merely the absence of light, so the most profound darkness can be eliminated with the light of a single candle. And so it is with victimhood. If people can just begin to realize that they're acting like victims, and if they can experience the early sensations of being unconditionally loved, they can build on that knowledge and on those feelings, and the destructive effects of a lifetime of victimhood can be banished.

❧ Chapter Nine ☙

Responding To Other People Who Act Like Victims

Victims are literally everywhere, so in an average day it's likely that we'll be required to respond to their behaviors on many occasions. Now that we understand victims, and we understand better how to eliminate victimhood in our own lives, it's time to discuss how to respond to other people when they act like victims.

VICTIMS ARE SO IRRITATING —AND CAPTIVATING

Victims tend to have a powerful effect on us, and most of us respond poorly to them. Let's examine the reasons victims have a negative effect on the people around them. Victims

- complain about everything.
- are endlessly demanding.
- are never satisfied with what you do for them.
- find fault with everything.
- whine at you when they're not happy about anything.
- are never wrong.
- love to point out your mistakes.

- can always think of something else you should be doing for them.
- seem to think that you exist for the sole purpose of pleasing them.
- never admit their mistakes.
- have a real knack for making us feel guilty and obligated.
- have an excuse for everything.
- are late all the time.
- love to talk to other people about how they've been hurt.

In the presence of these behaviors, most of us feel either threatened or angry or guilty, and then we respond by protecting ourselves from them or trying to please them. Let's discuss these reactions.

Protecting Ourselves from Victims

Many of us find the behaviors of victims quite threatening, so we react by

- withdrawing from them (avoiding them).
- getting angry at them.
- arguing with them.
- criticizing them.
- showing them all that we've done for them.
- proving how we have not injured them, as they had supposed.
- trying to show them how they're wrong.
- trying to show them how we are right.
- feeling like victims ourselves, and using all the above victim behaviors.

The way we respond to victims sets up an impossible cycle, which goes as follows:

- Victims behave as they do only because they don't feel loved.
- Each of their behaviors communicates to us the message *I don't love you*.
- If we don't have sufficient Real Love ourselves, we find *I don't love you* a threatening message, and then we respond with our own Protecting Behaviors.
- Each of *our* Protecting Behaviors also communicates *I don't love you* to the victim, who then feels even less loved.

- Feeling less loved, victims are then *more* likely to engage in their victim behaviors, and we're back at the beginning of the cycle, which steadily worsens.

Victims can be the most grating and abrasive people on the planet. They often say things that are so annoying that a response seems absolutely *required*. You may be overcome with an urge to supply this response, but I strongly recommend that you do not step onto the Field of Death with a victim. You will be sorry.

Enslaving Ourselves to Victims

Those of us who don't feel irritated by victims usually feel hurt or guilty because of their manipulations. Then we respond to them by

- agreeing with them, just so they won't attack us.
- trying to please them, so they will like us.
- trying to salve their wounds, so they won't be in pain.
- trying to make them feel better so we won't continue to feel guilty.

We feel obligated to victims, and they are often so successful in their manipulations that they virtually *own* us. Remember the example of my patient Martha on pages 118-19. I do not exaggerate when I say that the members of her family were emotional and physical *slaves* to her. When she acted like a victim, she controlled them like puppets on strings.

I received the following letter from a man who had read a manuscript of *Real Love and Freedom of the Soul*:

Dear Greg,

"After reading the book about victims, I can see my whole life more clearly. My mother was a huge victim, and I did *everything* she wanted so she wouldn't be in pain, so she wouldn't be mad at me, and so she would love me. Although I didn't realize it at the time, I was completely driven by guilt. My father reacted to her victimhood by avoiding her completely, so I was the one left to please her. I was her slave.

"Without understanding what I was doing, I then married a woman who behaved exactly like my mother, and it became my mission in life to please her and keep her from being angry. Once again I was stuck, but this time I added some of my father's behavior. When I get tired of pleasing my wife, sometimes I just run and avoid her. I've spent my whole life on the Field of Death. Now I'm grateful to see a way out of all this."

The Tar-Baby

In 1879 the Atlanta Constitution began to publish a series of folk tales written by Joel Chandler Harris, a young journalist at the newspaper. He used the voice of an aged black man to tell a number of humorous and provocative stories set in the culture of the Deep South. The two most frequent stars of these tales, Brer Rabbit and Brer Fox, were perpetual enemies, and perhaps the most beloved of their anecdotes was "The Wonderful Tar-Baby Story." Because the language Mr. Chandler chose for his stories was both old and peculiar to a certain Southern culture, it can be quite difficult for us to read today, and I therefore choose to render the story in modern English and in an edited form.

Brer Fox mixed some tar and turpentine and fashioned it into a figure he called a Tar-Baby, which he set on the side of the road. Then he hid himself in the bushes to see what would happen. Before long Brer Rabbit came prancing down the road with all the energy in the world, but when he saw the Tar-Baby he immediately stopped in front of it, quite astonished.

"Good morning!" said Brer Rabbit. "Nice weather."

When the Tar-Baby failed to answer, Brer Rabbit tried some additional small talk, and when the Tar-Baby still refused to speak, Brer Rabbit said, "Are you deaf? Because if you are, I can shout louder."

After no answer from the Tar-Baby, Brer Rabbit said, "Oh, so you're stuck up and think you're better than me. Well then, I'm going to cure you of that. I'll teach you to speak to respectable people when they talk to you if it's the last thing I do. If you don't take off your hat and say hello, I'll bust you wide open."

There was still no response from the Tar-Baby, and all the while Brer Fox was laughing to himself as he watched the spectacle. Brer Rabbit punched the Tar-Baby in the side of his head, and now the Rabbit's fist was stuck in the Tar-Baby's head.

"If you don't let me go," said Brer Rabbit, "I'll hit you again," and he hit the Tar-Baby with the other hand, which was then stuck fast. "You turn me loose," said the Rabbit, "or I'll kick the stuffing out of you." And then he kicked the Tar-Baby with both feet, which became stuck in the tar.

Blind with anger, Brer Rabbit demanded that the Tar-Baby let him go or he'd butt him with his head, which he did. Now that the Rabbit was completely immobilized, the Fox came out from his hiding place, laughing until he was sick.

Arguing with a victim, getting angry at a victim, trying to be right with a victim, trying to please a victim, or responding with other Getting and Protecting Behaviors with a victim is very much like hitting a Tar-Baby. It may be tempting. It may seem justified. It may seem unavoidable. But if you give in to your urges, you won't like the consequences. Let's talk now about other ways—much more productive ways—to respond to victims.

HOW TO RESPOND TO PEOPLE WHO ARE ACTING LIKE VICTIMS

As we learn to respond to victims far more effectively than in the ways outlined above, we will find a much greater measure of peace for ourselves, and in most cases we will also succeed in having more fulfilling interactions with those who act like victims.

The general pattern for responding to victims is simple:

1. Never respond with Getting and Protecting Behaviors.
2. Tell the truth about yourself.
3. Listen to what the victim wants.
4. Offer what is *needed* and what you can give *freely*.
5. Teach the truth about human behavior.
6. Occasionally describe what you are doing and the choices available.
7. Occasionally impose consequences.
8. Stay off the Field of Death.

You may use any one of the responses in this list with any given victim—or any combination of them—but generally speaking they tend to be most useful when used in the order listed. We'll review each of them now.

1. NEVER RESPOND WITH GETTING AND PROTECTING BEHAVIORS.

Always remember that people act like victims only because they are empty and afraid. Their behaviors are intended to protect themselves or fill themselves up with Imitation Love, or both. As I said at the beginning of this chapter, because victims are so demanding and angry—because they are so threatening to us if we don't have enough Real Love ourselves—it's quite natural for us to respond to them with Getting and Protecting Behaviors of our own. The instant we use *any* of these behaviors, however—as we discussed on page 31—the message we strongly communicate is *I don't love you*.

When victims hear any hint of *I don't love you*, they feel more empty and afraid, and then they respond with *more* victim behaviors, at which point any productive conversation is pretty much impossible. To make this absolutely clear, therefore, when someone is acting like a victim with you, you must absolutely never

- speak in anger.
- express anger in the many other ways we manage to do that without words.
- act hurt.
- avoid him or her out of fear or anger.
- act like you're being treated unfairly.

Does this mean you can't express how you feel? No. If you feel like a victim—or you feel hurt or angry—in response to a particular victim, you have every right to express your feelings. In fact, it's *healthy* to express how you feel, but *not* to that particular victim. If you express your victimhood or your anger to a victim, it will *never* go well.

So what can you do? If you're feeling like a victim, or you're feeling angry, it's only because *you* don't feel loved, so what do you need? You need to tell the truth about how you feel *to someone who is capable of seeing, accepting, and loving you*—to a wise man or woman, as we defined on page 35. It's *Real Love* you need, not to have a confrontation with the victim you believe is causing your present feelings. It is a terribly destructive misconception that when we get upset, we can get a sense of real satisfaction only by "working things out" with the person we are having—or have had—the conflict with. That is *not* the case. Real Love from *any source* eliminates emptiness and fear and Getting and Protecting Behaviors, so when we feel empty, afraid, frustrated, angry, or upset in any way, we just need to find *any* source of Real Love. If someone is acting like a victim it is *highly* unlikely that he or she could be that source.

2. TELL THE TRUTH ABOUT YOURSELF.

Paul and Deborah had been arguing for most of the years they'd been married. They came to see me because they were both getting tired of the nearly constant conflicts.

"He never spends any time with me anymore," Deborah said. "We did lots of things together when we were dating—we ate out a lot, went dancing, went to movies, attended plays, stuff like that—but now, *nothing*."

"Oh, come on," said Paul, "just last weekend I took you out."

"You're kidding, right? We went to the *auto parts* store!"

"Hey," he said, "I said I was going out to do some errands, and you asked if you could go with me. I said, sure. Just because one of the places we went was the auto parts store—some place that's not *your* favorite—it doesn't count? So if we go someplace *I* like, it's nothing? How am I ever supposed to satisfy you if everything I do counts as nothing?"

"See what I mean?" she said to me. "He's impossible. He calls a trip to the auto parts store a *date*—a night out. No wonder he doesn't understand what I want."

"I went with her to her parents' house too," Paul said. "*That* was something *she* wanted to do. I suppose *that* didn't count as taking her anywhere either."

"*Going out* means just the two of us going somewhere together, just for fun."

"See?" he said. "No matter where I go with her, it's not going *out*. It's never enough."

They had engaged in this argument—and others like it—on countless occasions. She vigorously complained—acting like a victim and attacking—and he reacted by lying, attacking, acting like a victim, and running.

Victims do not respond well to arguments or to reason. They're empty and afraid, and in that condition they don't listen to anything well. What they need is to be loved. One loving act we can share with victims is to tell the truth about ourselves. Why is that such a loving act? Because when we choose to tell the truth about ourselves, we're also making a choice to *refrain* from

- lying.
- attacking.
- acting like victims.
- running.
- clinging.

All the behaviors listed above are designed to get Imitation Love for *ourselves* and to protect *ourselves*. In short, all the Getting and Protecting Behaviors are selfish, and when we make a choice not to use them in any given interaction, we're choosing not to think of ourselves. We're choosing to think of the welfare of another person. That is exercising a degree of loving.

When I talk about truth telling in response to victimhood, I am *not* talking about *appeasement* or trying to please someone. I am not talking about admitting that we're wrong in a way that is *giving in* to the attitude of the victim. I'm talking about telling the truth just because it's the right and loving thing to do. Let's see what truth telling would look like in the interaction between Paul and Deborah.

"Deborah," I said, "I'm not disputing the validity of a single thing you're saying, and Paul, you're doing an excellent job of defending yourself. I do have a question, though. In all the times that you two have argued like this—no matter how expertly—have you ever felt closer to each other?"

There was a considerable pause before Paul said, "No, not really."

"Would you like to try something different here?" I asked. "Something that might actually make a positive contribution to your relationship? Something, in fact, that might revolutionize the way you live?"

"Sure," said Paul, "why not?"

"One loving thing you can always do," I suggested, "is to tell the truth about *yourself*—particularly about your mistakes and flaws. Paul, I realize that Deborah may be unappreciative of you generally, and I also realize that she's not being kind or thoughtful to you right now. But lay that aside and consider what might happen if instead of talking about what *she* is doing wrong, you simply told the truth about *your* mistakes. Forget about revealing *her* mistakes, and forget about defending *yours*. When you're talking about her mistakes and defending yourself, you're fighting her on the Field of Death. Would you consider moving to the Field of Life instead?"

He smiled. "I could try. I'm not doing all that well on the Field of Death."

"So when she says you never do *anything* with her, you *could* quibble about details—and you might even be right about some of them—but you've pretty much proven over years that that approach *never* works. So instead of arguing with her about how she's *wrong*, try telling the truth about how she's *right*. In what ways *is* she right? When she says you never do anything with her, what part of that is *true*?"

"Well . . . we don't go out as much as we used to."

"Perfect. So you don't go out together as much as you used to. That's about *quantity*. Now what about the *quality* of the time you spend together? When you first dated, you probably spent more time alone, with just the two of you, yes?"

"That's true."

"Now you spend more time together running errands, visiting parents, and other stuff. Would that be fair to say?"

"I guess it would."

"So as far as Deborah is concerned, you spend less *time* together now, and the time you do spend isn't as *personal*. From her perspective, that would be quite a loss, don't you think?"

"I guess it would."

"So tell *her* that."

"Deborah," he said with complete sincerity—not just to repeat what I'd said to him—"I don't spend nearly as much time with you now as I used to, and even when I am with you, it's not like we're really doing something *together*. You've been trying to tell me that for some time, but instead of listening and telling the truth about it, I've been defending myself and trying to be right."

Deborah wept. The argument was over. In following sections we'll be talking about where the conversation went from here.

Telling the Truth Can Be Frightening

In some circumstances, telling the truth about our mistakes can be especially frightening, as in the case of Matt and Cheryl, whose marriage had been crumbling for years.

As she saw their marriage falling apart, Cheryl talked to everyone she knew about what a horrible husband and father Matt was. Some of what she said was true, but her stories were mostly exaggerated and sometimes even fabricated for the purpose of allowing Cheryl to feel like a victim. When Matt lost his job, and their financial situation became difficult, Cheryl could see no reason to stay in the marriage. One day while Matt was out of the house, she bolted—taking the children with her—to live in the hometown of both their parents, several hundred miles away.

She filed for divorce and lined up allies by the dozen—including his parents—to support her lawsuit demanding sole custody of their two sons. In court, she planned to assassinate his reputation in every way she could. She would talk about his two years of prescription drug abuse, which had ended years before, and would have people testify to minor events that would cast ugly doubts on his fitness as a father.

Matt called me and asked what he should do. He knew he could join in the fight and find people who would say negative things about Cheryl—and he'd already begun the search—but he wondered if that was the right thing to do. I suggested that he abandon all efforts to smear the character of his wife—because such efforts could only make him feel hateful and unhappy—and instead simply tell the truth about himself in court. Of course that approach went against Matt's natural inclination to defend himself, but he was also wise enough to realize that all the attacking he'd done in his life had never made him happy.

When the custody hearing arrived, Cheryl brought out all her guns and viciously attacked Matt in front of the judge. In response, Matt calmly admitted to all the mistakes he'd made—his past drug use, his failure to sufficiently love Cheryl, some financial irresponsibility on his part, and so on—and added that he had always done his best to love his children and be a good father. After the hearing, and before he heard the judge's ruling, he called me to say, "I'm so glad I didn't fight her. I would have been bitter and angry, and I would have said and done things that would have caused unhappiness for myself and my family for a long time."

In court the judge—having witnessed many cases where both parties battled furiously on the Field of Death—expressed how favorably impressed he was with Matt's honesty and with his refusal to attack Cheryl. He further expressed his belief that Matt's honesty and loving attitude would have a favorable effect on the children, and he awarded Matt joint custody of his sons. The lesson here is not that being loving will always win you what you want in court, but that it *will* enable you to avoid the anger and bitterness that will uniformly destroy you.

3. LISTEN TO WHAT THE VICTIM WANTS.

Let's observe the continuation of my conversation with Paul and Deborah from above.

"Paul," I said, "your admitting that you've been defending yourself is huge. You saw that it made a big difference to Deborah to hear you tell the truth that you really haven't been spending as much time with her. So now you've admitted what you've *not* been doing with her. Do you want to consider moving to the next level with her?"

"Sure," said Paul. "This is working pretty well so far."

"You've admitted that you *haven't* really listened to her. The next step would be to actually *listen*. What is she really trying to tell you?"

"I don't know."

"Which is why you keep having the same arguments. By the way, *she* doesn't know what she's trying to say to you either. That's why she keeps pounding you with so many details. She can't get to the real meaning of what she's saying. The *words* she's saying are that you don't spend enough time with her, but that's not what's important. We've talked about this before. Whenever your partner talks to you with any heightened energy in his or her voice, it's always about *what*? What do we all want most?"

"Love?"

"Brilliant," I said. "When she says that you don't spend enough time with her, what she's really trying to say is that she *doesn't feel loved* by you."

Deborah began weeping again.

"That's all that matters to her. The rest is just *details*."

"Well, that makes sense out of a lot of things," Paul said.

"So what could you say to Deborah that would indicate you understand what's been going on in your relationship?"

Paul thought for a moment. "Deborah," he said, "all this time I've been arguing with you and not listening to you, and all you've been trying to tell me is that you don't feel loved by me. And it's little wonder that you wouldn't. I've been irritated at you and avoiding you and telling you in a hundred little ways that I don't care about you."

Deborah got out of her chair, sat in Paul's lap, and hugged him as she cried. When people genuinely listen to us, without defending themselves in the slightest, we feel loved. Just by Paul listening to her, she made the transition from feeling like a victim to feeling loved, all in a few moments. By way of comparison, no amount of arguing had ever led to any kind of positive progress.

In a following section, we'll continue this conversation between Paul and Deborah even further.

Listening to Victims in the Workplace

How we respond to victims is similar no matter where we encounter them: in marriage, in parenting, in the workplace, and so on. Let's observe Suzanne, a supervisor, as she responds to the victim behavior of Martin, one of the employees reporting to her.

As Suzanne passed by Martin's desk, it was obvious to her that he was irritated about something. She could easily have walked on and ignored his irritation—which would have been understandable, since he was well known to be a victim, and victims are no fun to talk to—but she stopped and spoke to him.

"How are things going?" she asked.

"Oh, all right, I suppose," he said, failing miserably in his attempt to hide his disgust.

"You do not have to talk about this if you don't want to, but it sure looks like something is bothering you."

"I spent all week gathering the information for the Curtis Corporation account, and I had it right here on my desk, but now it's gone."

"Oh," said Suzanne, "that was me. I moved those files, and I sent you an email that I had taken them. Shawn was finishing some negotiations with the Curtis Corporation, and he needed that information."

"I haven't checked my email," Martin said, "so I didn't know you had taken it." With obvious irritation, he continued, "I guess I would have preferred being *asked* for the information instead of having it taken from me."

Suzanne could easily have insisted that she was right—that she had informed Martin about removal of the files, that she needed the information, that he could not be found at the time, and that the negotiations could not be delayed while they waited for his permission—but she realized that Martin was feeling like a victim and that victims literally cannot hear reason and logic. She decided to take the first three steps we have discussed thus far in responding to a victim: Never respond with Getting and Protecting Behaviors, tell the truth about yourself, and listen to the victim.

"You're right," said Suzanne, "I should have been more thoughtful about that. I could have left a big note across your computer monitor, or any number of things, but I didn't. An email was far from sufficient. My mistake entirely. But I think I may have screwed this up even more. It's not just that I took the files off your desk. There's something else bothering you here. What is it?"

What Suzanne said here was remarkable. She didn't just listen to what Martin said. She listened carefully to what he was projecting with his tone, facial expression, posture, and other subtle signs. That's real listening, and Martin could feel it.

"Well," said Martin, hesitating at first, "I've put quite a bit of time and thought and creativity into this project, and . . . I don't know quite how to say it."

Suzanne was powerfully listening now, which is quite an active behavior. She understood that when people are irritated, it's always about Real Love. In the absence of Real Love, people want whatever form of *Imitation Love* is available—acceptance, recognition, praise, and so on—and *that* is what Martin was trying to say.

"You've put a lot into this project," said Suzanne, "and now it seems like I'm taking your *work* but leaving *you* out of it. Would that be a fair summary?"

Martin looked stunned. How often do people have a complaint that their supervisor can articulate before they can? Instantly Martin felt like Suzanne cared about him personally, and in that instant, he felt a taste of Real Love. That makes all the difference in the world.

"Well, yes, I guess that's part of it," he said. "I don't mean to complain. I'd just like to be more involved."

"I understand," Suzanne said, "and that's been my mistake entirely. I'll pay more attention to that. I'll talk to Shawn and have him get with you so you can more thoroughly explain to him the work you've done. Is that acceptable?"

Suzanne wasn't catering to a victim. She wasn't responding to whining. She wasn't dealing with Martin on the Field of Death. She simply made a decision to tell the truth about herself and to genuinely listen to him, activities that take place on the Field of Life. In that instant their interaction changed dramatically.

You can learn a great deal more about how to genuinely listen to other people in a powerful way in the books *Real Love for Wise Men and Women*, *Real Love in Marriage*, and *Real Love in the Workplace*.

4. OFFER WHAT IS *NEEDED* AND WHAT YOU CAN GIVE *FREELY*.

The particular argument that we highlighted between Paul and Deborah on pages 247-9 began with Deborah saying, "He never spends any time with me anymore."

The complaints of a victim can be very annoying, especially because when a victim complains about how things are, the rest of the message he or she communicates goes like this (and we *hear* the rest loudly):

- And because I have been treated so unfairly, so badly, so abominably, for so long, justice must be done *right now!!* I must have what I want *now, now, now!!*
- If *you* have had anything whatever to do with this injustice—or even if I *believe* you have—then you must immediately devote yourself to giving me what I want, no matter what the cost to you.
- If you don't give me what I want immediately, you shall be labeled a monster of the worst kind, and I will do my best to spread the word of your behavior.

Is it any wonder that we hate the complaining of a victim? They're loud, demanding, and grating, and they never go away until they get what they want. When Deborah would complain to Paul that he never took her anywhere, all he wanted to do was get her to shut up. He tried to do that by showing her how she was wrong, but that never worked. It never occurred to him to just try to love her, because he'd never been loved enough himself to have enough love to give her.

We really hate the feelings of obligation that victims give us, but the obligation decreases considerably when we remember the Law of Choice and the Law of Expectations from Chapter Two. Just as other people have the right to make their own choices, and we have no right to expect other people to do anything for us, so also *we* have the right to make *our* own choices, and other people have no right to expect *us* to do what *they* want.

Consider again the metaphor of the drowning man—which we introduced in Chapter One—but this time from a different perspective. People who act like victims are all drowning, but they do *not* have the right to demand that *you* save them. Similar to what we discussed on page 184,

- according to the Law of Choice, no one ever has the right to tell you what you must do. Just because victims are in a position of need doesn't obligate you to do anything. Their drowning is their problem to solve, and they have no right to make it yours.
- they don't have the wisdom to know whether you are *capable* of helping them out of the water in any given moment.
- they have an obligation to do all they can to get out of the water themselves. You didn't put them there, and it's not your job to get them out.

Should you *choose* to help a victim, you are still not obligated to help him or her in the way—or to the extent—that he or she might demand. As you consider helping or loving a victim, you might weigh two elements in your decision. Rather than giving the victim what he demands, you might consider

- what the other person actually *needs*.
- what you actually *choose* to give *freely*.

Let's examine these two considerations in turn and then in combination:

Giving People What They Actually Need

Victims often make angry demands for what they want, and they often insist that what they *want* is the same as what they *need*. That is often not the case, however. Imagine, for example, that a cocaine addict demands from you what he *wants*, which would be more of his drug. Would it then be prudent to give him what he wants, rather than what he *needs*, which is love, support, and perhaps some kind of drug rehabilitation? There is, in short, often great wisdom in refusing to give a victim what he wants, giving him instead what he needs.

Victims believe that happiness will result from their acting like victims to win the sympathy and attention of those around them. As we have discussed at length in previous chapters, however, acting like victims can lead only to more misery. Victimhood is a virtual institution in this country. We've been taught that we *must* give sympathy to anyone who demands it. We tend to support each other in the belief that victims are always justified in their anger and their claims of helplessness. As we do that, however, we fail to recognize the power of choice, responsibility, truth, and love. We often cripple people by giving them sympathy, thereby failing to satisfy their true need for telling the truth about themselves and feeling the genuine compassion found in Real Love.

Real Love vs. Sympathy, or Supporting vs. Rescuing

What victims *want* is sympathy. What they *need*, however, is Real Love, and we must learn to recognize the difference. On page 78, for example, I introduced to you the toddler who had learned to manipulate his mother for attention by acting like a victim when he fell down while running across the floor. I suggest you review that brief description, at the end of which I promised to describe in this chapter how a parent could handle the situation in a way that a child would not be encouraged to act like a victim. Let's observe one mother, Joan, who understands Real Love as she interacts with her toddler.

Joan watches as her toddler falls, smacking both hands hard on the floor. She does not get up from her chair, nor does she look startled or frightened. Sudden movement and a look of panic from parents are enough to make most children cry. "Wow," Joan says, "that was quite a noise. Come here and let me look at you."

The child walks over to Joan, where she lovingly touches his hands and face as she inspects them for signs of injury.

"Oh good," says Joan. "Everything is where it should be. Now go off and play. I love you."

Joan's child did not need to be picked up and treated like a baby. He was quite capable of getting up by himself. What he needed was to be reassured that he was safe and loved. We need to remember that principle as our children get older and fall down in other ways—physical, financial, academic, social, romantic, and emotional. If we rescue them, we teach them that they *are* victims and rob them of opportunities to learn responsibility.

We need to love our children as Joan did, teaching them that inconvenience and pain are a natural part of living—to be minimized where possible, but not to be feared. With that kind of healthy instruction, children won't foolishly expect everything to go their way. The inevitable discomforts of life become merely inconvenient, or even insignificant, instead of frightening. We give our children a great gift when we teach them to avoid the deadly trap of acting like victims.

Consider again the discussion between Paul and Deborah from pages 247-9 earlier in this chapter. Although Deborah was complaining that Paul didn't spend enough time with her, Paul wasn't the least bit obligated to give her what she *wanted*—and demanded. Instead he chose to tell the truth about himself and to genuinely listen to Deborah. In so doing, he gave her what she *needed*, which was his unconditional love.

Giving People What We Choose to Give Freely

Certainly Deborah felt greatly supported by Paul's choice to tell the truth about himself and to listen to her, but still she didn't feel entirely gratified. She still wanted to discuss the possibility of spending more time with him, and we approached that subject next as we continued their discussion from the pages mentioned in the paragraph immediately above.

"We used to go out to plays and go dancing when we were dating," she said, "but we haven't done that in the longest time."

At this point Paul looked like he was suffering from severe indigestion. "I've always hated dancing, and I never did like plays. Never did."

"But you *said* you enjoyed them," Deborah said with considerable surprise.

"Oh, I know. I said lots of things in those days. I guess I was willing to go just about anywhere you wanted back then. When you're in love, you'll say just about anything, you know?"

Deborah began to get angry, but I interrupted. "Deborah, you asked him a question, and he's finally telling you the complete truth. Now, do you really want to make him feel bad for being truthful? Is that what you want?"

"I guess not."

"Good thinking," I said. "Deborah, I know that what you say you want is to go to plays and to go dancing, but isn't your real desire actually much bigger than that? What do you really want from Paul? What do you want that isn't associated with a specific thing or activity?"

Deborah began to catch on. "For him to love me?"

"Right. That's what matters most, and you'll feel loved by Paul *only* if what he gives you is given *freely*. If he feels *forced* in any way to give you anything, you won't feel loved at all. Do you see that? In that case he wouldn't be *loving* you. You'd just be manipulating him. He'd just be your *hostage*. Clear?"

"Yes, I get it."

"So, Paul, if you don't like dancing, and you don't like going to plays, what *do* you like doing with Deborah? What would be a good start?"

"Well," he said, "I like going out to dinner. We could do that."

Vague discussions about what people might do in the future are usually worthless, so I helped them get specific. "How often would you be willing to commit to doing that?" I asked.

"Once a week," he said.

"What day?"

"Friday."

"Deborah, would that be acceptable to you?" I asked. "I know you'd like something more, but look where you've gotten with demanding more. Nowhere but miserable. *This* is what Paul is offering *freely*. He's offering to spend time with you—just the two of you—while you go out to eat with him every Friday. Would you be willing to accept that as an initial move to spend more time with you?"

"Yes, I think that would be nice."

And so they had begun to break out of their cycle of attacking and victimhood and withdrawal and a steady loss of intimacy in their relationship.

Giving People What They Need and What We Choose to Give Freely

In order to further illustrate what it looks like to give people what they need and what we choose to give freely, allow me to share with you a letter I once received, along with my reply.

Dear Greg,

"My neighbor doesn't have a car, so about once a week she calls and asks me to take her grocery shopping. The problem is that I don't have all day to take her places. When I drop her off at the store, I tell her that I'll be back in forty-five minutes (when I'm done with my own errands), but when I return she's never done. It takes her an hour and a half or more to finish her shopping, and by that time I'm pretty mad. She doesn't appreciate anything I do for her either. She hardly ever says thanks. When I bring up that it's taking too long, she just gets irritated. And she never wants to go shopping when I do my own, only when it's convenient for her. I'm getting really tired of this, but I feel guilty that she doesn't have anybody who can take her anywhere. I know I should help her, but when does it stop?"

My reply:

> We all have a responsibility to be loving toward the people around us. It's simply the right way to live, and it brings us lasting, genuine happiness. Other people, however, do not have the right to choose *how* loving we must be toward them. You're responsible to love your neighbor as much as *you* choose, not as much or in the way *she* chooses.
>
> In order to illustrate this concept further, imagine that I come to your door and tell you I really need some money. Out of a real sense of concern for me, you give me twenty dollars, but I say *no*, I want a thousand dollars instead, and then I come into your house and ransack the place until I get what I want. As a loving person, are you obligated to stand by while I do that? No, you are not.

In a similar way, you don't have to give your neighbor a single minute of your time, but you have nonetheless chosen to do that. You're offering her a gift of your time and energy and concern. In each case, she says with her behavior that your gift is not enough and that you're obligated to give her more. But you are not obligated. How much you give her is entirely your choice, and when you remember that, you'll feel less guilty. She is trying to manipulate you with anger and guilt to give her what she wants, but that obligates you in no way.

Your anger at her demonstrates that *you* also expect something from *her* in return—gratitude, appreciation, kindness—which means you're not entirely giving her a gift. You're making a trade with her. Trades usually end up being perceived as unfair by one or both parties, and trading is not a loving, rewarding way to live.

Instead of trading, make a decision about what you're willing to do for her, a gift of your time and resources that you can offer without any thought of return for yourself. Then offer your gift, fully prepared for her to be ungrateful, demanding, and irritated, which are routine reactions for a victim. If your gift is genuine—truly unconditional—you won't mind if she is ungrateful. If she demands more than you offer, clearly and lovingly re-state what you're willing to do.

Practically speaking, how will this actually look as you talk to your neighbor? There are at least a couple of ways you could approach this:

- The next time she asks you to take her to the store, tell her that you have exactly _____ minutes to give her. Don't bring up all the times she's been inconsiderate before. If you do that, she'll feel attacked and defensive. Just tell her what time you'll be coming to pick her up at the front of the store. Tell her that if she isn't finished when you come to get her, you have other places to be, and she'll have to get a taxi or other means of transportation home. Think about it: would the bus wait for her? Like the bus, you also have a schedule to keep and other things to do.

- Tell her that you'd love to help her with her shopping, but she'll have to go at the times you choose to shop for your own family. She'll also have to complete her shopping in the time you allot for your own. If she says that the times you choose are inconvenient for her, then she can find other means to get to the store.

As you learn to love your neighbor, you'll be happier. That love will bless both of you, however, only if you offer it freely. Give her what you can without a desire for your own reward, and without guilt or anger. By your own choices and experience, you'll discover what is the right amount of assistance to offer.

Practicing Real Love does *not* make you a hostage to victims who make demands on your time and attention. Being loving does not mean being a doormat. As you are trying to be loving toward people, give them what they need and what you can offer freely. If you try to offer more than that, you'll empty yourself to the point where you won't feel loving anymore, and then everyone is harmed.

The Complaining Parent

Jacob lived more than a thousand miles from his parents' home, and according to his mother, he never called enough, never visited enough, and never gave them enough attention of any kind. She reminded him of this in virtually every phone call, which she made almost daily. It was driving Jacob crazy, to the point where he avoided his mother whenever possible.

He talked to me about this situation one day, and I asked, "Why do you think she complains all the time that you never call or visit?"

"Because I *don't* call or visit?" he said.

"Think deeper," I suggested. "It's not about calls or visits. It's always about Real Love. Now, in view of that insight, why is she complaining?"

"Because she doesn't believe I love her?"

"Exactly."

"So what am I supposed to do?"

"As long as you are only responding to her *demands*, she'll never feel like you're offering your love *freely*, and she'll never be satisfied. That's one of the problems with acting like a victim. When she whines and complains, whatever she gets never satisfies her. When she acts like a victim, she makes it impossible for her to feel loved, no matter what anybody ever does for her. So the only way out of this horrible situation is for you to completely step off the Field of Death—where she lives—and offer whatever you have *freely*."

"Frankly," Jacob said, "I don't *have* very much to give her."

"That's pretty obvious," I said, "and I understand. I'm not suggesting that you give her what you don't have. So what *could* you give her? I know she can be pretty demanding, so you would have to decide what you could give her *without feeling obligated*. What you give her has to be an unconditional gift. Could you call her, for example, and talk to her for, say, three minutes without feeling pressured?"

"I think so. Sure. If I knew there would be an end to it after three minutes, I could handle it."

"So every day, before she can call you, you call her and just talk to her about whatever she wants to talk about for three minutes. Ask her how she's doing. Ask her about those pains in her joints that normally you hate hearing about. You'll be cheerfully offering her those three minutes as an unconditional gift—without any hesitation—and I think you'll be surprised at what happens."

Jacob called his mother as we had discussed. At first he called her for three minutes a day, then five, and in a couple of weeks he called me to say that she had become so much less demanding that he hardly recognized her. Love freely offered is worth a hundred times more than love given grudgingly.

5. TEACH THE TRUTH ABOUT HUMAN BEHAVIOR.

Sometimes miraculous effects can be seen from teaching victims about human behavior. I must emphasize, however, that in almost all cases we must teach victims about human behavior *in general* and must avoid lecturing them specifically about *their* behavior. If you attempt to point out to someone how he or she is acting like a victim, that person will rarely be grateful for the instruction. As an illustration of the benefits of discussions about human behavior, let me share a letter I received:

Dear Greg,

"I moved away from home years ago. I get along pretty well with both my parents, but every time I talk to my mother on the phone, she talks about my father. She complains about how he's thoughtless, messy, doesn't take her anywhere, doesn't do anything for her, and gets angry at her for no reason. She could talk forever. If I would put the phone down and come back an hour later, she wouldn't know that I'd been gone. For one thing, it's boring, and for another, I don't like her talking about my father like that. Sometimes I try to defend him, or tell her that I don't want to hear it, but that only makes her mad at me. How can I get out of these conversations with her?"

My response:

> Clearly, your mother doesn't feel loved, and in order to get brief periods of relief from her pain, she acts like a victim, from which she gets the sympathy of those around her. She also gets a sense of power as she makes her husband wrong. Being *right* is a powerful feeling.
>
> When she acts like that, you see only four choices:
>
> - Agree with her and feel like you're betraying your father.
> - Listen to her silently.
> - Defend your father.
> - Tell her you don't want to hear it.
>
> If you agree with her, or if you just listen silently, it will only fuel the fire of her victimhood. She would love that—she'd be only too happy to play the victim game with you forever—but it would never help her, because no matter how much sympathy she received, it would never feel like Real Love. Real Love can be felt only when it's freely given and received. Whenever we have to manipulate people for attention—by acting like victims, for example—whatever they give us can never feel unconditionally given.

If you defend your father, or if you tell her you don't want to hear it, all she will hear you saying is that she's wrong, and she won't be able to tolerate that. Being right is like a drug to her, and she will not allow you to take that away from her.

Fortunately, there is another option—a much better one—that you haven't been seeing. In relationships we must remember that happiness is always about telling the truth and loving people. In this case, tell the truth about your father's behavior, and be loving toward both your parents. How would that look?

Suppose your mother says, "I am sick and tired of the way that man treats me. I talk to him, and he just grunts. I say something he doesn't like, and he snaps at me."

Instead of the four choices you've been making, try something different. First acknowledge the truth of what she's saying—so she senses that you're really listening and that you care about her—and then help her see the truth about the *meaning* of his behavior. You could use any combination of the statements found below, but always including—and beginning with—the first on the list:

- "You're right, Mom. He really can be difficult."
- "I always used to get mad at people when they ignored me—that's what Dad is doing when he just grunts at you—or when they got angry at me. But I've been learning that when people behave badly, it's always in response to their own pain. It has little or nothing to do with me."
- "Dad is just drowning. He's never felt *unconditionally* loved—few people have—so he's in pain all the time, and then he responds by doing whatever protects him in the moment: attacking people, withdrawing, acting like a victim, whatever. That's what he's doing with you."
- "Drowning people really can't see the needs of others. They become completely selfish. I used to take that personally, but now I can see that they're really just trying to save themselves. When they behave badly, they're just thrashing and kicking to keep their heads above water, and in the process they affect the people around them in negative

ways—like Dad does with you. But his goal isn't to hurt you. It's just that when people are drowning, they really don't see clearly what they're doing to other people."
- "It must be hard for you when he acts like that. I can promise you, though, if he knew how to behave differently, he would."
- "He does that with me sometimes, too, but then I remember that he's just having a hard time—which has nothing to do with me—and then I try to love him as well as I can in that moment. That's the only thing I've ever found that helps me or him."

Now imagine a different situation. Suppose your mother says, "I am sick and tired of that man leaving his stuff all over the floor." You could use statements like the following—again always including first the first item:

- "He really can be a mess, that's for sure. In many ways, he just doesn't think of other people."
- "I've learned that when people are selfish—when they're not thoughtful and loving—it's always because they don't feel enough love in their own lives. Then they don't have any to give anybody else."
- "Mom, that's almost exactly the scenario in this book I've been reading, and you wouldn't believe the solution. It's up to you—I don't care if you read it—but I do suggest you give it a try. The book is called *Real Love—The Truth About Finding Unconditional Love and Fulfilling Relationships*, and that story is on pages 49-62."
- "And when you get mad at him about it, what does he do? In all the years that you've gotten mad at him, has it ever made a positive difference in his behavior or in your marriage? I'm not criticizing you, just wondering if it's time to look at doing something different."

As you speak to her, you can't feel the slightest bit irritated, disappointed, critical, or condescending, or she'll feel attacked. If you tell her the truth in a loving way, it's quite likely that she will react in one of two ways:

- She'll sense the truth of what you're saying, but she still won't like it. Once she senses that her victimhood is no longer justified in your mind, however, she will tend not to keep using you as a sounding board for her complaints. In this scenario, she loses someone to complain to, but you win, because you don't have to hear the gossiping anymore.
- She'll be utterly intrigued by this new way of seeing her husband, herself, and the world around her. She'll investigate Real Love, and will experience the joy that comes from living according to these principles. In this case, she wins and you win.

Notice that in both cases, you win. At worst, she could get mad at you, but she's done that hundreds of times before, so that would be nothing new for you. If you keep offering loving *explanations* for your father's behaviors—without *defending* him—one of the above situations will prevail, and in either one you'll be much happier than you are now.

Teaching Children About Victimhood

Most of us have a natural tendency to help anyone who is treated unfairly. We root for the underdog. Look at the sympathy and support we give to disaster victims, for example, as well as abused children, war-time refugees, and endangered animal species. To our credit, much of our motivation comes from genuine compassion. When children act like victims, however, our motivations become especially muddied, and we often give them what they want for selfish reasons.

If we don't already feel loved ourselves, we feel guilty when our children claim to be injured by us. We then give them what they want because we're afraid *not* to. We want to be seen as concerned and loving parents, and if we don't give them what they want, we're afraid they will judge us as unloving and will withdraw their approval and affection from us. We also tend to give in to our children because we don't want to look like unkind parents in the eyes of other people. In our society, it's quite politically incorrect for us to withhold our support from any person or group which claims to have been treated unfairly.

When our children claim to be injured by someone else, we have an especially good opportunity to look like loving parents. We feel important, even indispensable, when we rise to their defense, feeling self-righteous and powerful as we take the side of truth and justice. In these situations, we briefly feel more connected to them and less alone. In other words, we sometimes save our "victimized" children in order to feel more loved ourselves, as illustrated in the following story about a boy, Lewis, and his father.

When Lewis came home from school, he was quite upset and said, "My teacher is stupid. I was supposed to turn in my English paper this morning, but I didn't have it ready, because I was sick yesterday. I couldn't help being sick, but she still gave me a zero on the assignment."

"That's not fair," said Lewis's father. "You were in bed all day yesterday. Did you tell her you were sick?"

"I tried, but she wouldn't listen."

"Don't you worry about it. I'll call her and straighten this out."

It's tempting to save our children from injustice—it can seem like the compassionate thing to do—but sometimes when we do that, we teach them that the world is obligated to treat them "fairly," and that can be a crippling belief. Lewis's father thought he was being supportive, but instead his behavior was selfishly motivated—and produced harmful results—in ways he was not aware of:

- He helped Lewis feel like a victim. Unwittingly, he taught his son that we should always get what we think is fair, which is a foolish and dangerous notion. In the first place, our idea of fairness is often completely mistaken. We tend to define "fair" as whatever benefits *us*, which is rarely fair to everyone else. In addition, children need to understand that all our lives we function in relationships and systems—families, friendships, schools, jobs, and politically-defined societies—where it's entirely the right of someone else to define what is "fair." Employers and judicial systems, for example, often establish what is fair. If we allow our children to believe that they always have the right to define fairness, they'll experience endless conflict and disappointment in their lives.

- Lewis's father had often been treated unfairly in his own life, and he understandably hated the sense of helplessness and loneliness that had accompanied those incidents. Defending Lewis gave him a chance to vent his frustration and anger at all the people who had "victimized" him in the past. Sympathizing with Lewis became a selfish way for *his father* to feel more powerful, which distracted him from his true responsibility to love and teach his son. This is an example of the Vicarious Victim, which we discussed on pages 119-21.
- As Lewis's father offered his support to Lewis, he succeeded in winning Lewis's affection. He unconsciously *used* his son to feel more important and "loved." He saw that "love" immediately in Lewis's face when he said that he'd call the teacher and straighten things out. Lewis's father often used people in that way, saying and doing things so they would like him and make him feel better. Most of us do that, and we're mostly unaware of it.

By responding to Lewis as he did, his father missed a valuable opportunity to teach his son some important lessons about responsibility and about accepting the consequences of his own choices. We'll discuss these lessons shortly. He also missed the chance to teach his son about the right that all people have to inconvenience us as they learn from their choices and mistakes, a lesson we discussed on pages 55-7 and 183. In addition, he neglected to talk to Lewis about the fact that other people never make us angry (pages 26-7). Every time we interact with our children, we have the opportunity to teach them many important principles.

Not all parents respond to a child who is acting like a victim by giving him what he wants. Some parents become irritated by victim behaviors, and they punish a child when he whines and cries. When a child acts like a victim, however, it is certain that at least one parent in the family does reward victim behaviors occasionally, or the child wouldn't be motivated to use them. When parents sometimes reward a child's victim behaviors and on other occasions punish them, life can be very confusing for the child.

When children act like victims, what do they really need? No surprise here: They need to be loved and taught, as explained thoroughly in the book *Real Love in Parenting*.

We must learn to identify the victim behaviors of our children and help them see these behaviors in themselves. As we teach them, and as they feel loved by us, they will no longer have a need to get Imitation Love and protect themselves by acting like victims. Their victim behaviors will disappear without our ever doing anything to *make* them go away.

In the scenario above, when Lewis received a zero on his school assignment, he knew from past experience that he'd be criticized and would feel less accepted by everyone he knew, including his parents. Immediately and unconsciously he protected himself by angrily blaming his *teacher* for treating him unfairly, thereby using two Protecting Behaviors—acting like a victim and attacking. He also blamed his *illness* for his incomplete assignment, another way of acting like a victim.

Now let's change the interaction between father and son in one significant way. Let's suppose that months before this event occurred, Lewis's father had taken the steps to find Real Love for himself. He had also learned about victimhood and how to respond to people who act like victims. In this new scene, therefore, when Lewis complains about his teacher, his father feels loved and is not blinded by emptiness and fear. He is able to see his son clearly and give him what he really needs.

When Lewis came home from school, he was quite upset and said, "My teacher is stupid. I was supposed to turn in my English paper this morning, but I didn't have it because I was sick yesterday. I couldn't help being sick, but she still gave me a zero on the assignment."

"I know you were sick yesterday," Lewis's father said, "but how long ago did your teacher give you the assignment?"

Lewis paused before he answered, "Well, about a week ago. Maybe longer."

"So you could have done the assignment on the same day it was given—a whole week ago—couldn't you?"

"Well . . ."

"If you had done the assignment a week ago, it wouldn't have mattered that you were sick yesterday, would it? The work would have been done, and you could have turned it in on time. So the real reason you got a zero is that *you* chose to put off doing your assignment until the last minute. Your teacher actually gave you plenty of time to do your work, don't you think?"

"I guess so," Lewis responded weakly.

Lewis's father smiled. "I'm not picking at you. I've done this many times myself. We like to blame other people for our problems, don't we? It's easier than admitting that *we* made a mistake. We don't like to look wrong or stupid. This isn't the end of the world. You just made a mistake. Next time you get an assignment, you'll remember this zero, and you'll choose more wisely." Father hugged Lewis and said, "I still love you. The zero means nothing."

Lewis's father taught him a wonderful lesson. Without making him feel worthless, he taught him that he was entirely responsible for the consequences of his behavior. He taught him that he was not a victim.

6. OCCASIONALLY DESCRIBE WHAT YOU ARE DOING AND THE CHOICES AVAILABLE.

On pages 261-2 we talked about Jacob, who learned to give his mother the love she needed in the ways he was able. In some situations, however, she could still be quite demanding. On one occasion a business trip took him close to his parents' home, so he called to tell his mother that he'd be coming to visit. He knew, though, that he couldn't possibly be around her for as long as she would want. She was just too demanding and critical for him to handle, and he wasn't loving enough to react well to that yet.

It is important to note the *reason* Jacob chose in his head for not spending more time with his mother. He didn't blame *her*. His attitude wasn't that he couldn't be around her because *she* was demanding and critical. He simply *described* those qualities in her—without feeling victimized by them—in order to provide a *context* for his real reason for not spending a lot of time with her: He realized that *he wasn't loving enough yet* to respond to her in a loving way.

On a subsequent call she began to lay out her plans for his visit. "I've prepared food for two days," she said, "and of course you'll stay here with us."

"Oh, that's very kind of you, mother," he said, "but I'll be pretty busy, so I'll be staying at a hotel near my meetings, and I plan on coming by the house on Thursday from six to eight o'clock in the evening."

His mother began to protest that she had gone to great lengths to prepare for a longer stay, complaining that he never stayed long, and so on. Jacob interrupted in a gentle way.

"Mother, I really look forward to seeing you. I hope you'll enjoy my coming too. We really have only two choices here though. You can either resent my coming, or you can enjoy it. It's your choice, but either way, I'm coming Thursday from six to eight. I look forward to seeing you then."

If Jacob had tried to answer each of her objections and complaints, he would only have been jumping on the Field of Death with her, and nobody would have won. Instead he simply described what he was doing and gave her a simple choice. On some occasions that's all we can do with a victim.

7. OCCASIONALLY IMPOSE CONSEQUENCES.

Sometimes victims learn best from experiencing the consequences of their own decisions. If we attempt to reason with a victim, he can't listen because he's too empty and afraid. If we push him, he feels even more victimized. Victims see almost everything *we* do as a threat, after which they defend themselves. They take our behavior personally. Consequences, on the other hand, have no personality. Consequences teach people simply by virtue of their effects on those who made the choices that led to the consequences.

On pages 193-6 we talked about the effects of consequences in teaching punctuality to Joseph, an employee who was frequently late. Remember that when Joseph's supervisor made him feel guilty, reprimanded him, and reasoned with him, Joseph never learned anything, because he reacted like a victim to any *person* who attempted to show him anything at all. The imposition of consequences, however, proved to be quite an effective teacher.

We can see the teaching value of consequences illustrated once again as one mother, Joyce, interacts with her daughter, Kate. One Saturday morning Kate was leaving the house when she was stopped by her mother.

"Did you do those two loads of laundry I asked you to do yesterday?" asked Joyce.

"There wasn't time," said Kate, "and I can't do it now because I have to leave for cheerleading practice."

Notice that Kate was making three protests based on a belief that she was a victim:

- When she said, "There wasn't time," she was blaming something other than herself for her situation, and that's the definition of acting like a victim.
- When she said, "I *can't* do it now," she was stating her belief that in this situation she was helpless—that she was at the mercy of circumstances—another belief central to victimhood.
- When she said, " . . . because I *have* to leave," she was implying that any attempt to stop her from going to cheerleading practice would be *unfair*. She was threatening to become an even bigger victim if anyone dared to interfere with her righteous plans.

"Well," said Joyce, "please try to do the laundry when you get home."

Joyce was taking the easy way out when she accepted her daughter's excuses. Most of us hate conflict, and in order to avoid it we often allow our children to act like victims. We don't like to keep giving those repetitive, boring, and often difficult lessons in responsibility that our children hate as much as we do. When we fail to teach our children what they need to know, however—when we take the lazy course—we're running, a Protecting Behavior. We run because we're uncomfortable about confronting our children with their behavior. We have learned that when we teach and correct them, our children often resent that and then withdraw their affection from us, and it's understandable that we're afraid of that withdrawal.

On other occasions when our children make excuses for their behavior, we don't run. Instead, we become irritated. We express our anger at them so they'll stop making excuses and instead will do what we want them to do. But anger doesn't help them to become responsible and loving either; it only communicates to them that we don't love them.

Now let's suppose that prior to their interaction above, Joyce had already taken the steps to find Real Love and had learned how to lovingly teach her daughter with consequences. In the following interaction, therefore, she is happy and doesn't need to buy the approval of her daughter. She's not afraid to teach her daughter, even though she knows that Kate might not like it.

"Did you do those two loads of laundry I asked you to do yesterday?" asked Joyce.

As before, Kate said, "There wasn't time. And I can't do it now because I have to leave for cheerleading practice."

"I gave you that assignment more than twenty-four hours ago. In that entire time, did you watch television?"

"Yes, but—"

"Did you talk to anyone on the phone?"

"I talked to Kris for a little while, but—"

"And I remember hearing you talk to Sharon, too."

"I forgot about that."

"So you chose to do at least three things—probably more—instead of the laundry I assigned you. Your statement that there 'wasn't time' doesn't hold up very well then, does it?"

"I guess not."

"Another thing. When I asked about the laundry a moment ago, you told me you couldn't do it now because you *had* to leave for cheerleading practice. When Sharon called, did you tell her that you *had* to do the laundry before you could talk to her?"

"No."

"Do you see the point? We all *choose* what we do, and *you* have repeatedly *chosen* not to do the laundry. Your obligation to do your assignments here at home is at least as serious as your commitment to cheerleading. You've been neglecting a lot of your responsibilities lately, and we've talked about this before, but talking hasn't been enough. It's obvious that you need some help understanding the importance of the assignments you've been given, so I'll help you by requiring that you do the laundry right now. You may remember that a week ago, you agreed that if you didn't do the laundry on the same day it was assigned, starting the next day you wouldn't be able to go anywhere until you did the laundry. You agreed to that consequence."

"But I'll miss practice if I have to do the laundry now. They can't do the routines without me there. That would hurt the whole team. You can't do this to the team."

"*I'm* not doing this to the team. *You* are. If you had chosen to do your assignment when it was given—if you'd done what you were asked to do yesterday—this wouldn't be happening. You knew the consequence of not doing the laundry promptly, so when you chose not to do the laundry, you also *chose* to miss cheerleading practice. This is a result of *your* choice. You *could* tell the team this is *my* fault, of course, but *you* will know that that's not true."

"In the past," Joyce continued, "I have allowed you to go to practice many times when your work wasn't done, and all you learned from that approach was that you could do whatever you wanted. That was *my* mistake. I'm choosing not to make that mistake again this time. All your life, your choices will have consequences to you and to others, and this time I'm just allowing you to experience those consequences."

Kate was not happy about missing practice, but she found it difficult to stay angry at her mother when it was obvious that Joyce wasn't angry at Kate and when Kate remembered that she had agreed to this particular consequence.

This kind of firm and loving interaction is impossible for us as parents unless we feel loved ourselves. When we tell our children the truth about themselves and impose consequences, they often become angry and communicate that their pain and anger are all *our* fault. If we don't feel loved, we'll feel threatened by their accusations and will likely protect ourselves. At that point the possibility of a loving interaction will go straight down the drain.

In this situation Joyce could also have been creative and given Kate more than one choice for her consequence. She might have offered Kate any of the following options. "Because you haven't fulfilled your responsibility to do the laundry today

- you can't go to cheerleading practice today (the consequence she had previously agreed to)."
- you can still go to your practice today, but because I will have to do the laundry for you, you will be required to clean the kitchen for me when you get back." Remember, the purpose of a consequence is to make poor choices sufficiently *inconvenient* that a child will be motivated to make the right choices (pages 142-4). Mother knew that cleaning the kitchen would involve at least three times the work of doing two loads of laundry.
- your brother will have to do the laundry for you, but then you will be required to do all of his jobs for three days."

Again, the purpose of a consequence is to make poor choices so inconvenient that people will choose to make wiser ones. Consequences are powerful and clean teachers, because consequences of themselves don't get angry, don't act like victims, don't have personal agendas, and don't take things personally.

8. STAY OFF THE FIELD OF DEATH.

At the beginning of this chapter, I suggest that the eight numbered responses to victimhood tend to be most useful when used in the order listed. This particular response, however—Stay off the Field of Death—is an exception to that general recommendation. This response must be used at all times.

Victims live on the Field of Death. They're comfortable there—they're experts at trading and negotiating there—and they want to keep everyone around them on the same field. If you're not already on the Field of Death with them, they will do everything they can to *lure* you there. We can see this illustrated by an interaction between Blaine and his wife, Cheryl.

"You never do anything I ask you to do," Cheryl said.

"What do you mean?" asked Blaine. "Last Saturday I spent hours tilling up that space in the backyard because you said you wanted to plant a garden there. And now you're telling me I never do anything you ask me to do?"

"How long have you put off cleaning out the garage?"

"I've been working at that for months. It's just not finished."

"It'll never be finished, and how about the faucet that's been dripping in the bathroom for years now? When will that be *finished?* Are you *working on that* too?"

This exchange went on for some time, and you can imagine how productive it was. Cheryl made multiple accusations, and Blaine energetically defended himself. On the Field of Death, everything is *counted,* and by Cheryl's meticulous accounting, Blaine had not met her expectations of an adequate performance.

What Blaine didn't understand was that you can never make a victim happy, no matter how hard you try to meet his or her expectations. We talked about this somewhat on pages 73-4. Victims don't make requests. They issue demands and expectations, and in the process they make their own happiness impossible, because when you expect something, receiving it can never feel like Real Love. Blaine could have argued with Cheryl forever, and he would have accomplished nothing, because he was playing on the Field of Death with her.

So what can be done? I taught Blaine about Real Love and about victimhood, and he practiced telling the truth about himself in a Real Love group for several weeks. Then one day Cheryl came to him in a huff and said, "Do you ever do anything I ask you to do?"

Blaine remembered what I'd said about the Field of Death, and that nobody ever wins there, so rather than argue with Cheryl, he smiled—which instantly disarmed her—took her by the hand, and said, "Come with me." She'd never seen anything like this response before, so feeling thoroughly disoriented, she followed him. He led her over to the couch, laid her down, lay down beside her, kissed her, and said, "You're right. I don't listen very well. So right now I'm going to listen closely to what you want. Which would you rather I did first: make out with you here on the couch or fix the dripping faucet in the bathroom?"

Cheryl was completely out of her element by this time, and after a moment she said, "The faucet can wait."

All Cheryl really wanted was to feel loved, and in the absence of Real Love she had learned to settle for nagging Blaine about what he hadn't done, which gave her a feeling of power. On this occasion, Blaine absolutely refused to step onto the Field of Death with her, and as she felt his genuine concern for her, all thoughts of Imitation Love were driven from her mind.

By the way, Blake did fix the faucet later.

1-8. PUTTING ALL THE RESPONSES TOGETHER

We can learn even more from seeing all the above responses put together, as in the following scenario involving a man named Seth, who came to see me about the problems he was having at home.

"Overall," Seth said, "I'm happier than I've been in a long time. I've been studying Real Love for several months, I've been calling people and sharing the truth about myself, and I've been attending a Real Love group. I'm having more and more moments when I feel unconditionally loved. But I'm having a problem, and I can't seem to figure out a solution by myself."

"Tell me more," I suggested.

"I have four children," he said, "and all the way home from work I dread what's going to happen when I walk in the door. From the moment I get home, I'm assaulted by kids wanting something. One of them wants to play, one wants help with her homework, another wants me to listen to everything that happened that day, another wants me to look at a painting he did at school, and it goes on and on. I feel absolutely overwhelmed by all the demands. I just can't handle them all."

"And when you *can't* handle them all, how do your children respond to that?"

"They get loud and whine more and get more demanding."

"Then what do you do?"

"I feel more frazzled by all the noise and the demands, and before long I just give up. I either get in the car and take off, or I go back to my room and shut myself away from it all."

"I'll bet the kids love that."

"They hate it, but it just gets to the point where I can't stand being around them anymore."

"It sounds like you feel trapped."

"I *do* feel trapped, because I *am* trapped. What can I do with all those kids circling me like hyenas coming in for the kill?"

"First let's talk about what's really happening here, and with that insight you just might be able to change both the way you feel and the way you respond. But it all starts with how you see things. Look at the words you choose and how you feel:

- You say the kids make demands of you.
- You feel trapped by them.
- You feel overwhelmed by them.
- You feel like they bother you incessantly.
- They disturb your peace and quiet.
- Every day you dread what they're going to do to you.
- You see them as wild animals tearing you apart.

"In short," I continued, "you feel *victimized* by your children. You see them as doing things *to you* and not giving you what you want. In that condition—focused entirely on yourself as a victim—you couldn't possibly be loving your children, and they *feel* that. Your children, in turn, feel victimized by you, since they don't get from you the love they feel entitled to."

"Whatever you call it," Seth said, "I know it's not working out very well. So what can I do about it?"

"The truth is," I said, "that both you and your kids really *are* being victimized. All of you really are being inconvenienced against your will and are not getting what you want. So you are true victims (page 26). But that doesn't mean you have to *feel* and *act* like victims. How you feel and act is a *choice*, and that's what you can see differently."

"I don't get it. If I really am being victimized, how can I choose not to *feel* victimized?"

"Let me show you. As things are now, because you and the kids feel victimized together, you're doing everything on the Field of Death (pages 43-6), where Getting and Protecting Behaviors are the rules. The Field of Death is dominated by expectations, demands, disappointment, irritation, and endless manipulation. On the Field of Life, however, people don't do any of that. There are no expectations or demands or resentments or feeling pressured or feeling victimized. You don't know what that would be like because you've never been there."

"You're right. I can hardly even imagine it."

"Moving to the Field of Life is something you can *choose* to do all by yourself," I said. "You can't make the kids go there with you, but going there yourself will change everything in your interactions with them. Their behavior might stay the same for a while—they might still make demands, for example—but on the Field of Life you don't have to respond to them. You don't have to take their expectations and demands on your shoulders at all."

"Tell me more, because I'm still not quite getting the picture."

"On the Field of Life, instead of responding to expectations—and then feeling pressured and overwhelmed and trapped all the time, like you do now—we make a conscious decision to simply offer unconditionally whatever love we have to give. But we offer only what we can give freely and unconditionally—and *no more than that*. Anytime we try to offer more love than we have, we get completely emptied out, and then we become resentful and unloving. We think we're doing the right thing to try to satisfy everyone's demands, but when we go past our ability to love, we actually harm ourselves and others."

"It's starting to make sense, but I still don't know how to do it with the kids."

"I think you'll begin to see what I'm talking about if you do a mental exercise with me. Would you be willing to do that?"

"Sure."

"Close your eyes and imagine that you're in a place where you have chains fastened to your hands and feet, and the people around you are constantly tugging at you to pull you in whatever direction they wish. You are their slave. You can't make your own decisions. You're under constant pressure, you're being controlled all the time, and you're miserable. Does that sound familiar? Sound a lot like what you have now at home?"

"Yes."

"Now imagine that I come along and break all the chains and pick you up and carry you off to an entirely different place. In this place there are no chains, there is no one tugging at you or telling you what to do, and you get to make all your own decisions. Nobody can take anything from you or force you to do anything. Instead you give people only what you *choose* to give. How does that feel?"

Seth let out a long sigh of relief and said, "That would feel wonderful. For just a moment, I feel free."

"Open your eyes. You can have that feeling of freedom right now, just by changing the way you see things. So let's do this one small step at a time. Is it possible for you to do two things at once?"

"Well, some things. I can walk and chew gum."

"But can you do two *significant* things, like with your children? For example, can you help one child with his homework while you intently listen to another child's story about something she painted at school?"

"No."

"And I'll bet you've tried."

"More than once."

"So doing two of these tasks at the same time is literally impossible, wouldn't you say?"

"Yes."

"And yet you actually feel *guilty* when you can't do it. When two kids make their demands of you at the same time—or three or four kids—they actually make you feel guilty that you can't satisfy all their needs simultaneously. Just because they act like victims, you feel like you've done something wrong, like you're a bad parent, don't you?"

"Yes."

"Kinda dumb, huh?"

"So what can I do?"

"Instead of continuing to attempt the impossible, and feeling guilty when you can't do it, what if you just offer what you're capable of giving in any given moment? You can choose to give what you have as a *gift*, instead of responding to expectations and obligations. Just like the visualization we just did. Wouldn't that be fun?"

"I don't quite know how I would do that."

"What kind of work do you do for a living?"

"I'm a computer programmer."

"In any given moment, how many projects do you have to work on?"

"Several."

"Can you work on all of them at the same time?"

"No."

"So while you're working on one, what happens to the others?"

"They have to wait."

"Don't you feel guilty about that?"

"Not really. I know I'll get to them after I finish the one I'm working on."

"So why would it be any different with your children?"

There was a long pause before Seth said, "I'm not sure."

"The difference between your children and the computer programs is the Victim Factor. Computer programs don't act like victims. They don't whine and cry and make demands. They don't tug at your sleeves, look at you with pleading eyes, and say, 'Daddy! Daddy! Daddy!' And you don't feel victimized *by* the programs that sit quietly in the queue of things to do."

"I'd never thought about that. I think you're right."

"You just learned that satisfying all your children's demands simultaneously is simply impossible, so why do you keep falling for your children's acting like victims, and why do you keep feeling guilty for not doing the impossible?"

"Okay, so I can see why I don't need to feel guilty or feel like a victim, but what can I actually do when they all come at me like hyenas?"

"Do what you do with computer programs. Take care of them one at a time."

"That will never work. They all just get more and more demanding."

"And that bothers you only because you feel guilty. Now that you can see the foolishness of feeling guilty, you can deal with them much better. You don't have to do anything I'm suggesting, but if you'd like, I will propose something that has worked with many other people."

"I'd love it."

"When you walk in the door, you can adopt an attitude that you're not obligated to do a single thing. Because you're *not*. Instead, be determined to offer your time and love to your children as a *gift*. Then recognize that usually you can only do that with one child at a time. So at home you carry an index card with you, or you keep a pad of paper in a specified place, and on that card or paper you write what exact times you'll be giving to each child. You say to one child, 'I'll help you with your homework from 4:30 to 5:00.' To another child you promise 5:15 to 5:45. And so on. And each time you make a promise, you write it down. And it's critical that you do all of this with a completely giving, loving *attitude*. You can't be doing this just to get them out of your hair, or they will sense that."

"As you do this," I continued, "look at the miracles you will accomplish: First, you will eliminate your own feeling of being torn apart by a pack of hyenas, because you'll be separating the impossible onslaught of a million tasks into small, separate ones that you can do rather easily. Second, each time you write down a time and a child's name, that child will feel like he or she is important. He will *know* that in just a few minutes—or an hour or whatever—he'll be getting the time he wants with you. That's all they want, is to know that they matter to you. If they know their time is coming up in thirty minutes, or an hour, they can hang on and wait. They won't feel like victims, and you won't feel like one either."

"Perhaps the most important thing you will accomplish by doing things this way," I said, "is that you'll be moving off the Field of Death and on to the Field of Life. The way you're doing it now, your kids have to manipulate you for attention or demand it from you, so whatever attention you *do* give them doesn't feel like love to them, because it's not freely given. Whatever you give anyone grudgingly doesn't count for anything, so no matter how hard you work at satisfying your kids, they always feel unsatisfied. It's an endless cycle for victims. When you *offer* your time to them, though, you're creating opportunities for them to feel loved. That's huge."

"So what if I try this," he said, "what if I tell Hannah I'll help her with her home work at 5:30—thirty minutes from when she wants it—and she whines and complains and insists that I spend time with her right then? What can I do then?"

"Oh, that's easy," I said. "First, you refuse to respond with Getting and Protecting Behaviors of your own. You cannot become the slightest bit irritated, or you'll be back on the Field of Death, and then everybody loses. Second, instead of taking all the responsibility for the situation—which makes you feel like the bad guy and makes them feel like victims—you always give them a choice. Make them responsible for what happens next. So you might say something like this: 'I'm just giving you an opportunity to spend some time together in thirty minutes. You do *not* have to accept my offer. If you'd prefer, we could spend no time at all together. I'm offering you no time *right now*, because I'm busy with something else, but I am offering you some time in *thirty minutes*. Do you want that time or not? It's your choice.' Now the child has the choice of taking the time in thirty minutes or having no time at all. But whining about it suddenly makes no sense."

Seth began to implement what we had discussed, and within just a few days he called me again. "I can't believe the difference," he said. "I'm not spending a bit more time with them, but now I'm not feeling pressured. And because I don't feel pressured, I'm actually *enjoying* the time I spend with them. I'm liking this."

Briefly, let's examine how each of the responses to victimhood was used in the above scenario:

1. Never respond with getting and protecting behaviors.
    - I made no attempt to control or criticize Seth. Victims respond poorly to that.
    - I told Seth that whatever else he did with his children, he absolutely must not demonstrate irritation.
2. Tell the truth about yourself.
    - Seth recognized that he was acting like a victim with his children.

3. Listen to what the victim wants.
   - I listened to Seth and understood that he wanted primarily to feel understood and accepted, rather than to simply get sympathy.
   - I helped Seth understand that his children didn't really want all their demands satisfied at one time. They really just wanted to feel valued and loved.
4. Offer what is *needed* and what you can give *freely*.
   - Seth came to understand that he didn't have to satisfy every demand. What his children really needed was his love, and he only had to offer what he had.
5. Teach the truth about human behavior
   - I taught Seth about victimhood and Real Love, which had a significant impact on his understanding of the situation with his children.
6. Occasionally describe what you are doing and the choices available.
   - Seth clearly outlined with his children what he was doing with them.
   - Seth gave his children choices.
7. Occasionally impose consequences.
   - Seth told his children that one natural consequence of their rejecting his offer of his attention at a specific time would be to get no time at all.
8. Stay off the Field of Death.
   - Throughout my discussion with Seth the emphasis was to stay off the Field of Death.
   - Throughout Seth's discussions with his children, his goal was to stay off the Field of Death. This guiding principle helped me a great deal.

No matter how hard they work to make other people happy, or how hard they work to get other people to do what they want, victims are never happy. The only way to achieve happiness is to eliminate victimhood entirely and move off the Field of Death.

RESPONDING TO VICTIMS IN THE WORKPLACE

We generally fail to appreciate the terribly negative effects that victimhood has in the workplace. On pages 227-31 we discussed the cost of victimhood in the workplace, and the principles in that section are important to remember.

- An employee who feels like a victim will cause harm in so many ways: by resisting direction from superiors, by spreading malcontent among other employees, by carrying out instructions as slowly as possible, and often by feeling justified in stealing from his company.
- A customer who feels like a victim can react with considerable anger at the company he feels victimized by, and he will then cause all the trouble he can for that company and its employees.
- A supervisor who feels like a victim will fail to appreciate anything his employees do, will antagonize his employees, and will cause a general demoralizing condition in the company he or she manages.

Let's look at a couple of examples of how we might respond to victims in the workplace:

The Angry Customer

On pages 166-7, you participated in a mental exercise where you worked at the Customer Service counter. A customer stormed up to you, slammed a set of headphones down on the counter, and said, "I bought these from you, and now they don't work."

You tried to explain how the warranty had expired, and how the item had been obviously used in ways it had not been designed for, but the customer continued to vent his anger at you. In Chapter Six I said we would talk in this chapter about how to handle a case like this. Let's consider using some of the guidelines for responding to victims that we outlined above.

First, you recognize that this man is acting like a victim. He's empty and afraid, and in that condition, you would "Never respond with Getting and Protecting Behaviors." When someone is attacking you like this man is, it's quite natural to become afraid and defend yourself, but if you do that, you'll only make things much worse.

Second, you'll "Stay off the Field of Death." With each accusation this man makes, he's trying to drag you on to the Field of Death. You'll be tempted to respond to each of his accusations—you'll be tempted to show him how he's wrong—but you know that doing so won't work. No one wins on that field.

Third, you'll "Listen to what the victim wants." What does this man want most? Why is he yelling at you? It's not just about a broken product. He's empty and afraid, and he's responding with anger because *nobody* listens to him or cares about him: not at work, not at home, not anywhere. Because he purchased a product from your company, he believes he's found a legitimate excuse to *make* somebody—in this case, you—listen to him, and he's determined to milk it for all it's worth. Is that fair to you? No, but that's irrelevant, because you've decided to really help him and listen.

So instead of arguing with each of his statements, even though they're all accusatory and unfounded, you really listen. When he says, "This @#%& thing doesn't work," you respond with, "I know that feeling. It's very disappointing, isn't it? Once you buy something, and it works for a while, you kind of expect it to do its job forever, don't you? I know I do. Then when it breaks, you almost feel like you've been betrayed."

"Yes," the customer says. "That's it! It's like you've been betrayed."

The entire tone of the conversation has changed. You and the customer are not opponents anymore. You're both talking about an experience you have shared. This makes an enormous difference.

Fourth, you "Offer what is *needed* and what you can give *freely*." In the process of being loving toward people, you are *not* a hostage. You are not a doormat. You are not obligated to give people whatever they demand of you. What you give to people is still *your choice*, and in this case—where you are acting as an agent for your company—you may be limited by rules beyond your control.

What this man needs most is Real Love, and you've already given him a large measure of that as you

- made a choice not to respond to him with Getting and Protecting Behaviors. This is a very loving act.
- chose to listen to him. We offer people a real gift when we genuinely listen. Every time people speak, they are offering us a piece of who they are, and it is quite loving when we accept it completely by listening.

So you've already accomplished the greatest part of what is needed. In many cases you may be done at this point. In some cases, however, the victim may insist on more, so you may need to say more. You might say, for example, "Look, I really understand how frustrating it is to pay for something and then have it break. First, you have this thing that doesn't work. Then you have to go out of your way to get another one. It's a real drag. I get it. Understand, though, that these things really don't last forever. The item you got was warrantied for one year, and yours lasted for five. You got four bonus years out of it. If you'd like, I could recommend a replacement that has a warranty even longer than this one."

With all your listening and caring about him, this man might well be finished at this point. I've seen this approach be effective on many occasions, because his *real* issue is not the broken item; it's that he doesn't feel loved. In some cases, however, he might still have a residual need to be right about the broken object. In that case, you might say, "Four years after a warranty is over, we simply are not allowed to replace the item. The manufacturer just wouldn't go for it. If you'd like, though, I could find out if we could come up with a discount on a new one."

The Discontented Employee

We've all seen the employee who is unhappy about almost everything that happens at work. He sits silently through meetings, glaring with disapproval at those who speak. When he's asked to do something, he agrees to the assignment, but with his tone of voice and body language he virtually screams his irritation. He doesn't come right out and disagree with policies, but it's obvious he dislikes most of them. Supervisors tend to avoid these employees, because conversations with them are rarely pleasant.

Andre was one such employee, and his supervisor, John, had the wisdom to recognize that Andre wasn't intentionally trying to make problems for people; he was just feeling and acting like a victim because of his own personal emptiness. John understood that

- when victims are given a difficult assignment, they take it as a personal persecution of *them*, and then they respond with irritation and other behaviors that tend to push people away.

- when victims don't feel heard, they feel unloved, and in their pain they tend to lash out at people.
- victims need to feel seen, accepted, and loved.

John asked Andre if he had some time to talk, and as you read their conversation that follows see if you can spot the guidelines for responding to a victim that we have previously discussed.

"Andre," John said, "I've been watching you for some time, and I'm impressed with your abilities. You prepared the background information we needed for the Wilson account in a way that few people could do. You're also able to take a great deal of data and translate it into a few pithy statements that people can understand. That's a real gift and a real asset to the company."

"Well, thank you," said Andre. He was surprised. He had expected to be criticized for something.

"I do have a concern," said John.

Yeah, here it comes, thought Andre.

"I think you have another whole gear that we've never seen, and I think it's my fault that we've never seen it."

"I don't understand."

"You already do good work, and I hope you don't misunderstand me as I say this, but it seems like there's something holding you back. You just don't seem happy, and when people aren't happy there's no way they can be doing their best work. In your case I say it's my fault because I should have brought this up with you long before now. If there's something about your work environment that I can help with, something that would make your job more enjoyable, I'd like to hear about it."

"Well, I don't know," said Andre. All of Andre's life, nobody had ever really listened to him, so he'd played the role of the silent, sulking victim. Why bother to express your complaints openly when nobody really listens anyway? Of course, he still expressed his complaints behind the backs of his supervisors, thereby spreading discontent among other employees.

"I can completely understand any reluctance you might have to be completely honest about what you'd need. Many supervisors don't listen, or they get offended, and then you feel like you've wasted your time. All I can say is that I value what you do here, and I want to remove anything that's keeping you from realizing all your potential in this job."

Andre thought for a moment. This conversation really was going differently than anything he'd experienced before. John really seemed to be listening to him, so he decided to take a risk and say what was bothering him.

"I have some ideas about improving the performance of our department," said Andre, "but nobody seems to want to hear them."

"Entirely my mistake then," said John. "If you've made suggestions about improvement, I've somehow missed them, which means I wasn't listening. Would you be willing to state them again?"

"Well, to be fair, I made most of them with the supervisor who was here before you, but I did make a couple of them to you."

John listened carefully and took notes while Andre made several suggestions. John then asked questions about what resources—in materials and personnel—would be required to implement each of these changes. John suggested that they meet two days later to talk about which of them—if any—could be implemented. When they met again, John gave Andre the responsibility for implementing two of the changes he had suggested, and Andre was thrilled that John had paid such close attention to his ideas.

As a result of John's listening to Andre and genuinely caring about him—loving him—Andre's attitude at work changed considerably. No longer was he the reluctant follower or the grumbling employee. John had successfully taken Andre off the Field of Death and given him a much happier role on the Field of Life.

RESPONDING TO ALCOHOLICS AND DRUG ADDICTS

On page 163 we began an important discussion of a new understanding of addictions. For a moment let's focus only on drug addiction, which includes addiction to alcohol. One helpful definition of drug addiction is the use of drugs to the extent that individual happiness or healthy participation in family, work, or society is adversely affected. By this definition it is estimated that 10-20% of the adults in this country are addicted to alcohol or drugs. The latest estimate for the costs to society of illicit drug abuse alone is $181 billion (2002). The combined costs of drugs, alcohol, and tobacco exceed $500 billion, including healthcare, criminal justice, and lost productivity.

This widespread prevalence of drug addiction, and the enormous costs attendant to it, indicate both our society's generalized failure to understand addiction and the profound need for us to finally gain that understanding. Contrary to what is generally believed, addicts don't abuse alcohol and drugs because they're *fun*. Alcohol and drugs don't make you feel better than you do when you're healthy and whole physically and emotionally. No, addicts use these substances because they are in *pain*—because the relative lack of Real Love causes an emptiness and fear that are literally painful—and they'll do almost anything to diminish that pain.

In today's society and in today's medical community, the majority opinion at present is that drug addiction is a disease, an affliction that people just "get." The National Institute on Drug Abuse (NIDA), a member of the National Institutes of Health, states that "Drug addiction is a complex but treatable brain disease." Without any mention whatever about the cause, this definition has a sophistication reminiscent of the Middle Ages. On the NIDA home page, drug addiction is compared to diabetes, hypertension, and asthma, but the comparison is horribly flawed, because we know the causes of the latter diseases, whereas the NIDA proposes none for addiction.

Although the medical community lacks a cause for addiction, it has not hesitated—oddly—to plow ahead with treatment. The NIDA states, "Like people with diabetes or heart disease, people in treatment for drug addiction will need to change behavior to adopt a more healthful lifestyle." This treatment philosophy could easily be re-stated in the following way to any given addict: "You know, using drugs isn't good for you, so you really ought to stop." One would think that the depth of this insight would hardly require a medical degree.

Simply put, we have uncounted alcohol and drug treatment centers in the world attempting to "cure" drug addiction without understanding the basis of the disease. What the practitioners in these centers do is this:

- They tell their patients that they *should* stop using their drugs of choice.

- They crudely facilitate the process of separating the addict from his drug—one definition of "cure"—by simply removing drugs from the addict and providing a restrictive environment where no drugs physically exist.
- They often provide medical assistance to ease the process of physical withdrawal from the drug, a process called detoxification.
- They make some attempts at psychological therapy to help the patient understand other issues in his life and to construct a life without drugs.

I don't lightly offer my assessment of what treatment facilities do. I was a drug addict for many years myself. I was a patient at one of the more respected drug treatment centers in the country, and I have interviewed many hundreds of addicts who have also been to treatment centers. I have studied drug treatment for thirty years as a physician.

The success rate of alcohol and drug treatment clearly reflects our lack of understanding regarding the cause of addiction. Let me first state that gauging the success of treatment is difficult, because of a number of factors:

- How long does a patient have to be drug free before he or she is considered "cured?"
- Studies that measure success use different time periods for follow up, so they're difficult to compare with one another. Generally, however, follow up is one to two years.
- Profit-based treatment centers would have a natural tendency to inflate their statistics that indicate success.
- Addicts are well known for lying about their drug use.

Recognizing the above difficulties, Alcoholics Anonymous (AA)—easily the largest organization in the world concerned with helping drug addicts—has a success rate of about 5%. Those individuals who succeed in quitting drugs with the use of AA are quite fervent in their testimonials about the effectiveness of AA, but the actual statistics as a whole are really quite dismal. In defense of AA—having been a participant in the program myself—it is entirely voluntary, and people pass in and out of it at will, so for any given person the influence of AA is often very brief.

The success rate of formal treatment centers has to be somewhat explainable by the fact that 97% of them are based on the "twelve-step" program of AA. Drug treatment programs are successful in treating addiction in about 10-30% of cases. In some studies, both AA and treatment programs have demonstrated *no improvement whatever* over the natural course of the disease. In other words, patients treated by AA and some treatment centers were found to do no better than those left entirely alone, 5-10% of whom simply quit on their own.

So why is the success rate of traditional treatment centers so abysmal? Because they ignore the central need that we all have for Real Love. As we discussed in Chapter Six, addiction is not a disease. Addiction is a response to *pain*, primarily the pain of not feeling unconditionally loved.

The primary approach to drug addiction, therefore, *must* include attention to supplying this critical ingredient that is missing in the lives of addicts and which is the cause of their pain. In order to meaningfully approach any treatment for drug addiction, we must talk about how we will go about providing the addict with Real Love. To talk about treating drug addiction without involving Real Love would be like talking about solving a drought without talking about water.

Traditionally, when addicts leave treatment programs, they may remain sober for a brief time, but they are still so miserable in the absence of Real Love that their return to the anesthetizing effects of drugs or alcohol is highly likely. I had the same experience myself when released from a drug treatment center. When addicts feel sufficient Real Love, on the other hand, the emptiness and pain in their lives decreases markedly, and then they gradually lose their *need* to use alcohol or drugs. Without a need to use drugs, an addict finds recovery quite a different affair. In Real Love groups across the country, we have had the opportunity to supply Real Love to thousands of addicts, and so far the results have been very encouraging.

It is my hope that in the near future, we will be able to perform controlled studies that demonstrate the effect of Real Love on drug and alcohol addiction.

RESPONDING TO OTHER ADDICTIONS

Most people associate the word *addiction* with alcohol or drugs, but that association severely and inappropriately limits the extent of addiction in our society. A new definition of addiction is needed, one which will give us a better grasp of the nature of addiction and will enable us to approach its treatment in a far more productive way. I proposed the following definition in Chapter Six:

> Addiction is the compulsive use
> of any substance, person, feeling, or behavior
> with a relative disregard of the potentially negative
> social, psychological, and physical consequences.

This definition creates a much broader—and more accurate—picture of addiction, which will enable us to meaningfully and effectively address a great number of behaviors that have been neglected heretofore.

All addictions are pretty much the same. We can become addicted to any substance, person, feeling, or behavior that gives us some sense of relief from the pain of our not feeling loved. We can become addicted to

- alcohol.
- drugs.
- our careers.
- money.
- control.
- power.
- anger.
- being right.
- acceptance.
- being a victim.
- sex.
- praise.
- safety (withdrawal, running).
- gambling.
- shopping.
- entertainment.
- adrenalin.

Regardless of the specific addiction, the *cause* is the same. Addiction is a response to the pain of emptiness and fear, so the *solution* to all the individual addictions is primarily the same: Real Love. This understanding revolutionizes our approach to addiction.

RESPONDING TO VICTIMS OF FATE

I first introduced this special classification of victim on pages 64-6 and I discussed these people again on page 127-9. We need to know how to respond to victims of this kind.

I spoke one day to a couple, Harold and Charise, about the conflicts in their marriage.

"Harold gets so angry," said Charise, "just because I can't do something."

"Like what?" I asked.

"Yesterday he yelled at me because I made a mistake in balancing the checkbook."

"And we had to pay two hundred dollars in fees to the bank for bounced checks," said Harold with some animation in his voice.

"I just made a mistake," said Charise. "I told him a long time ago that I'm too stupid to balance the checkbook, but he wants me to do it anyway."

"Anytime I try to talk to her about *anything* she does wrong," Harold said, "she gives me that excuse. 'I'm just stupid,' she says, and that's supposed to be the end of it."

I excused Harold from the room, because I knew Charise wouldn't enjoy having him in the room for what I was about to say. After he'd left, I said, "Charise, did you graduate from high school?"

"Yes," she said. "Actually, I graduated from college."

"Really? So you've done basic math in the past?"

"Yes. I don't like it much, but I've done it."

"So you don't *like* doing math, but the truth is that you're not truly stupid. Isn't that right?"

"I suppose."

"But when you claim to be stupid, you're claiming to be victimized by something beyond your control, and then you don't have to be responsible for your behavior. You're off the hook, right?"

Charise smiled. "I'd never thought of it quite like that, but I see what you mean."

We talked for a few more minutes, and when Harold returned Charise said, "Harold, I don't especially like balancing the checkbook, so I don't devote my full attention to it. Then when I make mistakes, I try to get out of trouble by claiming to be stupid, instead of telling you that I was irresponsible. I didn't realize I was doing that—it was mostly unconscious—but I still was, and I'm sorry I've made things inconvenient for you."

As I simply pointed out to Charise the truth of her victimhood, while unconditionally accepting her, she was able to see her victimhood and change her behavior. We can apply this general approach to almost all Victims of Fate.

RESPONDING TO SELF-INFLICTED VICTIMS

On pages 66-67 I introduced the subject of people whose victimhood is self-inflicted, and I mentioned two categories of such people: those who beat themselves up with guilt and those who simply feel worthless. Let's look at how you might respond to people in each of these categories.

Responding to People Who Are Excessively Guilty

A woman named Cynthia had been having a terrible time with her children for years. As she studied Real Love, she began to realize how unloving she had been toward her children, and she came to my office to talk about that. My first glance at her revealed that she was in considerable pain.

"I've been a terrible mother," she said.

"Yes, you really have," I said.

Cynthia looked very surprised, and understandably so. When we say something so self-condemning like that, when we are so obviously wracked with guilt, we virtually obligate the people around us to deny our self accusation or at least comfort us. So they usually say something like, "No, no, you haven't been a terrible mother."

The problem with that denial is that it's simply not true. When we're not dealing with the truth, two things happen:

- We can't change our behavior. As long as we believe in a lie, what would ever motivate us to change our behavior to conform to the truth?
- We can't feel loved. We can't feel loved unconditionally until we feel accepted for who we really are.

I let Cynthia sit with my sentence above for only a second before I added, "But who ever taught you how to be a loving mother? Who did? Who unconditionally loved you?"

"Nobody," she said.

"So what are the odds that you would have been able to give to your children what you never received yourself?"

"Well—"

"The odds were pretty much *zero*. We can't give what we don't have."

"But I've really hurt my children," she said.

"Yes, you have, and it couldn't have been any other way."

"I don't understand."

"The only way in the world for us to learn anything is through the process of making mistakes, and as we make those mistakes, it is absolutely unavoidable that we will affect the people around us. There is *no other way* for us to learn. As I learn how to become loving, I will inconvenience and possibly even hurt you, if you are close enough to me. As you learn to become loving, you will do the same to me. And that's the only reason you hurt your children, not because you *wanted* to hurt them. Was it ever your *goal* to hurt them?"

"No."

"And at the time you didn't know any of the information you now know about Real Love, right?"

"True."

"So at the time you did the best you could with the information you had, which was simply flawed. What sense does it make for you to feel guilty for simply *not knowing then* what you know now?"

More time and discussion were required, but Cynthia eventually understood how insane it was for her to continue feeling guilty. We make our mistakes from emptiness and fear and ignorance. How delightful it is that we can cure those conditions with learning and Real Love.

Responding to People Who Feel Worthless

As we just discussed, in the process of learning, we unavoidably make mistakes, and most of us make a great many of them. Some people make so many mistakes, and are so severely criticized for them—or otherwise suffer such great consequences because of them—that they become severely discouraged, to the point that they believe they have no worth. Such feelings can become quite paralyzing.

One day I spoke to a man named Joshua, who was deeply discouraged about his life. "I've made so many mistakes," he said. "I've screwed up two marriages. I've hurt my kids. I don't think I've done any good in the world. I've wasted my life."

"That may be true," I said, "but the real question is, How do you *want* to feel?"

"I don't know what you mean."

"Do you want to stay miserable, or would you like to be happy?"

Joshua paused before saying, "Well, I guess it would be nice to be happy, but I don't see how that's possible."

"How would you? You've never *seen* real happiness in your whole life, and part of you is discouraged because you've been unhappy for *so long*. All those years of unhappiness seem to pile up like a mountain, don't they?"

"Yes."

"But you could learn to see them differently. All these years you've been looking for happiness while you've been *blind*, but the time you spend looking for something while you can't see doesn't even count. How can you say you've really looked for something when your eyes have been shut? Now that you understand what Real Love is, though, and how to find it, you're beginning for the *first time* to look for happiness with your eyes open. So it's really like you're starting your life all over. It's harder to be discouraged when you're just beginning, you know?"

Joshua began to understand, and as he experienced his first moments of Real Love, his discouragement also began to melt away. People feel worthless only because they don't feel loved and because they feel no hope of ever feeling loved.

If someone continues to feel worthless even after steady exposure to Real Love, a diagnosis of depression—or some other mental illness—must be considered, and I recommend an evaluation by a health care professional.

RESPONDING TO WHAT VICTIMS SAY

Victims are so demanding and persuasive that we often don't know how to respond to them. They also have quite a repertoire of victim statements, and it can be helpful for us to look at a few of them, so we're better prepared to respond. Following are some of the statements victims commonly make, followed by possible responses, which are indented.

"I couldn't help it." Victims always have an excuse. To be sure, circumstances often do arise that are beyond our control, but only victims emphasize those when they make mistakes, while non-victims freely admit the factors they *did* have control over when they make mistakes.

> "I'm sure," you might say, "that there *were* factors beyond your control. There always are. What *could* you have done, however, to be better prepared for this job or event, so it could have gone better than it did?" An example of a discussion like this is found on pages 269-70, between Lewis and his father.

"Why do *I* have to do that?" When a task has to be done, it can't be given to *everyone*. *Somebody* has to do the job, which means that in that moment everyone else "gets out" of doing the job. Victims don't mind when *other people* get an assignment, but they have a fit in the moments when the "wheel of fortune" falls on their number.

> "Who would you suggest I give the job *to?* You're quite right that in the single *moment* you do this job, you might be doing more work than someone else, but the same would be true of anybody else I gave it to. So until you give me a better solution, this job will be yours."

"You did *what?*" Victims say this when something is particularly distressing to them, and their real meaning is, "You did *what* to *me?*"

> Victims say the above in the hope of getting either an argument or an apology. You simply respond with neither. Restate what you have done, with an explanation where warranted, with none where it's not. Then you're done. Imagine, for example, that you invited your mother over for Sunday dinner. Unknown to you, this was *not* what your wife wanted, so she says, "You did *what?*" Do not step on to the Field of Death and offer an answer for all

her objections. You will not win. Simply re-state that you issued the invitation, and then you might say, "Next time, I'll talk to you before I invite her."

"But you *said* _____" Victims say this when they perceive that other people aren't giving them exactly what they believe was promised. Victims can't imagine how anyone could dare not keep his or her promise to *them*.

"I probably did say that, but since then circumstances have changed. Simple as that. So in the face of changing circumstances, my position has also changed. That's the whole idea of gathering up-to-date information, so we can change our minds to fit the information we have. If that has inconvenienced you, I regret that."

"There wasn't time." Oh, the excuses we think up. We choose to put off doing a job day after day, and then at the last minute—surprise!—there isn't enough time to complete it, and we blame it on the *clock* rather than taking responsibility for our own choices to procrastinate.

You might try some variation on the approach taken by Joyce with her daughter Kate on pages 271-5.

(Sigh) How many times have we done this? Something happens that inconveniences us, or someone gives us an assignment we don't like, and we react by rolling our eyes and letting out a long, exasperated sigh.

A sigh can be like an infection, spreading skepticism and victimhood. We must respond to it. You might say, "You're clearly unhappy about something. Can you put it into words so I can better understand what's bothering you?" Victims like to hide their dissatisfaction behind grumblings, and it's often uncomfortable for them to express their grievances clearly.

"How could you do this?" The implication, of course, is "How could you do this *to me?*"

Simply explain your reasons, which is quite different from justifying yourself. Explanations are calmly made *once*, whereas justifications are repeated again and again in an atmosphere of fear and contention.

"How could you say that?" How dare you have said something accusing or inconsiderate to *me?*

Victims love to make you take the defensive position. Don't do that. Simply say something like, "Tell me what part of what I said was either unclear or troublesome, and then I can respond to the specifics of what was confusing or a problem for you."

"Did you see what he gave me for Christmas?" Most of us don't give genuine Christmas—or birthday or anniversary—*gifts*, which are given unconditionally. Instead we make Christmas *investments*, giving to people with an expectation that we'll get something in return: gratitude, appreciation, loyalty, or a gift. We prove that we have these expectations on the occasions when we *don't* get what we expect and then we become disappointed or irritated, as in the victim's complaint quoted above.

"So when you gave him his Christmas gift, did you make it clear that his gift to you had to come up to a certain standard or you'd be irritated? I just wondered if you'd given him a note or anything about your expectations." You have to do this without the slightest hint of criticism, or the listener will almost certainly be offended.

"*But* _____ " How quickly we protest what we don't like, certain that our rights have been violated, that eternal justice has been offended in some way. When we're given a task to do, the first word out of our mouths is often *but*. We say that word when we feel *we* have been victimized, but how often do we employ it in the defense of others?

"Hey, I'm sure there are lots of other ways to do this than the way I've proposed, so it only makes sense that you'd have some objection. If you have a way that is clearly, undeniably better than what I've proposed, I really want to hear it. Really. But if you don't—if you just don't like what I've proposed—somebody had to make this decision, and that would be me, so in the absence of a better way I just need you to do it this way."

"Why does *he* get to have that?" Heaven forbid that someone else would ever get to have more of something than we do. That would be unfair. Only a victim sees the world in this way.

Similar answer here to "Why do *I* have to do that?" above.

"Look at this mess!" How could you make a mess that inconveniences *me!*

Victims want you to pay in blood for mistakes you make. No need. Just go straight for a solution. "That's a mess, all right. What can I do to help clean it up?"

"There's so much to do." The meaning here is "I carry such a burden. Woe is me. Does anyone do as much work as I do?"

"You're right. There *is* a lot to do. You might not even get it all done. But who knows? What matters is what you choose to do right now. Do you want me to stay out of it? Or is there some kind of help or advice you'd like?"

"I never get any help around here." This has the additional meaning of "No one appreciates me. I do so much for everyone else, but I never get any help in return. It's so unfair."

Stay away from the complaints. Do not respond with sympathy, and don't try to persuade the victim that he or she has indeed been getting help. That won't work. Simply respond to the core meaning of the complaint. You might say, "Is there some specific thing anyone could do to make your job easier?" By asking this question, you are *not* obligated to give the assistance requested, but you have required the victim to clearly state a solution, rather than just complaining.

"She didn't even remember my birthday." The implication in this statement is clear: "I am so giving and thoughtful toward *her*—and everyone else, for that matter—but does anyone ever return *my* graciousness? Oh no."

Before you respond to this, you would *have* to be feeling loving and be filled with a sense of humor, or it would be perceived as an attack and backfire on you. You might say, "So let me get this straight. You don't really do things for people because you genuinely care about them. You don't give people gifts unconditionally. You do things for people so they will pay you back, and heaven help them if they don't. In fact, they'd better pay you back at least as much as you gave them in the first place, or more. That has to be a drag for you, keeping score like that all the time, eh?"

"My son never calls." After all I've done for him—brought him into the world, nursed him, changed his diapers, took him to school, tucked him in at night, and so on—he is completely ungrateful. How could he do this to me?

> I wouldn't recommend the following unless you feel loving and perhaps know the speaker well: "So, all during his childhood did you give him an invoice every time you did something for him? Each time you changed his diapers or tucked him in at night, did you give him a bill telling him how exactly he'd have to pay you back when he got older? If you didn't, it seems a little unfair to give him a bill for all that now, doesn't it? In business, you have to bill the customer at the time. You have to tell him what it costs at the time you provide the service. But the important thing is that from what you're saying, you never loved your son. You were just *investing* in him. You were doing things for him so he'd pay you back in the future—with interest. I'm not telling you what to do—not at all—but I'm guessing that this would make your son feel very unloved and probably more than a little resentful."

"How many times have I had to tell you_____?" The arrogance of this question is clear. The further meaning is, "Do you not understand who I am? If you did, you would never require that I ask for anything more than once. In fact, I shouldn't have to ask at all. You'd just *know* what I want."

> 1. If a child had the insight and the courage to answer this question—which he or she never would—he or she might say this to a parent: "I'm sure you've had to tell me this many times. The problem is, every time you tell me, you're angry, and each time you're angry I hear only four words: *I don't love you.* When I hear those four deadly words, I become completely devastated. I become paralyzed and deaf, so then I don't hear the content of what you're saying. In short, you have to keep telling me the same thing because you're incapable of speaking to me in a loving, productive way, a way I can hear."
>
> 2. As an adult, I *have* heard these words and actually responded with, "Oh, I'm just stupid. So, recognizing that I'm retarded, would you be willing to say it again for me, very slowly?" This response removes all the victimhood from the attacker. How can

a victim feel victimized by someone who acknowledges that he is stupid?

"She always has a headache." Further meaning: "Why did we even get married? She promised to love me, but all she does is ignore me all the time."

"I can't tell you *all* the reasons she avoids sex with you, but I do notice that you're angry as you talk about her. I can only imagine that when you're with her you're even more angry, and when you're angry all she hears is *I don't love you*. Why would she want to have sex with somebody who didn't love her? Really, think about that."

"All he ever wants is sex." The implication is, "All he ever does is *use* me."

"Has it occurred to you that he really does want to be close to you, and that sex is the only way he knows to be intimate with you? Most men are raised without intimacy of any kind. They don't talk with each other about anything sensitive. They don't phone each other and ask how their day is going, as women often do. They don't go shopping together. For many men, sex is the only time they ever feel really close to *anyone*. It's not just about physical gratification. Consider the possibility that he's trying to feel closer to you, rather than just using you."

"We never do anything together anymore." Translation: "You never pay attention to *me*. You promised to love *me*, but you don't. You never keep your promises to *me*."

"You're right, I don't spend nearly the time with you that I used to, and because of that you must feel pretty alone sometimes. Let's talk about what we can do on a regular basis so we spend time together. Would that be acceptable to you?"

"That's not fair." Victims are not talking here about true justice at all, only about their not getting what *they* wanted.

"You might be right. In the short term, you might be asked to do more than others, and if *fairness* were the goal in life, I'd be concerned. But it's not. Fortunately, we're here for much higher reasons: to learn to be responsible, to grow, to learn to be loving in spite of injustice and injury, and so on. So this might *not* be fair, but if you'll do it anyway, the potential rewards are great. Whether this is rewarding or irritating, however, is entirely up to you and how you see this."

"You have to go out of town again?" As a victim you wouldn't consider the behavior of other people in terms of what *they* needed. You would see their behavior only in terms of how it affected *you*. Victims see everything that way.

It's very tempting to defend yourself here. You'll want to say, "It's my *job*. You want me to lose my job?" But instead, you tell the truth, listen to your partner, and offer a loving act: "You know, I really have been gone a lot lately. What would you like to do together when I get back?"

"If it weren't for you . . ." The implication is that a project or event would have gone well if it were not for your mistakes.

"Oh my, if it weren't for me the world would turn more smoothly on its axis in many ways. My flaws are without number." Victims want to be right, to rub it in, to get a sense of power. Simply tell the truth about yourself, and all that is over.

"People *should* _____ " Victims always seem to know how everyone should behave. They enjoy the position of being right.

"There are *so many* things people *should* do. Now, the question is, how do we either change human nature or educate everyone as to what they should do? I've been working at that all my life. Let me know if you come up with a way." Victims enjoy complaining, and by saying this, you're stating in a subtle way that complaining is worthless. A much better goal is to find a way to actually accomplish change. Victims aren't interested in real work, just complaining.

"So you're on *his* side?" Victims see everything in terms of *us* and *them*. They gather allies like votes—the more votes they get, the more right they are—and they are offended when you don't cast your vote with them.

You don't have to play the voting game. Stay off the Field of Death. "Oh, I'm not smart enough to take sides. That's too complicated. I try to stick with understanding and following *principles*, which is much more reliable."

"You're saying this is *my* fault?" Victims simply cannot tolerate being blamed for anything, because if they are at fault, they can no longer be victims. If they are at fault, there is a possibility they could be identified as perpetrators.

"I wasn't really talking about fault. I was identifying who was responsible for specific behaviors. Can you identify what part of this event or task was your responsibility?" Instead of defending yourself—exactly the position victims are trying to put you in—you are requiring the victim to identify *his* responsibility for an event or task. You're not playing on the Field of Death.

Anger. Victims really enjoy getting angry. They enjoy the rush of it, the self-righteousness of it.

Do not respond to anger. Don't feel responsible for the anger of the victim. Instead look for meaning. "You appear to be angry. If you're willing to talk about it, I'd like to hear what's bothering you." The victim will respond with one of the many other victim statements in this section, and then you can respond sensibly to those.

"I'm so disappointed in you." When a victim says this, you're supposed to feel guilty and worthless.

Don't play this game. Just tell the truth and listen. "Oh my, I've lived with disappointment in my performance for a lifetime. Would you be willing to tell me exactly what is disappointing you, so we can figure out what can be done about it?"

"I can't forgive him for that." Victims love to be wounded, and, where possible, they love to hang on to their wounds for as long as possible.

"What he did was certainly inconvenient, maybe even inconsiderate and thoughtless. But be realistic, people make mistakes like that every day. They always will. If you choose not to forgive him, you're choosing to hang that piece of rotting emotional garbage around *your* neck forever. It will make very little difference to him, but it will make you miserable for a very long time. Do you really want to do that?"

Being demanding. Victims are fond of saying, "Bring me that," or "Give me that," or "Do that for me," or "Come over here." They are, after all, the center of the universe.

The victim's belief that he is the center of the world obligates you in no way. Remember that. You have the right to choose what you *wish* to do in each case, and if you choose not to do what is demanded, simply say so. You might say, "I'm busy right now, so you may have to get that for yourself or get someone else to do it." At that point, victims will almost always ask you *why*. They'll ask, "Well, what are you doing?" You are *not* obligated to answer. The more you answer, the more questions you'll get. You'll never win an argument with a victim. Just answer, "I'm busy doing something else."

Examples of children acting like victims:

When we tell them they can't buy something, they say, "But all my friends have one; it's not fair." They're claiming to be victimized by us in the hope that we'll feel obligated to eliminate this grave injustice by giving them what they want.

"I believe you, that your friends all have one, and if my goal were to make you like all your friends, I'd get you one too. But that's not my goal. My goal is to help you become as responsible and loving as possible, and I don't see how buying this item fits into that goal. If you can see how it does, let me know."

When we tell them they can't go somewhere, they counter with, "But everybody else is going."

Same answer as above.

When we tell them they can't do something, they get that pathetic look on their faces as they say, "Pleeease." They imply that if we continue to ignore their pleas, we are unbelievably selfish and cruel.

"If you can give me a genuine reason how this is important to your genuine happiness—not just something you want—let me know, but begging would be pretty irrelevant."

When we ask why an assigned task isn't done, they say, "I didn't have time."

We talked about this on page 298.

When children act hurt, and when they sulk, they're acting like victims. They've learned that the more wounded they appear, the less likely we are to punish them, and the more likely they are to get what they want and get away with unacceptable behavior.

> "I can see you feel wounded in some way. Explain to me how you've been cheated (or hurt). Don't tell me how you just didn't get what you wanted, but how you really didn't get what is truly fair (or right)."

Children often choose to wait till the last minute to study for a test in school. Then when they're poorly prepared and get a bad grade, they blame the teacher for giving a "hard" or "unfair" test. They falsely portray themselves as victims.

> You might respond in a way similar to that used by Lewis's father above on pages 269-70.

The whining child. Children are born into this world with a right to expect one thing above all else. They have a right to be loved, and when they don't get that—when they are not loved unconditionally—they are truly victimized, and they *feel* like victims. In that condition, they respond with whining, complaining, resisting, and so many of the activities we abhor in children.

> Children need to be loved and taught, a subject treated extensively in the book *Real Love in Parenting*.

TEACHING CHILDREN HOW TO RESPOND TO OTHER PEOPLE WHO ACT LIKE VICTIMS

All their lives, our children will interact with people who act like victims. We need to teach them enough about this behavior that when they encounter it, they will recognize it, understand it, and react to it in healthy ways. In the scenario that follows, Jason learned about victimhood from his father, Bruce.

> Jason came into the room with an obvious scowl on his face.
> "What's bothering you?" asked Bruce.

"Vanessa (his sister) is mad at me."

"About what?"

"She's going out with her friends, and she wants to take my Xbox (a video game machine) with her."

"So what did you say?"

"The last time she used it, she left a couple of the games at her friend's house, and she didn't put the machine back where she got it. So I told her she couldn't take it, and she had a fit. She said I was being stingy and selfish, and I didn't care about her, and I never let her use anything of mine."

"So she was really acting like a victim."

"Yes."

"Made you feel kind of guilty, didn't it?"

"Yeah, kind of."

"That's the whole reason people act like victims. She hoped that if she made you feel bad enough for how terribly you were treating her, you'd give in and let her have what she wanted."

"So do I have to let her use the Xbox?"

"Whose Xbox is it?"

"Mine."

"Then it's entirely up to you what you do with it."

"But would it be *nicer* of me to let her use it?"

"Frankly," said Bruce, "it's pretty nice of you to even ask. You obviously want to do the right thing. It *might* be the most loving thing to let her use the Xbox, even though she's been irresponsible with it in the past. After all, your relationship with her is more important than any video machine. On the other hand, how will she ever learn to be responsible if people keep letting her be irresponsible with their things? *And* you're not obligated to be as loving toward her as she *wants*. You're only obligated to keep trying to be as loving toward her as you *can*, as loving as you choose to be each day. It's a tough call, and only you can make it. But her acting like a victim should have nothing to do with your decision. She's acting like you hurt her feelings, isn't she?"

"Yes."

"We've talked about this in family meetings. Does anybody ever *make* us angry?"

"No."

"Exactly," said Bruce. "Vanessa is mad because she's not feeling enough Real Love in her life—mostly because of *my* failures as a father—and this Xbox thing is just another irritation to her. So she's blaming her unhappiness on you. If she doesn't have the Xbox, do you think she could think of other things she might do with her friends to have fun?"

"Probably."

"So if you don't let her have it, you're not *making* her unhappy. And if she felt completely loved, would she be angry about this?"

"Probably not."

"So is it your fault that she's mad at you?"

"I guess not."

"No, it's not. So, are you done feeling guilty about it?"

Jason was smiling. "Yeah, I guess so."

"All your life," said Bruce, "people will try to tell you that you're responsible for making them unhappy, but that doesn't make it true. Remember that. On the other hand, that doesn't mean you shouldn't care about their happiness. We should always *care* about the happiness of other people and do all that we can to *help* them be happy. But that doesn't mean we're responsible for *making* them happy—or for giving them what they want or doing what they want.."

"Just keep doing your best to be nice to Vanessa," continued Bruce. "She's acting like this only because she doesn't feel loved. If she wants to stay angry, she will, but, hopefully, in time, she'll get over this."

When we love and teach our children, we can help them see why people act like victims. We can help free our children from the chains of guilt, obligation, and manipulation that characterize so many unhappy relationships.

WE ARE NEVER RESPONSIBLE FOR THE CHOICES MADE BY OTHERS

We have established that we are always responsible for the choices we make, but in our society it is commonly taught that we are also responsible for the choices made by other people. If you say something unkind, for example, and someone's feelings are hurt, it is almost uniformly accepted that you are responsible for hurting that person's feelings. You are responsible for how he or she feels, as demonstrated by the well-accepted phrases "He makes me so mad" or "You make me angry."

On pages 26-7 I demonstrated that other people never make *us* angry. I address that subject at much greater length in other Real Love literature. It is equally important to understand that *we* don't make *other people* angry either—nor do we *make* them feel or act in *any* particular way. People always have a choice about how they feel or behave. To illustrate this, let me share a metaphor.

Let's suppose that I take a walk on a path in the woods, and I'm so preoccupied with my enjoyment of the beauty around me that I'm not watching very carefully where I'm walking. As I walk, I accidentally bump into four men—one after the other, several minutes apart—who are also walking on the path. I don't bump them hard, just enough to jostle them a bit and alter their course a little. Although I bump into each of them exactly the same way, their reactions are quite different:

- The first man is deep in thought—much like me—enjoying the beauty and peace of the outdoors. When I bump him, his thoughts are briefly interrupted, but he's delighted to meet someone who is also enjoying the beautiful surroundings. We talk for a few minutes, and he expresses his gratitude for our conversation.
- The second man is talking to a friend and is so thoroughly enjoying his conversation that he doesn't even notice that I've bumped into him.
- The third man came to the park angry at the world. He feels like he's been unfairly treated at work, at home, and everywhere else. When I bump him, he falls back in an exaggerated, almost theatrical way. He jumps up and down and screams at me, and in the process he turns his ankle and breaks it. Cursing me the whole while, he's carried out of the woods on a stretcher.
- The fourth man is deeply discouraged and boiling over with anger. When I bump him, he pulls a gun from his pocket, screams at me, "Why don't you watch where you're going?" and shoots me in the leg. As the recoil of the gun knocks him backward, he loses his footing, stumbles off the path, and falls over the edge of a cliff to his death.

The third man blamed me for breaking his ankle—as most people would—and the fourth man—had he lived—would have blamed me for his tantrum and for his falling off the cliff. Are they right? Did I cause their anger and violent behavior? If my bumping people *makes* them angry, then it would have to make *everyone* angry. But did it? No. My bumping the second man, for example, produced no reaction at all, and when I bumped the first man, he responded with delight.

In each of the four interactions, I did exactly the same thing, and each man made a *choice* (though mostly unconsciously) about how he would behave. I didn't *make* the first man happy, nor did I make the fourth man lose his life. In each of the four interactions, I was responsible only for *my* behavior, which was the same each time: I carelessly bumped a man on the path. *That's all* I was responsible for. I was guilty of carelessness, but no more. I was *not* responsible for any of the *reactions* that followed.

We are not responsible for the reactions of anyone. We're responsible only for what *we* do—even when other people blame us for their reactions, which they often do.

When I say that we are not responsible for the choices made by others—including their feelings—I do not intend that we use this as an excuse to be inconsiderate of others' feelings, nor to be intentionally unkind or thoughtless. My desire is only to allow us the freedom that comes from not being burdened with guilt for consequences that are not our responsibility. If we don't understand this principle, we will become captive to the false claims of victims all our lives, a burden we do not need to carry.

OUR RESPONSIBILITY TO HELP VICTIMS

People act like victims as a response to fear, and fear is destroyed by Real Love. The solution for victims is the same as for people who use any of the Getting and Protecting Behaviors. Victims need to hear the truth, tell the truth, and be seen by those capable of accepting and loving them. They need to realize that they always have a choice and then take responsibility for the choices they make. Until they do that, they can never see themselves and others clearly. They can never feel accepted and loved.

Even though acting like victims can only lead to unhappiness, the people who use this Getting and Protecting Behavior get a lot of Imitation Love from it—that's why they've been using it for a lifetime—and therefore will understandably resist you if you make attempts to point out the truth about it in their lives. Don't be surprised by their defensiveness and righteous indignation. Just love them and tell them as much truth as they can hear. Also remember that you're not responsible for changing anyone's life, as illustrated in my following interaction with Anne. For some time Anne had been feeling loved and had been practicing loving other people.

"I have a friend whose life is a wreck," Anne said. "She hates her husband. She's a huge victim about everything. She's depressed and drinking more than she should. I've talked to her a little about Real Love, and she seems to understand that she needs it, but then she withdraws and never calls. What can I do?"

"How long do you think she's felt unloved?" I asked.

"Probably all her life."

"You're not going to change that in a big hurry, and if *she* doesn't have a sufficient desire to change, you probably won't be able to help her at all. Remember that having a desire to change is the first step to finding love and happiness (Chapter Four of *Real Love*)."

"But she *needs* this. She's miserable. Her whole family's falling apart."

"It's not your responsibility to make her happy, and if you push her to accept something she doesn't want, it's actually intrusive—even though you mean well."

"So what can I do?"

"Keep being her friend. Keep accepting her. Be available to her. When she acts like a victim, you can remind her that *she* can make different choices, and that she's not helpless. But don't feel responsible for the choices she makes."

As wise men, we have a powerful *opportunity* to contribute to the happiness of other people, but we are not *responsible* for their happiness. When we understand that, we won't stumble as often on either of two stones which can be quite a distraction for any wise man: pride and discouragement.

౨ Chapter Ten ᭣

Infamous Characters Created by Victimhood

For generations we have debated how men and women could be capable of some of the heinous deeds recorded in history, and as I suggested in Chapter Six, it should be no great surprise that victimhood would be involved. In Chapter Three I quoted the old saying, "Hell hath no fury like a woman scorned" and said that this is really a statement about victimhood, *not* women. In Chapter Two I quoted W. H. Auden, who said, "Those to whom evil is done, Do evil in return." Once someone feels sufficiently wounded—especially if intentionally or unfairly—he or she will often feel justified in doing almost anything to protect himself or herself, or to get revenge on those who hurt him or her.

In this chapter we'll look at a couple of prominent historical examples of men we have come to regard as extraordinary villains, whose behavior may be explained on the basis of their feeling victimized.

INFAMOUS HISTORICAL CHARACTERS AS VICTIMS: ADOLF HITLER

In all the history of mankind there have been few names, if any, that have been more widely known—or provoked more emotional response—than that of Adolf Hitler. He dramatically affected the lives of tens of millions of human beings and has been characterized, among other things, as a

- murderer.
- tyrant.
- despot.
- psychopath.
- genocidal maniac.
- madman.
- monster.

Although we have ample justification for applying these labels, each of them can also become a self-deceptive and harmful dead end in our search for a genuine understanding of Hitler, of ourselves, and of human behavior as a whole. Allow me to illustrate what I mean with a discussion of just one of these terms: *monster*.

Imagine that you and I have a conversation where your behavior toward me is undeniably critical and angry. Hours later, when I'm reviewing in my mind what happened between us, I decide that you were unkind, mean-spirited, and singularly abominable. I conclude, in fact, that you were a *jerk*, even a *monster*.

Is my characterization of you justifiable? In some ways, perhaps. My reasoning—almost always carried out unconsciously—might go as follows:

- In order to be happy what we all need most is Real Love, as we discussed in Chapter One. Specifically, what I needed from you in our conversation was Real Love.
- When we're angry at other people, we're loudly communicating that *our* needs aren't being met. Anger is an obvious indication that we're focusing on *ourselves*, and in that moment we couldn't possibly have a primary interest in the happiness of others. In short, as we've discussed elsewhere, the message we convey with anger is *I don't love you*. Specifically, when you

were angry at me in our conversation, you were not loving me unconditionally, and I felt that.
- Because our need for Real Love is so great, telling people we don't love them is the most hurtful thing we could do. It's wounding. Specifically, you wounded me with your anger.
- The essential characteristic of monsters is that they hurt other people.
- Because you injured me—because you chose to hurt me instead of loving me—you qualify as a monster.

Labeling you a monster has some significant advantages:

- Clarity. When we don't understand what's really happening in a relationship, we feel lost and confused. We hate those feelings. And if we're also in pain, confusion keeps us from seeing a way out of our pain, and that's a terrible, hopeless sensation. If we can label another person the monster in a relationship, however, much of the confusion is then gone. Now at least we know *why* we're in pain—or we think we do. Specifically, when I label you a monster, I don't wonder anymore why our conversation was painful. Now I know that it's *your fault*, and from that certainty I can derive a perverse sense of comfort.
- Morality. Once I've labeled you a monster, I can feel morally superior to you. We discussed this somewhat on page 176-7.
- Power. After I label you the monster, I can often enlist the aid of others who will then help me in my defense against you. People tend to rally around the banner of those who are unjustly persecuted. We love to rally together against monsters.

Although there are many advantages to labeling people monsters, the disadvantages are enormous. If I condemn you as a monster in the above conversation, for example, I

- miss out on a valuable opportunity to *learn* anything at all from the experience. Once I label *you* as the problem, I remove all motivation to examine my own behavior, and now I'm really stuck. If my own behavior doesn't change, I will keep having the same miserable interactions with anyone who behaves like you did. Sure, I can keep blaming you and everyone else for

my unhappiness, but I'll still be unhappy, and that is a terrible price to pay.
- miss out on the opportunity to learn how to love you and thereby change both our lives.
- miss out on a golden opportunities to feel loved unconditionally that can be created only as I tell the truth about *myself*, not as I tell the truth about you or anyone else.

In this section we'll be attempting to genuinely *understand* Hitler, rather than simply labeling and condemning him. Specifically, we'll be examining how profoundly his life—and the lives of millions of others—was affected by his belief that he was a victim. Most important, by far, although this section on Hitler is fascinating both from a historical and psychological perspective, the true benefit to us—and a potentially enormous one at that—is the opportunity to understand *ourselves*.

As we study the lives of men who achieved singular notoriety—such as Hitler, Stalin, Saloth Sar (better known as Pol Pot, leader of the Khmer Rouge), Hussein—there is a natural tendency on our part to react by pursing our lips, sighing, shaking our heads, and responding with a self-righteous "Tsk, tsk." While this reaction is understandable, if we give in to it we rob ourselves of an invaluable, indispensable opportunity to learn about ourselves, since we are all united by the same humanity, the same need for Real Love, the same emptiness and fear, the same addictions to Imitation Love, and the same use of Getting and Protecting Behaviors. Certainly these men used Imitation Love and Getting and Protecting Behaviors in more dramatic and more visible ways than most of us do, and their addictions affected the lives of more people than most of us ever will, but we are not so terribly different from them as we would like to suppose. They still have much to teach us about ourselves.

These men all began as we did, as small children who were wounded by the absence of that which they needed most. Unlike you and me, they rose to positions where their behaviors affected millions rather than a few. When I as a parent speak unkindly to a child, in that moment I inflict the same kind of wound that Hitler did upon millions. In a moment of anger I am telling that child that I don't love him, and the damage done by that unkindness is not to be dismissed just because it pales in *quantity* with the actions of a man who was simply capable—by virtue of position and abilities and historical fate—of affecting a greater number of people.

As we read about Adolf Hitler in the light of our understanding of Real Love and victimhood, we create an opportunity to learn about our own victimhood:

- We can more easily see how we too act like victims and in our own ways cause our own kinds of destruction to spouses, lovers, children, friends, co-workers, and so on.
- We can better understand the vast numbers of other people around us who feel and act like victims.
- We can take giant strides toward replacing the fear and anger and pain in our lives with peace, love, and happiness. This reward alone should be enough to entice us to take steps in this new direction of understanding.

In this and in the following section I will discuss the effects that victimhood has had on the lives of two well known individuals: Adolf Hitler and Saddam Hussein. As I do that, keep in mind that

- I am *not* attempting to *excuse* anyone's behavior. At no point—and in no way—am I saying, for example, "Poor Adolf, he was a victim, so he just couldn't help himself. It wasn't really his fault that he killed millions of people."
- I am not proposing that there were no other factors that contributed to the behaviors of these people. In addition to acting like a victim, for example, Hitler and other infamous characters may also have been influenced by a psycho-affective disorder or paranoid personality. I am talking about the role of victimhood because historical records provide more certainty about this factor and because there is more we can do about this problem in our own lives. Let's say, for example, that I could state with authority—which I cannot—that 37% of Hitler's behavior was dictated by a well-defined psychiatric disorder, one which today could be marginally controlled with medication. And suppose we could say that 50% of his behavior originated from his belief that he was a victim. There is little reason to talk about the disorder for which there is only some hope of treatment at best, when we can talk about victimhood

instead, which can be profoundly affected with understanding and with Real Love.

I've been a student of history for many years, so I've drawn on a variety of sources read over a lifetime for information about Adolf Hitler. For this section, however, my primary reference has been a thorough study of *Adolf Hitler: The Definitive Biography* by John Toland, 1976, Anchor books, 1035 pages. The quotes in this section are all from that book.

Childhood and Adolescence

Hitler's father was a dictatorial man who had no patience with his children and harshly insisted that Adolph become a civil servant like himself. According to an old friend, his father gave Hitler a "sound thrashing" every day—sobering words in light of the fact that Austrians were already well known for their corporal punishment of children—and the boy became very resentful of his father and anyone else in a position of authority. Hitler's mother, on the other hand, babied and spoiled him, allowing him to do whatever he wished.

As a high school student he was described as lacking in self-discipline and as willful, arrogant, irascible, sulky, and surly, all traits that are prominent in victims. One teacher remarked, "He reacted with ill-concealed hostility to advice or reproof; at the same time, he demanded of his fellow-pupils their unqualified subservience."

A close adolescent friend once asked Hitler if he planned to work, but Hitler said, "Of course not," explaining that an ordinary job was not for him. That's a typical response for a victim, who feels entitled to get a greater reward for less work. The same friend observed that Hitler could tolerate only approval, never criticism of any kind.

Adolf dealt poorly with anything that remotely resembled rejection. At age seventeen he fell in love with a girl who was unaware of his existence. He imagined that her failure to return his affection was an intentional rejection, so he orchestrated a dramatic suicide scene, in which he and his lover would jump from a bridge, after exchanging some sentimental dialogue he had written. A friend talked him out of presenting this proposal to the young lady.

Opera

Hitler was obsessed with the music and operas of Wagner, and he had a particular fascination with the opera Rienzi. A young friend who attended the opera with Hitler said that Adolf was transformed by the experience, that he literally *became* Rienzi, the lead character of the play. As we briefly examine an outline of this play, therefore, we can learn much about the man who admired it.

Rienzi's goal is to unify Rome and lead it to greater glory, just as Hitler's goal was to unify Germany and lead her to world domination. As Rienzi works to accomplish his mission, many people rally to his cause, but many others are equally dedicated to betraying and defeating him. His rise to success is all the more remarkable because he is not a nobleman but a commoner who rises to leadership from nothing. It became something of a theme song during Hitler's life that he rose to a position of virtual godhood despite very humble beginnings and despite innumerable betrayals from within and without his organization.

Rienzi survives multiple betrayals—even an assassination attempt—and lives to save all of Rome from invaders, just as Hitler survived numerous attempts on his life. Rienzi finally succumbs to the attack of a mob, but he dies in grand style—like a grand victim—telling his murderers that they are unworthy of their glorious heritage. Although Hitler didn't realize it at the time he first saw the opera, his own life would become almost a replication of the story created by Wagner.

The Artist in Vienna

Hitler spent several years in Vienna, trying to establish himself as an artist but failing miserably. He couldn't sell his work. He couldn't even get accepted as a student at the art academy. For two years he lived in a bug-infested room, but eventually he couldn't afford that, and then he was homeless for several months, sleeping in parks and doorways. He was even a failure at begging. In the winter, he found refuge in a homeless shelter that had been established, ironically, by a Jewish philanthropist.

During most of his time in Vienna Hitler was friendless, penniless, and unwilling to work. As any good victim would, he blamed his condition on others. He spoke bitterly about the "splendid mansions of the nobility" in Vienna "with garishly attired servants in front and the sumptuous hotels." He railed frequently at the social injustice of all that unearned wealth, especially on the part of the Jews.

On one occasion he befriended a man from Germany and enjoyed hearing stories about that great country. His friend later spoke about how Hitler became animated when they sang patriotic German anthems with words like "We Germans fear God but nothing else on this earth." These two themes learned in Vienna—German nationalism and hatred of the Jews—would determine most of Hitler's thoughts, words, and actions for the rest of his life.

World War I

When the first world war broke out, and Germany declared war on Russia, Hitler was delighted. Years later he wrote about this day, saying, "Even today I am not ashamed to say that, overcome with rapturous enthusiasm, I fell to my knees and thanked Heaven from an overflowing heart for granting me the good fortune of being allowed to live at this time." Why would he be so thrilled at the outbreak of war, of all things? Because it was a means of his acting out on a pattern of victimhood that was already firmly established in his life:

- His father consistently mistreated him from birth until he left the house. I cannot overstate the effect on a child of hearing from his parent *I don't love* you over and over during the years when Real Love is the absolutely essential ingredient to happiness and the ability to form healthy relationships for the rest of his life.
- His mother spoiled him, which, ironically, is another way to be unloving to a child. Parents spoil children for one reason: to win the approval of the child. That places on the child the burden to make the parent happy, and that burden is crushing.
- In many respects, he was a different sort of child, an "odd kid" with interests different from those of most other children—he enjoyed art and philosophical discussions while his classmates enjoyed sports—so he experienced the ridicule and exclusion of his peers, which can be devastating to a child.

- Against the wishes of his parents, and against the trend of social expectations for an Austrian young man, he decided on art as a career. He experienced considerable ridicule for that choice. Then he was told repeatedly by the Art Academy and by art buyers in Vienna that he lacked the requisite talent to succeed.
- For his lack of success and lack of money, he was snubbed by all of "good society" wherever he went.

So what does all this have to do with war? War gave him a chance to *act out* on his feelings of being victimized in ways that had never been available to him previously:

- War is a violent affair. As a solder he could lash out in untempered and unrestrained ways that would simply not have been possible otherwise. He had his own gun and grenades and an enemy that had been delivered to him as a target. To a victim, lashing out at anyone can be quite fulfilling. When you feel helpless and downtrodden, any feeling of power and revenge will do. For a victim, war is a opportunity-rich environment.
- For several years Hitler had fallen in love with the idea of a "Greater Germany," a more powerful country that could right all the social and political wrongs of the past. This war would be an opportunity to create that Greater Germany, and he could then become a part of it. Victims love the idea of greater power.
- He had been a loner most of his life, and now—as a member of the army—he would finally *belong* to something. Moreover, that organization to which he would belong would have the official sanction—the adulation, really—of the entire country. Sweet.
- He had a genuine moral cause. Being a victim on one's own can be lonely. People can accuse you of being selfish, or of whining. But if you join with hundreds of thousands of others in a moral *cause*, your victimhood attains a level of untouchable righteousness. Joining the army and fighting for the Fatherland had that effect for Hitler.

From the beginning of the war, Hitler was involved in actual combat, and he saw a lot of action. Toward the end of the war, his regiment was involved in one battle in Belgium where they lost 80% of their 3600 men during the first *three* days of fighting. In that battle he was the victim of a mustard gas attack by the British, which left him seriously injured for weeks.

While recovering from the above attack in a German hospital, Hitler observed what he believed was the true cause of Germany's losing the war. Everywhere he looked, he was enraged to see civilians who not only failed to appreciate the efforts of himself and his comrades who were suffering and dying in the trenches but who, in many cases, even undermined the execution of the war. He wrote diatribes against war profiteers, malingerers, and traitors, most of whom, he observed, were Jews. When he was in the hospital, he noted that all the safe jobs away from the battlefront—clerks and the like—were filled by Jews, while the Jews were poorly represented in battle. He was also convinced that "Jewish finance" had seized control of Germany's industrial and munitions production. "The (Jewish) spider was slowly beginning to suck the blood out of the people," he said.

Conditions in Germany had become severe. Civilians were eating dogs and cats (roof rabbits). Bread was made from sawdust and potato peelings. 400,000 workers walked out of their shops in Berlin to organize a strike committee. The government was leaning toward surrender, and the soldiers felt betrayed. When the Kaiser—the German version of a king—ordered peace negotiations, one of the highest generals protested that there must be "more vigorous conscription of the young Jews, hitherto left pretty much alone." Four years of dehumanizing trench warfare had engendered in Hitler, as in so many other German patriots, an abiding hatred of the pacifists and slackers back home who were "stabbing the Fatherland in the back."

After four long years of heavy losses in the war, many factions in Germany pressured the Kaiser to abdicate so an armistice could be signed. While Hitler was still in the hospital, a group of Communist German sailors came into his ward and attempted to convert the patients to this revolution against the Kaiser. This event heightened Hitler's feeling that both he and his Fatherland were being betrayed. Three of the Communist leaders were young Jews, which further contributed toward his belief that Jews were trying to destroy the nation that was sacred to him.

The Fatherland

As a boy, Hitler was lost and confused. He wasn't a great student, nor did he excel in athletics. His father—along with the rest of the family—disapproved of his career as an artist, so he felt even more isolated. He had aspirations of greatness, but he didn't seem to have the talent or other means necessary to achieve his dreams.

Then, at age eleven, began the first of many steps that would lead him to the means for achieving acceptance and greatness. He found two illustrated magazines devoted to the Franco-Prussian War of 1870 and became completely immersed in their contents. He said it wasn't long before the great historic struggle of Germany became indistinguishable from his own. He found the means to greatness— and a solution to his isolation— in his nearly total identification with his beloved Fatherland. He and Germany became one in his mind. If you betrayed one, you betrayed the other. He created a world where anything that adversely affected Germany would personally victimize him.

When the Kaiser was deposed at the end of World War I, therefore, and replaced by a republic, Hitler felt that everything he had fought for in the long four years' war had been betrayed. The shock was so great that he experienced a period of total hysterical (psychological) blindness. When Germany then surrendered, Hitler felt personally shamed. Within twenty four hours of Germany's surrender, while in horrific despair as he lay on his cot, he experienced a "supernatural vision" in which he heard voices calling on him to save Germany. At that moment, he dedicated himself to become a politician and to save his beloved Fatherland. With this decision he was certain to be a victim or a savior or both all his life.

For about a year after the war, there were numerous Communist uprisings all across Germany, and Germany very nearly became a Communist state. After Germany was saved from the Red threat, the Allies forced Germany to sign the Treaty of Versailles in June 1919, with terms that utterly humiliated Germany. Germany was forced to pay exorbitant reparations, and huge chunks of German soil were cut off and given to France, Belgium, and Poland. Parts of the country also remained under military occupation. It was as though Germany were castrated and chained simultaneously, and the shame of this was unbearable to many Germans, but especially to Hitler.

He would spend the rest of his life fighting for the glorification of his beloved Fatherland. He believed that if Germany had a need, she immediately had a divine right to fill that need. He often spoke, for example, of a principle called Lebensraum (living space), which was Germany's God-given right to have enough land—breathing room, natural resources, and so on—for her people. Hitler spoke about how unfair it was that some nations—referring especially to Russia—should occupy nearly entire continents, while a world power like Germany should be cramped, living 360 people per square miles (for reference, the United States at that time had a population density of 43 people per square mile).

Hitler was so committed to his task of saving Germany—and himself, since the two were interchangeable—that he refused to marry, saying that marriage would distract him. He had many invitations to marry, especially from Eva Braun, but he didn't marry until hours before his joint suicide with Eva in 1945. "My only bride is my Motherland," he said.

The Jews and Communists

Hitler was responsible for killing six million Jews in Europe during a relatively few years—mostly the last three years of the war. Such dedicated hatred deserves an explanation. We already established in Chapter Three that once victims establish that you are the cause of their pain, they feel entirely justified in defending themselves in virtually any way available to them, and they feel justified in taking their revenge on you.

By age twenty, Hitler already had acquired quite a list of grievances against the Jews, enough in his mind to pay them back venomously for the rest of his life:

- It was a Jewish doctor who had treated his mother for cancer and failed to save her life.
- It was Jewish art brokers who had the responsibility for selling his paintings, and they failed.
- When he was homeless and starving in Vienna, it was rich Jews who ignored him and failed to take him into their homes. To be sure, non-Jews didn't take him in either, but any slight from a Jew was more noticeable to him.

- When he was penniless in Vienna, he had to sell his coat to get money for food. He felt that the Jew who bought his coat took advantage of him.
- He suffered on the front lines in World War I for more than four years, only to learn that the government's support of the war had been undermined by significant factions at home, most prominent of which Hitler believed to be the Communists and Jews.
- It was Hitler's experience that the Jews were considerably under-represented at the battle front, which he found quite a betrayal in light of the tribulations he experienced there.

In his book, *Mein Kampf*, Hitler said that in Vienna he discovered that the Jew was the "cold-hearted, shameless, and calculating director" of prostitution; that the music and art worlds were controlled by Jews; and, most important, that the Social Democrat press was directed by Jews." Anti-Semitism was very common then. There were many trash magazines that filled the newsstands that spouted such doctrines, and Hitler was an avid reader of them.

For reasons I established earlier, Hitler already felt thoroughly victimized at a young age, and victims *must* have a perpetrator to blame their pain on and to vent their anger against. As he matured as a politician and eventually as a dictator, the Jews became a perfect choice as a group to blame everything on. Consider the options. He could have chosen to blame

- the aristocracy, but that would have isolated him from their money, which he needed as a politician.
- the middle class, but they were far too numerous, and he needed their support.
- big business, but he needed their whole-hearted support in the industrialization and militarization of Germany.

Immediately after the end of the Great War, as mentioned earlier, Germany was engulfed by a terrifying series of Marxist-inspired uprisings that threatened to destroy the fabric of German existence. Many of these uprisings and conspiracies—in and out of Germany— were known to be led by Jews, so Hitler and millions of other Germans came to fear Jews and Communists almost as a single unit.

Germany would have gone Communist except for the Free Corps, groups of idealistic activists from the armed forces dedicated to defending Germany from the Reds. They studied philosophy and yearned for action of any kind, and often they gathered around campfires, under the direction of a Führer, a leader, who would teach them how to overcome their adversities. It was very much a victim-oriented philosophy, and in this atmosphere anti-Semitic literature sprang up everywhere. The language was rabid and victim-oriented and all-encompassing. They taught that the Jew stood behind all the world's evils. They believed that the Jews had planned the Great War and the Red Revolution, and that they were plotting to take over the world. Hitler read these newspapers and magazines.

As far back as 1919, long before he became a household name, Hitler talked about making legal attempts to deprive Jews of certain privileges on the grounds that they were a foreign race. "But the final aim must unquestionably be the irrevocable removal (also translatable as amputation or elimination) of the Jews."

After he spent six months in the Landsberg prison, where he wrote *Mein Kampf* and where he honed his victimhood to an even finer edge, he was asked if his position on the "Jewish question" had changed. "Yes, yes," he said. "I have been far too *soft* up to now! I have finally come to realize that the harshest methods of fighting must be employed in the future if we are to win. I am convinced that this is not only a matter of life and death for our people but for all peoples. The Jew is a world pest." The language here is pure victim.

Like all victims, Hitler was careful to come up with justifications for his actions toward the Jews. We've discussed many already. Unwittingly, other nations provided another. From the time the Nazi party came to power in 1933 until 1939, only about 100,000 Jews had left Germany to find homes in new host countries. This exodus actually aroused great *resistance* in America, France, Holland, and Norway to more Jews coming into their countries. Hitler interpreted their resistance as further ratification of his position that Jews were vermin worthy of eradication.

The Führer was even careful to instruct those entrusted with the Final Solution that the killings should be done as humanely as possible. This enabled him to maintain his position that he was simply doing God's work. "After all," he claimed, "have I not always been fair in my dealings with the Jews?" He claimed to have given them fair warning and to have treated them fairly and with dignity. He was only purging the world of the "Jewish poison," an "essential process of disinfection . . . without which we should ourselves have been asphyxiated and destroyed. We have lanced the Jewish abscess, and the world of the future will be eternally grateful to us." Again, this is all classic victim language. Victims are always entirely justified in their behavior, no matter how abhorrent.

Soliciting Allies

As we discussed in Chapter Four, victims gain enormous advantages from gathering supporters in their "cause," which advantages you might want to review on pages 116-19. The ability to gather and sway supporters was perhaps Hitler's greatest single power. He wasn't unusually sociable or sensitive or intelligent, nor did he possess what we would normally call leadership qualities. In fact, despite long and rather decorated service during the Great War, he rose only to the rank of corporal, because, according to one of his officers, he "lacked the capacity for leadership."

And yet he singlehandedly led an entire nation in lockstep wherever he wanted them to go. Was that not leadership? No, it was the ability to appeal to the same sense of fear and victimhood in others that controlled him. He was an absolute master at that. Transcriptions of his speeches are not impressive. He was not logical and persuasive in his reasoning, but in person he appealed to fear and victimhood in ways that could sway hundreds of thousands at a time and hold them spellbound for hours.

Throughout history many such "leaders" have swayed the opinions of dozens, thousands, even millions, in a similar fashion, by appealing to their fear and sense of victimhood. A few examples:

- Gang leaders often inspire their followers by describing what has been *done to them* —by the police, by others in authority, and by other gangs. They also keep their followers in line by instilling a fear of what will happen to them if they dare to disobey.
- Religious leaders throughout history have controlled people by making them believe that they *must* obey or they will be

offending God or God's messenger (the religious leader). Many other religious leaders inspire their followers to hate other groups by pointing out how those other groups have offended *them* or *God*. Some of the misguided leaders of Islam—not true followers of the Quran, who do not teach hatred—come to mind, as well as those of the fundamentalist right who preach hatred against gays or any other group.
- Many political leaders carry the banner of victimhood for some oppressed group and thereby rally people around them, when their real goal is approval and power for themselves. These leaders are vicarious victims, whom we discussed on pages 119-21.

At an early age, while still in grammar school, Hitler gathered people around him so he could practice sharing his ideas with them. By the time he was in his late teens, he was doing this regularly, testing how this mode of speech or that was most effective in influencing people's minds. He concluded early in his experimentation that the truth was irrelevant. All that mattered was controlling people. Once when he saw a particularly persuasive piece of advertising in a newspaper, he said, "That is what I call advertising. Propaganda, only propaganda is necessary. There is no end of stupid people." He said propaganda could make believers out of doubters.

Said an associate about his speeches, "He knew how to fire up the people, not with arguments, but with the fanaticism of his whole manner, screaming and yelling, and above all by his deafening repetition."

In 1936 he marched troops into the Rhineland, taking back territory given up after the Great War. Because he portrayed this act in a way that appealed to the national sense of victimhood and honor—"Look what they did to us, and we're getting them back!"—in the election held three weeks later he received 98.8% of the votes in the country.

War

Most human beings tremble at the very prospect of war. In the face of the unspeakable consequences—the loss of life, physical suffering, emotional anguish, the devastation to family ties, the loss of irreplaceable cultural artifacts, and so on—the vast majority of us will go to any lengths to avoid war. Hitler simply was not restrained by such concerns. War was just another tool available to him in the accomplishment of his goals, primarily

- to eliminate those who had hurt him (victim).
- to eliminate those who *might* hurt him (victim).
- to eliminate those who were simply disliked by others—like the Jews—thereby giving him more general political power. With this, he again had more ability to prevent anyone from hurting him (victim).
- to punish those who had hurt him or who even might hurt him (victim).
- to increase his power—and the admiration given him—in any number of ways, thereby giving him what he had always deserved (victim).

He once told two adjutants that war was the father of everything. "Every generation must experience war once." In Hitler's perverse world this actually made sense, and he tried to convince others that it made sense, so he would have allies when he acted in accordance with this belief.

Even though Hitler had no moral difficulties with waging war, somehow he nonetheless recognized that other people *did* require a justification for war, so he was *always very, very careful* to provide that justification in detail. No matter how naked and unprovoked his aggression, Hitler could always demonstrate that *he* had been *mercilessly victimized* in some morally reprehensible way.

Austria

All his life Hitler had wanted to see Austria—the land of his birth—united with Germany, the Fatherland. In 1938 he felt he had the political and military capability to simply force that unification. As a victim, however, he needed a moral justification, and, as usual, that required that Austria offend Germany in a significant way. To most men that would have been an insurmountable problem, because Austria simply hadn't done anything offensive to him or to Germany.

But Hitler was a creative victim, and when a victim needs to find a reason to feel offended, he or she *will* find one. In 1933, at Hitler's insistence, Germany had withdrawn from the League of Nations, and in 1938 he decided that anyone who didn't support Germany in every way would by definition be Germany's enemy. This shouldn't be surprising. We've all seen such behavior from the victims in our lives on many occasions. We've done it ourselves. With victims, everything is *us* and *them*, and everyone else is required to choose sides. In any argument, victims require that you choose a side: Do you support *them* or the morally bankrupt *other guy*? In order to influence your choice, victims run campaigns, count votes, and never forget which side you chose.

Hitler simply did on a larger scale what we do in our daily lives quite often. He threw down the gauntlet to Austria, claiming that Austria's continued presence in the League of Nations was an intentional and insufferable insult to Germany, to the German people, and to himself personally. He didn't stop there. He claimed that Austria's presence in the League of Nations was undeniable proof that she had *never* supported Germany, and, come to think of it, Austria's entire history was one uninterrupted act of high treason. Fueled with this moral rectitude and weeping from the pain of all those years of untold suffering at the hands of the Austrians, Hitler then ordered his infantry and tank divisions to march in and take over the country, feeling entirely justified in his actions.

On the off chance that he hadn't validated his actions sufficiently, Hitler added three additional flourishes: First, he told the world that Austria had fortified her borders and illegally mined the roads between the two countries, which was not true. Second, he instigated a crowd of Nazi supporters that swelled to 100,000 in number outside the Austrian executive mansion, chanting the name of the Führer in the glow of smoking torches. Third, he ordered a Nazi-controlled leader in the Austrian government to send a telegram to Berlin requesting troops to put down the disturbance that was caused by the Nazis in the first place. In every situation, from every perspective possible, Hitler was the aggrieved party and justified in his reaction.

Hitler was fond of saying "Might makes right," but just in case there might be people who didn't agree with his unassailable logic, he always prepared plenty of evidence that the "other guy" had wounded him to the point where defending himself was the only reasonable course of action remaining. The hypocrisy of "Might makes right" is particularly astonishing in Hitler's case, because he detested that attitude and viciously attacked it when it was found in others, such as his father. Victims, however, are never bothered by little things like hypocrisy. In their world, the only thing that matters is *their* pain, *their* needs, and *their* beliefs.

When Hitler marched into Vienna at the head of columns of heavily-armed troops, he was able to partially satisfy some long-held needs for victim-inspired vengeance. As he delivered a triumphal speech in the Hotel Imperial in Vienna, he recalled his years in the city while he was a youth: "I could see the glittering lights and chandeliers in the lobby (of the Hotel Imperial), but I knew it was impossible for me to set foot inside." One night he was paid for shoveling snow outside that hotel with a gang of men, and they took their hats off every time the aristocrats came and went. "They didn't even look at us," he said, "although I still smell the perfume that came to our noses. We were about as important to them as the snow that kept coming down all night, and the hotel didn't even have the decency to send a cup of hot coffee to us. I resolved that night that someday I would come back to the Imperial Hotel and walk over the red carpet in that interior where those aristocrats had danced. I didn't know how or when, but I have waited for this day, and tonight I am here." This is a speech of triumph and revenge for a victim.

Czechoslovakia

In the 1930s Czechoslovakia was a relatively new country, cobbled together after World War I from a collection of several cultures, languages, and political backgrounds. Geographically, Czechoslovakia created an indentation in the middle of the eastern border of Germany, rendering that border more vulnerable to attack.

But Hitler's reasons for wanting to annex Czechoslovakia were not geographical. They were reasons based on victimhood:

- In the western portion of Czechoslovakia—called Sudetenland—lived 3.5 million people of German origin. Hitler claimed that these Sudeten Germans were being severely persecuted and that he had a moral obligation to free them from their condition. Hitler actually compared the situation of the Sudeten Germans to that of the Palestinians being persecuted by the Jews in Israel. The German newspapers even published accounts—which, suspiciously, could not be confirmed—of the mistreatment and killings of these Germans.

- The Sudetenland was created as a result of the humiliating defeat of Germany in the Great War, so Hitler felt compelled to right that terrible wrong by bringing the Sudeten Germans back into the fold where they belonged. In addition, Czechoslovakia contained 70-80% of the industrial capacity of the former Austro-Hungarian Empire, and it was almost entirely owned by Germans. So Hitler felt further justified in taking it back into Greater Germany.
- The Sudeten Germans themselves were demanding to be annexed to Germany, as Austria had been only months before. How, in good conscience, could Hitler deny full fellowship in Greater Germany to these deserving few?
- At one point the Western press spread the story that the Führer had been forced by foreign pressure to call off his invasion of Czechoslovakia and by so doing made the mistake of humiliating him. From then on he was emphatically in favor of settling the Czech question by force of arms, to uphold his sullied honor.

At one point Hitler received a report that England was prepared to give the Sudeten territories to Germany without any military action, which was just what he said he wanted. But England didn't comprehend how thoroughly Hitler was motivated by his victimhood. He had been wounded by the British and their arrogance during the first Great War, and so for him a simple ceding of territory wasn't enough. He wanted revenge and humiliation, so he rejected the British offer. Victims *need* perpetrators, and where there are none they will create them.

Hitler's cries of injustice inspired tens of thousands of Sudeten protesters to demand independence, upon which state police opened fire on them. Martial law was proclaimed, and now Hitler had more than enough excuse to march into Czechoslovakia. The country surrendered to him at the mere threat of his crossing the border.

Poland

After the Great War the Allies gave significant portions of Germany to Poland. Hitler proposed a return of these territories, and when Poland refused, Germany began to publicize unconfirmed accounts that Poles were molesting German women and children in the streets and smearing houses and shops with tar. Once again, he was playing the victim to justify his planned aggression.

Before he invaded Poland, he also ordered German newspapers to publish accounts that Germans were being murdered. Lying to a crowd, he said, "Tens of thousands were carried off, mistreated, and murdered in the most gruesome manner." Finally, he sent German troops disguised as Polish soldiers to attack German outposts and create a provocation for his invasion.

As we discussed in Chapter Two, the only justification any victim really needs for taking something from another person is *need*. As a victim, when I have a need, my discomfort is reason enough to alter the priorities of everyone else on the planet. They *must* give me what I want, and that's how Hitler reasoned. He didn't hide it. He said, "I need the Ukraine (for its fields of grain) so we can't be starved out as we were in the last war," and he needed Poland as a gateway to the Ukraine.

As was the case with Austria and Czechoslovakia, peaceful negotiations for what Hitler wanted in Poland would have been possible, but that wouldn't have satisfied Hitler's victim mind-set. He said, "Basically I did not organize the armed forces in order *not* to strike. The decision to strike was always in me. Sooner or later I wanted to solve the problem (militarily)."

France and England

Before attacking France and England, Hitler emphasized repeatedly that the French and English must be told that it was *they* who had declared war on *him*. Technically that was true, but they declared war on Germany only in support of their allies—Austria, Czechoslovakia, and Poland—who had been consecutively invaded by Hitler. With laughable hypocrisy, Hitler said, "It was *their* war which was now bursting upon them. On no account must we allow ourselves to be maneuvered once more into the role of aggressor." Victims are always very careful to place the blame for their aggressive and hurtful behavior on other people.

When the French surrendered to Hitler, he forced them to sign the documents in the same railroad car and in the same woods near Compiegne where the Kaiser's representative had surrendered to the Allies at the end of World War I with the Treaty of Versailles. It was a vindictive as well as historic choice, one that only an inveterate victim could have made. By choosing that spot Hitler was retaliating in a highly symbolic way for the humiliation suffered by the German people and by himself.

Russia

After Germany took Poland, Hitler's unabashed goal was to take possession of Russia, a country that dwarfed Germany in both size and population. Hitler's invasion of Russia was a truly massive affair, involving more men than any military campaign in the history of the world to that point. In the battle for Stalingrad alone, over two *million* Russian and German soldiers were lost.

I mentioned previously that Hitler spoke a great deal about *Lebensraum*, Germany's divine right to have adequate living space for her people. Of course the meaning of *adequate* would be determined by Hitler, and there would be no appeal to a higher court once he had made his judgment. He openly declared that he could not "allow" the Russian people to make any decisions that might conflict with the needs of Germany. "I need empty space," he declared, and in order to satisfy that need he would move into Russia. "Policy," he continued, "is made not with illusions but with facts. Space is the deciding question for me in the East (Russia)!" Hitler lived in a world where his needs became "facts." In such a world, he could easily justify *any* course of action. So it is with any victim.

During his youthful days in Vienna, Hitler read many inflammatory pamphlets that described the Slavic people—the Russians among them—as a lazy, primitive, and hopelessly second-class race. If you're going to forcibly take something from someone to satisfy your needs, identifying them as sub-human makes your task all the easier. As even further justification for initiating his actions in Russia, Hitler told his soldiers before the invasion that he was reacting to the Russian build-up on the German frontier and to numerous border violations on the part of the Russians. He was always the victim.

Honing his Victimhood

In Hitler's first major political speech, hecklers began to interrupt him, but truly practiced victims—like Hitler—prepare for their victimization. They anticipate it. Hitler had brought along his military friends, and within minutes the agitators "flew down the stairs with gashed heads." This pattern became a trademark for Hitler. Everywhere he went he was accompanied by his thugs, who routinely carried rubber truncheons and riding whips, or worse. Victims feel justified in doing whatever it takes to protect themselves, no matter how aggressive their actions.

In Hitler's first party-controlled newspaper, his targets were Jews, the unfairness and devastating effects of the Treaty of Versailles, and the Communists. He chose these targets because he knew they would be most popular with other people who also felt like victims, which described the vast majority of the people of Germany. Victims simply love feeling victimized *together*, as well as planning together their joint vengeance.

Most victims live in worlds where emptiness and fear rule continuously. In these conditions virtually everything becomes a threat until proven otherwise. Victims are constantly afraid, especially of events and situations that are unfamiliar or unplanned, because then they are least prepared to defend themselves. Hitler regarded anything out of his control as an actual or potential violation. A friend of his, for example, described a New Year's Eve party where a pretty girl maneuvered Hitler under some mistletoe and kissed him. "I shall never forget the look of astonishment and horror on Hitler's face!" said his friend. "Bewildered and helpless as a child, Hitler stood there, biting his lip in an effort to master his anger . . . An uncomfortable silence reigned," and he left the party.

He did not like being confronted either, as illustrated in a heated argument that once developed between himself and his Foreign Minister. As he was defending himself, he stopped in mid-sentence, clutched his heart, and sank into a chair. "I thought I was going to have a heart attack," Hitler said to the Minister. "You must never again oppose me in this manner."

In any unpleasant situation, Hitler always believed himself to be the victim of someone else's unfair and unkind behavior, as illustrated by the following examples:

- To friend he said, "I am lied to on all sides." Increasingly he came to believe that everyone was out to hurt him.
- As the Germans were retreating before the advance of the Allies toward the end of the Second World War, Hitler ordered his commanders to blow up bridges, so the Allies couldn't use them in their progress toward Berlin. One particular bridge was seized intact by the Allies before the German army could destroy it, and Hitler regarded this as a personal betrayal. Enraged, he was determined to punish every man remotely responsible for this insult to him.
- Toward the very end of the war, Hitler screamed that he was surrounded by traitors and liars. Everyone was too stupid and too vulgar to be capable of understanding his glorious purposes. "The army has betrayed me, my generals are good for nothing, my orders were not carried out. It is all finished. Germany was not quite ready or quite strong enough for the mission I set for the nation." He was the consummate victim.
- When things went badly in battle, and his commanders were trying to tell him about the woes of the civilians and the wounded military men, he was more interested in complaining about those who had betrayed him.
- Hours before Hitler died, he summoned his personal secretary to take down his "last political will." She was sure it would be a confession, but his entire message was composed of blaming and accusations.
- To his personal pilot he said, "I want them to write on my tombstone: 'He was the victim of his generals.'" Hitler was a victim first, last, and always.

When Hitler did have the opportunity to get revenge for his injuries, he could be quite vicious and thorough, as many victims are:

- He was the object of many assassination attempts. In one case, a trusted aid and war hero, a Colonel von Stauffenberg, led a conspiracy to kill him with a bomb. "The Stauffenberg family

will be exterminated, root and branch!" Hitler said. Many of these conspirators committed suicide. The eight principal conspirators were hanged with piano wire, and their hangings were filmed so that Hitler could enjoy them over and over. *Five thousand* other men and women were executed in association with this one attempted murder.
- Toward the end of the war, when the German army showed signs of falling apart, Hitler threatened to arrest and shoot the entire extended family of any deserter.
- His desire for vengeance against the Jews alone led to the deaths of more than six million of them.
- In retribution for the humiliation of Germany in the Great War, Hitler eagerly initiated and perpetuated conflicts that resulted in the deaths of at least *fifty million people.*

Messiah

Victims manipulate others for sympathy. They protect themselves for safety. They think primarily of *themselves*. Another way a victim can focus everyone's attention on him or her is to come to the rescue of other victims—to be a savior or messiah recognized as indispensable by all. If you take the job of savior or messiah in a given situation, the potential rewards are great:

- You get a lot of positive attention (praise).
- People will often rally around you to assist you in your lofty calling (power).
- People are less likely to attack you while you are occupied in the selfless task of saving others (safety), because that would be considered socially unacceptable on their part.

Hitler consistently set himself up to occupy the position of savior for his people. Earlier in this section I mentioned that while still a young man he experienced a "supernatural vision" in which he was "called" to save his beloved Fatherland. He took this calling seriously, and he felt that it gave him the right to demand absolute loyalty from everyone.

It has long been the pattern in nations ruled by law—including Germany as it was before Hitler—that civil servants and members of the armed forces take oaths to support and defend the laws of the land, or the constitution, or the country itself. In Nazi Germany, however, everyone pledged an oath of allegiance to Adolf Hitler personally.

School children were taught to sing the following song before they began their day:

> Adolf Hitler is our savior, our hero,
> He is the noblest being in the whole wide world.
> For Hitler we live,
> For Hitler we die.
> Our Hitler is our Lord,
> Who rules a brave new world.

Another song these children sang went as follows:

> Führer, my Führer, bequeathed to me by the Lord,
> Protect and preserve me as long as I live!
> Thou hast rescued Germany from deepest distress,
> I thank thee today for my daily bread.
> Abide thou long with me, forsake me not,
> Führer, my Führer, my faith and my light!
> Heil, my Führer!

It's understandable that with this kind of sweeping support, he felt he could do anything he wished. "I will successfully lead the German people in their fight for freedom," he said, "if not peacefully, then with force." And he made it clear that he was willing to sacrifice his own life in the cause of saving the Fatherland. In one conference of party leaders—before he had come to power in Germany—he pled for their complete loyalty, and then he said that if he couldn't have it on the spot, he would kill himself. This is a move that only a consummate victim could make.

When it came to his role in criticizing, controlling, and eventually even exterminating the Jews, Hitler saw his Messianic role in an increasingly divine way. Early in his political career, he described a visit to Berlin in this way: "The luxury, the perversion, the iniquity, the wanton display and the Jewish materialism disgusted me so thoroughly that I was almost beside myself. I nearly imagined myself to be Jesus Christ when he came to his Father's Temple and found the money changers." And then Hitler brandished his whip and exclaimed that it was his mission to descend upon the capital like Christ and scourge the corrupt.

With time, Hitler's belief deepened that he had been called of God to carry out his particular mission, as demonstrated by the following statements he made:

- "Therefore, I am now convinced that I am acting as the agent of our Creator by fighting off the Jews, I am doing the Lord's work."
- "Christ was the greatest early fighter in the battle against the world enemy, the Jews . . . The work that Christ started but could not finish, I—Adolf Hitler—will conclude."
- He predicted that in five or six hundred years the name of Hitler would be honored in all lands as the man who once and for all exterminated the Jewish pest from the world.

It's not difficult to imagine, then, that when the Pope sent his personal congratulations to Hitler on his fiftieth birthday, Hitler would have taken that as ratification of his divine mission. Any victim would.

Being Right

As we discussed in Chapter Four, an essential part of being a victim is never, ever admitting that you're wrong. Victims cannot admit they're wrong, because their victimhood *depends* on making *other people* wrong. Remember the three credos of a victim:

- Look what you did *to* me (which makes *you* wrong).
- Look at what you should have done *for* me (which again makes *you* wrong).
- It's not my fault. So whose fault is it? *Yours*, of course.

If I admit that *I'm* wrong, I can't make *you* wrong, and the foundations of my victimhood fall apart. At some level Hitler understood that, so he never admitted to being wrong. Said a friend of Hitler, "Absolutely no one could ever persuade him to change his mind, once it was made up."

When victims are criticized, they

- act hurt.
- defend themselves.
- hold grudges.
- attack those who are criticizing them.

In short, victims make it so unpleasant for people to offer suggestions or criticism that most people won't. They give up. People avoid victims. Hitler had a profound need to be right. According to several people closest to him:

- "Hitler wants things his own way and gets mad when he strikes opposition."
- "As a rule, Hitler never converses, he either listens, or—more commonly—preaches, making his utterances as though they were endowed with the authority of revealed religion."
- "Nothing irritates the Führer more than people who were right when he was wrong."

This insistence on being right had terrible consequences for Hitler, his associates, and others:

1. He ignored useful input and advice, which caused him to make bad decisions.
2. He ignored useful input and advice, which resulted in a high incidence of subordinates who were frustrated and who then resented him or even betrayed him.
3. He was slow to make decisions, and he made decisions based on fear rather than what was right.
4. He often perceived betrayal where there was none.
5. He reacted with anger and violence where none was required.
6. He couldn't establish an intimate relationship with anyone.

Let us now examine each of these consequences of Hitler's extreme need to be right, and let us hope that we learn something about the consequences of our own need to be right.

1. He ignored useful input and advice, which caused him to make bad decisions.

At one point Hitler had planned an invasion of England, and his anticipated point of departure on the French side was the port of Calais, which would provide the shortest route from England to

France. That invasion never happened, but years later, as the Allied invasion day (D-day) approached, Hitler was certain in his own mind that the Allies would take the reverse of the route *he* had planned, so that they would *arrive* in Calais, France. He therefore made the strongest fortifications on those beaches and at that port, and when word arrived that the Allies had actually landed at Normandy—230 miles by road to the west of Calais—he simply would not admit that he had been wrong and would not allow tanks and guns to be diverted from Calais for the critical effort of repelling the invaders along the Normandy coast. The cost to Germany was enormous.

Hitler often ignored the information he was given if it conflicted with conclusions he had already made. On one occasion when someone was trying to get him to change his mind about a policy, he said, "I cannot turn back now. Any change in my attitude would certainly be misunderstood as giving in."

How many times in your own life have you been reluctant to take the advice of others, because that would have required admitting you were wrong, and as a result you've made bad decisions? I've done this so many times I've lost count. Parents are especially prone do this with their children. Children have great ideas, but parents don't want to be "misunderstood as giving in"—just as Hitler said—so they stand their ground and make poor decisions as a consequence. Spouses, in their pride and need to be right, ignore the input of their partners, and thereby doom themselves to poor choices. To be sure, our poor choices don't affect as many people as Hitler's did, but the basic prideful process is quite similar.

2. He ignored useful input and advice, which resulted in a high incidence of subordinates who were frustrated and who then resented him or even betrayed him.

A leader who always has to be right tends to come across in a number of negative ways to those he leads:

- Self-righteous. Nobody likes to work for a boss who never admits to a mistake. One man who worked closely with Hitler talked about how he always had to be right, and he added, "And he doesn't realize how he can wear on one's nerves."

- Blaming. This is a natural extension of the consequence listed immediately above. In any endeavor, no matter how carefully planned and executed, mistakes are inevitable. If I believe I am above making mistakes—or at least that I must never admit them—then whom shall I blame when mistakes are made? I can't hold myself responsible, and certainly *someone* must be blamed, so there's no doubt that the object of blame had better be you than I. I will blame you without regard for who actually made the mistake, and if I inappropriately blame you on enough occasions, you'll come to resent me. Many of Germany's leaders resented Hitler for that reason.
- Ungrateful. When a leader is always right, he can't give credit to others for creativity or anything else. This attitude can really chafe subordinates after a while. Hitler took credit for everything good that happened and blamed his subordinates for every mistake.
- Controlling. Most of us have a strong need to have ownership over some aspect of our lives. We need to have some responsibility that is really ours. We need the sense of accomplishment and fulfillment that comes from successfully managing our own stewardship. If a boss constantly meddles in the affairs of those he leads, and if he controls them, they *will* come to resent that. Meddling and controlling are exactly the styles Hitler used to "lead." His military experience, for example, was limited to four years as an enlisted man following orders in the trenches, and yet he continually countermanded the plans and orders generated by his generals, *each* of whom had decades of the most advanced theoretical and practical military education available in the world.

Because Hitler always claimed to be right, the negative effects described above were seen in abundance among his subordinates, and many men came to resent the Führer deeply. It was said that he was easy to worship from afar, but the closer one approached him, the more the glow around him disappeared. These resentments ran deep. Many attempts were made on Hitler's life, usually carried out or spurred on by people who knew him quite well.

Most of us cause effects among those we lead similar to those caused by Hitler among his followers. Parents who are always right breed resentment in their children. Corporate leaders who are controlling and ungrateful create environments of discontent that affect productivity far more than they realize.

3. He was slow to make decisions, and he made decisions based on fear rather than what was right.

As we've discussed, victims simply cannot be wrong, so making decisions is difficult for them, because with every decision comes the frightening possibility of making a mistake. Hitler hated making decisions. His personal adjutant could hardly get him to read the files containing information prepared for making important decisions. "Hitler was of the opinion," said his aide, "that many matters took care of themselves as long as one didn't stir them up." So he waited and waited in hope that the decision would be made for him by fate or circumstances.

Once a decision was made, Hitler drove his generals crazy by vacillating back and forth on decisions constantly. This caused numerous postponements in matters of critical importance. Victims can't stand being wrong.

Hitler himself said, "The question to me is never to take a step that might have to be retracted. I always go to the very brink of boldness but not beyond. One has to smell out, 'What can I get away with and what can't I?'" He said he tried never to take a step until he was absolutely certain of positive results, and that approach would certainly have paralyzed him on many occasions.

I have seen this approach to decisions enacted in every aspect of life, but perhaps most commonly in marriage. One partner—the more victim-prone of the two—is quite reluctant to make decisions. So he—in this case we'll make it the man—waits and waits, making no decision at all, but recognizing that one must be made. Finally, his wife does make a decision, and the second something goes wrong, he leaps in to criticize and loudly proclaim how he *would* have made the decision. Often he even tells her that he had "told her so." Again, just as Hitler used to do, but on a smaller scale.

4. He often perceived betrayal where there was none.

Hitler thought himself so far above the possibility of making a mistake that he believed himself a holy instrument in God's hands.

He believed the world revolved around his needs, which is a common belief among victims. Imagine then how he felt when someone else made a mistake or—heaven forbid!—actually made a conscious choice not to conform to his wishes. To someone as self-important as Hitler—and all victims qualify for that designation—any action contrary to his or her wishes wouldn't just be a mistake but would constitute a personal betrayal.

Hitler felt wounded and betrayed continually. As I stated on page 336, he was heard to say, "I am lied to on all sides." He further said that his generals had betrayed him, nobody did what he wanted, and everyone wanted to see him fail. At various times he made public and private accusations of betrayal involving almost everyone he had ever known. Many of these people—some of his most effective associates—were executed or exiled, despite their having done nothing to merit their punishments. This created a pervasive atmosphere of fear that motivated many people in the short term but caused resentment and disorganization overall.

Ironically, the promises *Hitler* made to others—written and oral, direct and implied—meant nothing to him. He didn't hesitate to violate treaties, break promises, and unilaterally dissolve friendships, and yet if others did anything remotely similar to him, his reaction was volcanic. On one occasion, he organized a violent coup against the German government, kidnapped a group of important government leaders, and extorted from them—literally at gunpoint—a promise of cooperation. When these leaders were mistakenly released from their involuntary custody, they understandably failed to honor their extorted promises to Hitler, at which point he expressed outrage at *their* "betrayal."

5. He reacted with anger and violence where none was required.

Because of his need to be right, Hitler saw mistakes where there were none and betrayal where there were only simple mistakes. This tendency toward severe judgment naturally affected his reactions to situations. Instead of reacting appropriately to a mistake or a difference of opinion with guidance or correction or perhaps even tolerance, he felt compelled to put down "rebellions" or to punish "betrayals," so his reactions were far angrier and more violent than necessary. In his own words, Marxism and Judaism, for example, had to be fought "not according to middle-class standards but over corpses!"

In the world of a victim, everything becomes a threat, so a state of constant hyper-vigilance is required. On one occasion a lone man set fire to the building where the German Parliament met, and the chief of police confirmed that this man had acted alone. Hitler was certain, however—based on no evidence—that it had been a conspiracy, so "for the protection of the German people" (translate: for his *own* safety and power) he suspended free speech, free press, sanctity of the home, secrecy of mail and telephone conversations, freedom to assemble or form organizations, and inviolability of private property. He also authorized the central government to seize control of any state government that couldn't maintain order. With scarcely a protest, democracy was instantly eliminated from Germany.

Albert Einstein's bank deposits were seized when authorities found a bread knife—paranoically classified as a lethal weapon—in his home. In the mind of a victim, his reaction is never overdone, because his assessment of the situation is always correct.

The more you study any of the Real Love literature—as described at the end of Chapter One—and practice the principles therein, the more you'll discover that nearly all of us share the characteristic of this particular sub-section with Herr Hitler. We use anger where none is required, and we vastly over-react to people and events. Anger, for example, as we discussed in Chapter Five, is always selfish and destructive. It communicates *I don't love you* to the people around us and is never the best way to communicate *anything*. The more we learn about Real Love, the more we can replace anger with Real Love and happiness.

6. He couldn't establish an intimate relationship with anyone.

Hitler had brief liaisons with a number of women but avoided serious relationships with all but one, Eva Braun. Even with Eva, though, he refused to assume the responsibilities of a genuinely committed relationship, and he didn't marry her until less than two days before their joint suicide. In public he said that he didn't marry because the Motherland was his bride, but in a private moment he admitted that he couldn't possibly have been a good husband. He recognized that marriage "created rights" for a woman, such that she could expect her husband to give her the time she needed in order to be happy. He realized that he didn't want to be tied down in that way and that at some point a wife would have become dissatisfied with him and would have confronted him with "the sullen face of a neglected wife." He decided it was "far better to have a mistress" he could neglect at will.

And he did neglect Eva most of the time. He would leave her alone for weeks at a time, and on two occasions she tried to kill herself to eliminate the pain of her loneliness. When he did see her, he never apologized for his long absences. On one occasion she wrote, "I had to sit next to him for three hours without being able to say a word. At parting he handed me an envelope with money. How nice it would have been if he had written a greeting or a nice word with it. It would have made me so happy. But he does not think of such things."

Hitler saw no hypocrisy in his openly neglecting her as he did but becoming enraged himself if anyone dared to slight him in the least degree. He was dismissive not only toward Eva but toward most of his visitors. He commonly kept people waiting outside his office literally for days without the slightest feeling of regret.

Selfishness

Victims manipulate other people to get sympathy for *themselves*, and they protect *themselves* to achieve a measure of safety, and in doing so they demonstrate perhaps the most important quality of all victims: simple *selfishness*. The center of the world to a victim is himself or herself, and Hitler certainly had an abundance of that quality.

Whenever possible, for example, he stole the credit for good ideas from those around him. Said one close associate, "Though he often does what we advise, he laughs in our faces at the moment (about the suggestion) and later does the very thing as if it were all his own idea and creation. I've never seen a man so magnificently unaware that he is adorning himself with borrowed plumage."

While stealing the credit of others on the one hand, on the other hand he also didn't hesitate to dispense harsh criticism to others for the very flaws which he himself possessed in great abundance. Hitler once said, for example, that negotiating with Churchill would be useless since he was "guided by hatred and not by reason."

Continuing the theme of selfishness, he seemed to have no concern for the suffering of others. If the misery and deaths of other people showed any possibility of giving him even a moment of relief or pleasure, he didn't hesitate to allow or to order that suffering or those deaths.

Toward the end of the war, Hitler said, "If Providence should actually deny us victory in this battle of life and death, and if it is the will of the Almighty that this should end in catastrophe for the German people, then you, my generals and admirals, must gather around me with upraised swords to fight to the last drop of blood for the honor of Germany—I say gentlemen, that is the way it actually must be!" On more than one occasion he actually gave orders for entire armies of a hundred thousand men each to fight to the last man instead of surrendering.

When it was obvious that the war was lost, Hitler made plans to blow up as many buildings, airports, and roads as possible. He said that if the war was lost, the people would have proven that they weren't worthy of being saved anyway, so why leave them anything?

The Lesson

Hitler demonstrates so many qualities that are easy to criticize, but before we condemn them, we might benefit from seeing the same tendencies in ourselves. We do have them, and if we don't acknowledge them, they will cause as much destruction in our personal lives as Hitler's qualities did on a grander scale.

Why did Hitler's victim behaviors cause so much more destruction than those of most of us? The potential answers to this question are legion, but mostly he had abilities, propensities, and a place in time and location that greatly magnified the consequences of his behaviors:

- Hitler came to manhood in a nation that—from its perspective—was severely victimized at the end of The Great War by the rest of the civilized world. Even though Germany in great part precipitated that war, the Fatherland was severely penalized in money, land, pride, and resources for many years to come, and the German people were truly devastated by these penalties. This historic stage was uniquely ripe for a man of Hitler's abilities and tendencies.

- Hitler happened to choose a complete identification—almost a pathologic merging—with the Fatherland, whereas you and I identify with ourselves, perhaps our families, or maybe even a religion or ethnic group, and often that identification is intermittent. His identification was fanatical, and it opened unique doors in his future.
- Most young men choose sports or academics or women or drinking or collecting baseball cards —something like that— as a means of gathering Imitation Love. Hitler chose the rather unique hobby of manipulating the opinions of the people around him. Beginning at a tender age, he gathered groups of people around him solely for the purpose of practicing his craft, and in time he became one of the greatest masters of human persuasion to ever live.
- He had a great ability to remember details and to reduce great mountains of information to the simplest statements, which made him look like a man of great vision and clarity. These are qualities that people look for in a leader.

When you and I act like victims, and when we try to persuade others to our view, we might influence two people, or four, or even forty to follow us in beliefs or behaviors that are less than loving and productive. Because of the abilities and circumstances described above, when Hitler persuaded others to his view, he was able to influence *millions*. I caution us to consider, however, that this is a difference in *quantity* and in abilities and circumstances, and that we must remember that victimhood of any description is still terribly destructive in our lives—to ourselves, to our families, to those we work with, and so on.

INFAMOUS HISTORICAL CHARACTERS AS VICTIMS: SADDAM HUSSEIN

Most of the data in this section was gathered from Saddam Hussein, a Biography, by Shiva Balaghi, Greenwood Press, 2006. The quotes in this section are all from that book.

Saddam Hussein's father died before he was born, and his mother went to her brother's home for the delivery of her child. Saddam always regarded himself as a victim of his father's loss, and in later life, as dictator of Iraq, he favored poets who referred to similarities between himself and the Prophet Muhammad, whose father had also died before he was born.

Shortly after Saddam was born, his mother re-married, and her new husband beat Saddam and called him a "son of a dog" and "son of a whore." The stepfather also didn't talk to Saddam much and certainly didn't show him any affection. At a young age, therefore, Hussein had already been victimized severely, and he soon reacted to his pain by *acting* like a victim.

Saddam was raised in Tikrit, a very poor and harsh place, and at a young age he became what the Arabs called a "son of the alleys" or what we might call a hoodlum or young gangster. An old friend remembered that at an early age Saddam carried with him an iron bar to protect himself from stray dogs or other people, and he grew up believing that the only thing he could trust was that iron bar. This is how a victim sees the world, as something he must protect himself from constantly. When his friends gathered and talked about growing up to become doctors and poets, Saddam talked about having a jeep, a gun, and binoculars.

At age ten Saddam moved to his uncle's house, where he received his education. His uncle had been intimately involved with the 1941 Iraqi rebellion against the British occupation of the country, and for his efforts he had spent five years in prison. He too felt thoroughly victimized, and he powerfully conveyed that attitude to his nephew. He once wrote a pamphlet, *Three Whom God Should Not Have Created: Persians, Jews, and Flies*. Saddam wrote of him, "He always inspired us with a great nationalistic feeling." To Saddam nationalism meant a reaction to centuries of victimization by outsiders. Note the similarities here to the life of Hitler.

Saddam felt victimized personally, but he also lived in a country and in a household and in a culture where victimhood was preached daily as a form of patriotism. The Ottoman Turks had occupied Iraq for hundreds of years, and then in 1917 they were replaced by the British, who promised not to occupy the country. But the Brits stayed, and they installed as king a man who wasn't even Iraqi, which really irritated his subjects. The Iraqis made many subsequent attempts to throw the British and their puppet leaders out, and on each occasion when they failed—with the increased political oppression that followed—it was regarded as another victimization of the country.

Hussein learned to read at a late age, and in school he intensely resented the authority of teachers. Once he even slipped a snake into the robe of a teacher while he was pretending to embrace the man. When Saddam was fourteen, one teacher gave him a beating, and one witness testified that later that night Saddam went to the teacher's house and shot the first person to open the door, who happened to be the teacher's brother. The man lived.

Saddam's earliest political activities consisted of organizing street gangs in support of the Baath party. At age twenty-one he served six months in prison for murdering a local communist leader, and with every passing year his sense of personal and national injustice was building.

A year later Saddam was part of the assassination team that tried to kill the president of Iraq, and his escape from the country was both dramatic and well-used as propaganda material for many years afterward. In his absence he was sentenced to death, but he simply remained in Syria as an exile for four years. When Saddam returned to Iraq, he was soon involved in another plot to assassinate a new Iraqi president, and this time he was caught and put in prison. In prison he read a lot, and his favorite work was Hemingway's *The Old Man and the Sea*. It's worth pausing here to note the themes of victimhood in his favorite book

The Old Man and the Sea

The Old Man and the Sea is a story of an old fisherman who had an extraordinarily bad run of luck, catching nothing for eighty-four days. His "sail was patched with flour sacks and, furled, it looked like the flag of permanent defeat . . . Many of the fishermen made fun of the old man." Right from the beginning, the old man is victimized by the ocean, by fate, and by other fisherman.

One day when he sailed especially far out on the ocean, "He was sorry for the birds, especially the small delicate dark terns that were always flying and looking and almost never finding, and he thought, the birds have a harder life than we do except for the robber birds and the heavy strong ones. Why did they make birds so delicate and fine as those sea swallows when the ocean can be so cruel?"

This is such a commentary on the victimhood in Saddam's own life. Poor Saddam, such a "delicate" little thing, picked on by the "robber birds," the "heavy strong ones," and the big "cruel" ocean. All his life he saw himself being picked on by so many: stepfather, teachers, superiors, other political parties, law enforcement officers, and so on.

Finally, the old man caught a fish, the largest he had ever seen or even heard of. He fought the fish for two days and two nights, and in the process the fish tossed him about, dragged him all over the ocean, and made him suffer horribly. By the time he brought the fish in and killed it, he was far out to sea, and during his long journey home the sharks came and took the old man's prize, piece by piece, despite his valiant attempts to fight them off. The old man fought against all the power of the ocean, just one man against everyone and everything. "I'll fight them until I die," he said. Saddam saw himself in that way, victimized and picked on and therefore justified in pitting himself against everyone.

At one point in the old man's journey home, he thought, "Perhaps it was a sin to kill the fish. I suppose it was even though I did it to keep me alive and feed many people. But then everything is a sin. Do not think about sin. It is much too late for that and there are people who are paid to do it. Let them think about it . . . I killed him in self-defense, and I killed him well."

The old man decided that in his struggle, the concept of sin wasn't worth agonizing over. Let others think about that. Certainly Saddam let go of the ideas of right and wrong early in his life, concentrating instead on doing whatever it took to defend himself and to "kill them well." Once people are convinced they are victims they can justify almost anything.

In the space of ten years, four government coups took place in Iraq, so Saddam was part of a tumultuous political landscape where justification of extreme behavior came easily. In his early speeches, he talked about fighting imperialism and making his country a safe place for the Arab struggle. He saw the world in terms of himself and *them*, everyone that he must defend himself against.

"When I was a child," Saddam Hussein once told a reporter, "a man walked through my village without carrying a weapon. An old man came up to him and said, 'Why are you asking for trouble?' He said, 'What do you mean?' The old man replied, 'By walking without a weapon, you are asking for people to attack you. Carry a weapon so that blood will not be spilled!'"

When Iraq's president retired, Saddam succeeded him and summoned four hundred Baath party members to a televised meeting. There he announced that he had discovered a plot to overthrow the party, and he began to name traitors who were hauled away one by one, until one man stood to sing the praises of Saddam, at which point everyone joined in. Five hundred officials were later executed, not just at Hussein's orders but in many cases at his personal hand. After the executions were complete, Saddam stood on the balcony of the Presidential Palace in Baghdad and saluted a crowd of 50,000 who shouted, "Death to the Traitors!" All of this was right out of the Victim's Handbook: a plot (against *him*), motivating the leaders to sing *his* praises, *his* personally exacting revenge for offenses against *him*, the crowd of 50,000 (to worship *him*), the chant "Death to the Traitors" (who betrayed *him*).

At one point Hussein became personally offended—as victims do—at the *language* of Ayatollah Khomeini of Iran, and in retaliation he launched the longest war of the twentieth century, which resulted in 1.5 million casualties.

After invading Kuwait, he said, "Arabs, Moslems, believers in God, this is your day to rise and spread quickly in order to defend Mecca, which is captive to the spears of the Americans and the Zionists . . . who want harm for your families." Victims see harm everywhere, and they commit their atrocities in the name of defending themselves and others. He then changed the Iraqi flag, adding the words *God is great* written *in his own hand* in the middle of the banner. Victims have no limits to their self-centeredness. He referred to the battle with Western forces as "the great duel, the mother of all battles, between the victorious right and the evil that will certainly be defeated."

As with all victims, Hussein was not concerned with the cost of his behavior to others. In 1989, Iraq's gross domestic product (GDP) per capita was $2,840. By 1997—under his leadership—it had dropped to $200. His decisions to involve his country in wars to salve his sense of victimhood had nearly destroyed his entire country. But he didn't let these conflicts affect his personal wealth. He was worth billions and lived in fifty palaces, just one of which was big as all of the District of Columbia.

Conclusion

In order to calculate the area of a rectangle, we multiply the length of one side by the length of an adjacent side. We can calculate the approximate overall effects of a disease in our society in a similar way, by multiplying the number of people who are affected by the disease times the seriousness of the effects of that disease on an average individual. AIDS, for example, has rather serious effects on individuals, but it affects a relatively small number of people in this country—about one-third of one percent—so the overall effects on our society are not great. The common cold affects a great number of people, but its effects on individuals are usually not serious, so the overall effects on society are still small. Heart disease, on the other hand, affects a large number of people and has serious individual effects, so the overall societal effects are large.

I bring up this assessment of the impact of a disease because in most cases, our society devotes its greatest resources to the diseases and problems that have the greatest overall destructive effects. Our attitude toward victimhood, therefore, is especially peculiar, because victimhood demonstrates the deadly combination of both serious effects on individuals and a widespread distribution amongst us. Let's examine these two characteristics of victimhood now.

First, the number of people affected. As you have read the examples of victimhood presented throughout this book, it should have become obvious that victimhood affects very close to 100% of the population, and most people exhibit significant signs of the disorder many times every day. Victimhood is an illness more prevalent than the common cold or tooth decay.

Second, the seriousness of the effects of the disease on individuals. All through *Real Love and Freedom for the Soul* we have demonstrated that when an individual is afflicted by the attitude and behavior of victimhood

- he cannot feel unconditionally loved.
- he cannot be happy.
- he cannot participate in a loving marriage.
- he cannot be a loving parent.
- he can't cooperate effectively with his co-workers.
- he sows seeds of dissension in his family, among his friends, and in his workplace.
- he makes the people around him miserable with guilt and contention.
- he causes the employees he supervises to feel controlled and resentful.
- he strangles his relationships.
- he makes sure that everyone around him is at least as unhappy as he is.

In short, each victim makes himself miserable and spreads his misery to as many of the people around him as possible. When we multiply the severity of victimhood's effects on individuals times the number of people affected, we can say with confidence that victimhood—along with emptiness and fear, from which victimhood is spawned—is the cause of more unhappiness on the face of the planet than any other affliction.

It is painfully ironic, then, that when we look in the medical journals, or in the mental health literature, or in the newspapers and magazines and television news programs we read and view every day, we find almost no mention of victimhood whatever. After a review of all these sources of information, we would think that victimhood didn't exist, despite its nearly universal presence and horrifying negative effects.

It is absolutely essential, therefore, that we learn to identify victimhood in our own lives. As we do, and as we find more Real

Love, we can eliminate this behavior that is destroying our individual happiness and making healthy relationships impossible. We must also learn to identify victimhood in the lives of those around us, because then we can respond to them so much more positively.

As you study the principles in this book, and as you fill your life with Real Love, you will consistently discover the following benefits:

- The anger that has caused you so much unhappiness will steadily disappear, and it will do so with virtually no conscious effort on your part.
- The long held resentments that have poisoned your relationships will evaporate.
- Your marriage will become increasingly free of disappointment, irritation, and frustration.
- Dating will become consistently fun and productive, instead of confusing and frustrating.
- You'll become more productive in the workplace, and you'll enjoy what you do far more.
- You'll enjoy teaching and loving your children, instead of being annoyed at them.
- You'll feel a sense of contentment and power at work that you've never known before, even when people are being demanding and otherwise difficult.
- You'll discover a sense of peace that you never imagined, despite all the turmoil and contention swirling about you.

Although victimhood has devastating effects on us individually and as a society, the outlook for the future need not be the least bit discouraging. As we increase our awareness of this problem, we gain a power to eliminate the effects of victimhood in our own lives and to be an enormous asset for peace and happiness in the lives of those around us.

Index

Abandoned wife, 153-4
Addiction:
  cause, 163-5
  causes proposed by society, 163
  definition, 162, 292
  drug, cause, 288-91
  drug, definition, 288
  drug, incidence and cost, 288-9
  drug, responding to, 288-91
  list of, 292
  not disease, 163
  not just about alcohol or drugs, 162
  responding to, 288-91, 291-2
  variety of, 292
AFTERIOTIDPG, 117
Alcoholics, responding to, 288-91
Alcoholism, see Addiction, drug
Anger (and angry):
  choice, 145, 147-8
  distinguishes Real Love from conditional love, 12-14
  eliminating by understanding Getting and Protecting Behaviors, 32-4
  eliminating with Real Love, 35-6
  expressing alone not effective, 217-18
  "I don't love you" the message of, 13, 153-4
  incompatible with Real Love, 13-14

Anger (cont.):
  makes happiness impossible, 144-5
  makes us prisoners to people if we believe they make us angry, 147
  "me-me-me" the message of, 13
  not caused by others, 26-7
  right to be, 145
  selfish, 144-5, 215-16
  "venting" not effective, 217-221
  wrong, 144-5
Attacking:
  anger, see Anger
  definition, 23
  evolution of, 23-4
  examples, 23-4
  negative consequences of, 24-5
  see Getting and Protecting Behaviors
Auden, W.H., 70
Blaming, makes us prisoners, 146
Boss, critical, victimhood in, 167-8
Brer Rabbit, 244-5
Burn, reacting to, compared to Getting and Protecting Behaviors, 85-6
Canyon hike, metaphor of, 41-3
Children:
  anger and rebellion caused by victimhood, 162
  lying, taught to, 20

Children (cont.):
   speaking like victims,
      examples of, 305-6
   teaching about the Law of
      Choice, 191
   teaching about victimhood,
      191, 266-70
   teaching how to respond to
      victims, 306-8
   teaching how to tell the truth
      about their victimhood,
      204-5
   victimhood leads to anger
      and rebellion in, 162
Choice (choices):
   always have, 135-7
   controlling, see Controlling
   Law of, see Law of Choice
   none we can see in absence of
      Real Love, 145
Civil conflicts and victimhood,
   172-9
Clinging:
   definition, 28
   examples, 28, 94
   see Getting and Protecting
      Behaviors
Commitment, why men (and
   women) fear in relationships,
   154-7
Conditional love:
   definition, 11-12
   distinguished from Real
      Love by presence of
      disappointment or anger,
      12-14
   earned, 146
   examples, 11-12, 146
   vs. Real Love, 12-14

Consequences:
   characteristics, 142-3
   purposes, 143
   vs. punishment, 142-4
Contracts, see Promises
Controlling:
   caused by victimhood, 77-8
   dangers of, 67-8, 70-1
   disregard for Law of Choice,
      77-8
   disregard for Law of
      Expectations, 77-8
   effects of, 76-7
   examples, 75-6
   interferes with learning, 76-7
Customer, angry, victimhood
   in, 166-7, 284-6
Dating:
   fear of commitment in, 154-7
   victimhood in, 154-62
Details, don't get distracted by,
   200, 251-2
Difficult experiences, required
   for learning in life, 186-7
Disappointment:
   distinguishes Real Love from
      conditional love, 12-14
   incompatible with Real Love,
      13-14
   "I don't love you" the
      meaning of, 13
   Me-me-me the meaning of,
      13
   see Anger
Dogs fighting, 107-8
Drowning:
   metaphor, application of in
      real-life situation, 218-19

Drowning (cont.):
  metaphor for people using Getting and Protecting Behaviors, 32-34, 58-9
  metaphor to understand victimhood, 183-4
  people do not have the right to demand that you save them, 255
  we use Getting and Protecting Behaviors when we are, 32-4
  when see people as, can choose to love them instead of defending ourselves, 32-4

Drunk drivers, two, 141-2

Employee, discontented, responding to, 286-8

Employee, unappreciated, victimhood in, 167-8

Emptiness, cause of victimhood, 49

Expectations:
  caused by lack of Real Love, 72
  disappointment proof of, 74
  examples of, 71-72
  make happiness impossible, 73-4, 140
  make love impossible, 140
  not effective motivation, 74
  roses metaphor, 73
  selfish, 71-74
  wedding vows and, 73

Fairness:
  our obsession with inappropriate, 67-8
  victim's demands for, 254
  victim's idea of, 59-61

Fairness Enforcing Device, 67-8

Faith:
  definition, 216
  required for truth telling, 216-17

Falling in love, addiction of, 17-19

Fear:
  effects of, 50-3
  leads to Protecting Behaviors, 53
  makes us blind and insane, 53
  physical effects of, 50-1
  power of, 50-3

Field of Death:
  defined, 43-6
  examples, 44-9
  stay off, 236-8, 275-6, 284-5, 288

Field of Life, defined, 43-6

Gandhi, 202

Getting and Protecting Behaviors:
  can't feel loved when using, 30-31
  cause more getting and protecting from others, 53
  cause the emptiness and pain they're designed to avoid, 30-1
  caused by emptiness and fear, 19, 53
  caused by lack of Real Love, 19
  competition of, 46-9
  consequences of, 29-31

Getting and Protecting
Behaviors (cont.):
  eliminating by seeing others
    clearly, 32-4
  eliminating by understanding
    drowning metaphor, 32-4
  eliminating by understanding
    Getting and Protecting
    Behaviors, 32-4
  eliminating with Real Love,
    35-6, 87-90
  examples, 46-9
  Field of Death and, 45-6
  founded on victimhood, 86-94
  futility of, 44-5
  greatest obstacles in
    our interactions and
    relationships, 29-30
  "I don't love you" the message
    of, 29
  irony of, 30-31
  learned, 98-100
  make Real Love impossible,
    53
  moving from one to another,
    92-3, 97-100
  patterns of, 97-100
  negative consequences of,
    29-30
  response to emptiness and
    fear, 53
  selfishness of, 29-30
Guilt:
  eliminating with an
    understanding of the Law
    of choice, 191-2
  responding to people who
    demonstrate excessive, 294-5

Happiness:
  choice, 147-8, 185-7
  comes from Real Love, 144
  definition, 11, 144
  goal of life, 11, 144, 148
Handicapped people and
  victimhood, 169-170
Harris, Joel Chandler, 244-5
Hatzfeld, Jean, 173
Hitler, Adolf:
  being right, 339-46
  general, 314-48
  how he teaches us about our
    own behavior, 314-17,
    329, 332-3, 339-46, 346-7
  messiah, 337-9
  selfishness of, 346-7
Hurt, victims act, 57-9
Hurting other people:
  secondary result of protecting
    ourselves when in pain,
    85-6
  unavoidable consequence of
    learning, 68
Hussein, Saddam, 348-52
Hutus, 172-9
"I don't love you," the message
  of disappointment or
  irritation, 13
"I love you," possible meanings
  of, 155-6
Imitation Love:
  addictive nature of, 16-19
  caused by emptiness and fear,
    14
  competition for, 2-3, 46-9
  examples, 46-9
  Field of Death and, 43-6
  futility of, 44-5

Imitation Love (cont.):
  trading, 161-2
  used to fill our emptiness, 14
Inconveniences:
  price of life, 54-5, 57
  see Pain
  taken as personal insult by victims, 55-7, 57-9
International conflicts and victimhood, 172, 179
Israel, and conflict with Palestine, 179
Justice, see Fairness
Law of Choice:
  definition, 68
  effects of violating, 182-4
  essential to happiness, 68
  examples of what we say in terms of, 69
  involves mistakes and hurting other people on occasion, 68, 183
  negative effects of violating, 70-71
  price of, 68
  selfishness of violating, 182-4
  teaching children about, 191
  understanding helpful in eliminating guilt, 191-2
  understanding helpful in eliminating victimhood, 182-92
  victims attitude toward, 68
  victims violate, 182-4
  violating, reasons for not, 184
  world without, 68

Law of Expectations:
  defined, 71, 196
  exception to, 198-9
  illustrated, 196-8
  follows from the Law of Choice, 196
  understanding of can help eliminate victimhood, 196-8
  victimhood founded on disregard for, 196
  victims' disregard for, 71-4, 196
Law of Responsibility:
  defined, 71, 74, 192
  illustrated, 208-209, 192-6
  victims disregard for, 71-4
Learning:
  hurting other people unavoidable consequence of, 68
  mistakes unavoidable consequence of, 68
  requires difficult experiences, 186-7
Listening, loving act, 285
Love, conditional, See Conditional love
Love, see Real Love
Lying:
  buys approval, 20-1
  can't feel loved while, 22-3
  common, 19-20
  eliminating with Real Love, 87-90
  examples, 20-21, 87-90, 92-3
  frequency of, 23
  Getting and Protecting Behavior, 19-22

Lying (cont.):
  makes it impossible to feel loved, 145
  negative consequences, 22
  see Getting and Protecting Behaviors
  taught to us as children, 20
  unconscious, 19-21
Machete Season, 174
Malaria, compared to victimhood, 3
Mark and Susan, 2-3, 6-9, 17-18, 20-1, 23-4, 27, 46-9
Marriage, victimhood in, 152-4
"Me-me-me" the message of disappointment and anger, 13
Memories, false or repressed, 112-15
Mistakes:
  judging by Victim Factor, 141-2
  of others not our business, 211
  price of learning, 140-41
  reaction to, Real Love vs. conditional, 12-14
  unavoidable, 140-41
  victims want to punish people for, 140-42
Monsters:
  disadvantages of labeling people as, 314-17
  why we label people as, 314-15
  without Real Love, identifying easy, 176-7

Mr. Fine and Mr. Whine, 206-7
Munchausen syndrome, 115
Munchausen syndrome by proxy, 116
Needs vs. wants, 255-6
Pain:
  attitude toward a choice, 185-7
  causes selfishness, 54
  increased by victimhood, 165
  influenced by perception, 165
  justification for victimhood, 54, 70
  learning opportunity, a, 185-7
  not necessarily to be avoided, 185-7
  price we pay for the Law of Choice, 55
  reaction to involuntary and complete, 85-86
  sources of everywhere, 54-55, 185
  unavoidable consequence of Law of Choice, 185
Palestine, and conflict with Israel, 179
Path, in woods, metaphor, 309-10
Perpetrator, victim's need for, 106-7
Pleasure, form of Imitation Love, 15-16
Power:
  benefits of, 117
  form of Imitation Love, 15
  victims manipulate people for, 116-21

Praise, form of Imitation Love, 14-15
Promises, exceptions to Law of Expectations, 198-9
Protecting ourselves, natural response to fear, 53
Punctuality, 193-6, 207
Punishments:
  characteristics, 143
  victims want them for others, 140-42
  vs. consequences, 142-4
Real Love:
  benefits of, 355
  compared to twenty million dollars emotionally, 26
  connection from, 12
  definition, 11
  distinguishing from conditional love, 12-14
  effects of, 87-90, 218-21, 221-4, 236-8, 355
  effects of in workplace, 227-30
  eliminating victimhood with, 209-39
  finding compared to physical training, 35-36
  finding, resources to help with, 37-39, 233
  finding, truth telling, 35, 225-226
  freely given and received, 257-8, 259-61, 261-2
  how it looks, 225-7, 231-5, 284-8
  never speak without, 235-8
  power of, 221-4

Real Love (cont.):
  vs. conditional love, 12-14
  vs. rescuing, 256-7
  vs. sympathy, 256-7
Real meaning of what people say and do, see What people say and do (real meaning)
Relationships, reason for failure, 21
Rescuing vs. Real Love, 256-7
Responsibility (and Responsible):
  Law of, see Law of Responsibility
  other people are not for our happiness, 147-8
  ours toward victims, 310-11
  see Consequences
  teaching with Real Love, 192-3, 193-6
  we are to be loving, 148
  we're not for the choices made by others, 308-10
  we're not for the happiness of other people, 146
Running:
  definition, 27
  examples, 27, 92-3
  see Getting and Protecting Behaviors
Rwanda, civil conflict in, related to victimhood, 172-9
Safety, form of Imitation Love, 16
Self-help, tends to encourage victimhood, 170-2, 217
Selfishness, caused by pain, 54, 69-70

Sex:
   as illustration of mutual victimhood, 233-5
   can become distraction too early in a relationship, 158
   evidence that men see women as objects for, 158-9
   husbands who complain they don't get, 152-3
   men who complain women they date don't give them, 157-8
   used as basis for victimhood, 302
   why people resist, 157
   women use to trade with men, 159-62
   women who complain they're treated like objects for, 158-62, 302
Sex-starved husband, 152-3
Sexual abuse, case of, 221-4
Spoiled, victims are, 140
Starvation, compared to lack of Real Love, 72
Stealing food, metaphor of, 41-3
Stop sign, 199
Sympathy:
   rewards of, 110-111
   victims manipulate people for, 109-16
Tar-Baby, The, 244-5
Tardiness, 193-6, 207
Therapy, tends to encourage victimhood, 170-1, 217
Toddler, learning victimhood, 78

Toilet seat, 55-7
Training, athletic compared to trials of life, 186-7
Truth → Seen → Accepted → Loved, described, 22, 209
Truth telling:
   about our anger and selfishness thereof, 215-16, 217-21
   about our mistakes, 213-15
   about ourselves, not others, 210-11
   about what we get from being victims, 202-4
   as often as possible, 213
   eliminating our victimhood with, 199-202
   essential to feeling loved, 22, 209-10
   example, about our own victimhood, 199-202
   example, about the victimhood of another person, 199-202, 218-21
   faith required for, 216-17
   gradually, 211-13
   how, 35-36
   not to people who allow us to be victims, 211-13, 235-8
   purposes of, two, 212-13
   results of, 212-13, 213-14
   risk of, 216-17, 249-51
   role in eliminating victimhood in our lives, 199-205
   see Truth → Seen → Accepted → Loved

Truth telling (cont.):
  teaching children how to about their victimhood, 204-5
  teaching other people how to about their victimhood, 199-202, 204-5, 218-21, 235-8
  to people who are capable of accepting us, 211-13
Tutsis, 172-9
Two dollars (and twenty million):
  examples of using metaphor, 25-7
  compared to the inconveniences of daily life, 26
  metaphor of, 25-6
Victim:
  being vs. acting like, 25-6
  definition, 26
  true, 25, 26
Victim Factor, 141-2
Victimhood:
  accepted as normal in our society, 10
  addiction caused or worsened by, 162-5
  beliefs of, 4
  benefits of, 5
  benefits of eliminating, 263
  caused by a lack of Real Love, 10-26
  caused by emptiness, 41-3
  children's anger and rebellion caused by, 162
  choice, 25-6, 148-9, 185-6
  civil conflicts and, 172-9

Victimhood (cont.):
  common to the point of being accepted as normal, 10
  controlling and, 75-8
  cost of in society, 352
  cost of in workplace, 227-31
  creates a role for people to occupy in the world, 124-6
  definition, 4-5
  disease of, 1-2, 3-4
  effects of, 3-4, 181-2
  eliminating by telling the truth about ourselves, 199-202
  eliminating with Real Love, 35-6, 209-39
  eliminating with understanding, 181-208
  emptiness motivation for, 41-3
  examples, 2-3, 6-9, 46-9, 64, 79, 80, 80-84, 91, 92-3, 97-8, 103-4, 106-7, 118-19, 122-4, 133-5, 135-7, 137-40, 147-8, 152-3, 153-4, 157-8, 159-60, 166-7, 167-8, 187-91, 247, 276-83, 306-8
  examples, spoken, 80-4, 297-306
  examples of children speaking like, 305-6
  exchanging, 2-3
  excuses for, 41-63
  foundation for other Getting and Protecting Behaviors, 86-94
  foundations for, 41-63

Victimhood (cont.):
handicapped people and, 169-70
incidence of, 182
injury at the core of, 102-4, 106-7
international conflicts and, 172, 179
justification for revenge, 70
justifications for, 41-63, 49
Law of Choice, understanding of in eliminating, 182-92
learned, 78-80, 94-7, 110, 125-6, 149-50
marriage and, 152-3
negative consequences of, 131-50
other Getting and Protecting Behaviors and, 85-100
patterns of behavior of, 5
power of, 238-9
provokes Protecting Behaviors in others, 185
rewards of, 5, 101-29
rightness at the core of, 102-4, 106-7
see Getting and Protecting Behaviors
self-help encourages, 170-2
selfishness of, 6-10
seriousness of, 3-4
sex as claim for, 152-3, 157-62
stupid, 148-9
teaching children about, 191, 266-70
therapy encourages, 170-1
unproductive, 148-9

Victimhood (cont.):
tools of, 5
why we use, 101
workplace and, 166-8
worshiped in the United States, 1701
Victims and acting like victims:
act hurt all the time, 57-9, 102-4, 106-7
also liars, 145
angry, 144-5
arguing with, 244-5
arrogant, 34
attacking, 43
beliefs and behaviors of, 43, 55-70
blaming of, 63-4, 106-7, 133
can't be free, 146-8
can't be happy, 148-9
can't be loving, 133-5
can't feel loved when, 132-3
can't grow, 135-7, 137-40
can't have intimate relationships, 133-5
characteristics,
cost of, 131-50
dangerous, 43
demanding, 43, 49-50
eliminated by Real Love,
eliminating irritation toward by understanding them as drowning, 32-4
enslavement by, 243-5
examples, 64
fairness, concept of, 59-61
false, 111-16
feeling imprisoned by, 243-5

Victims and acting like victims (cont.):
  guaranteed to be angry, 144-5
  guilt a tool of, 107-9
  guilt of, 66-7
  how we protect ourselves from, 242-3
  inconvenienced, belief that they are by others, 55-7
  injuries proudly displayed by, 102-4, 106-7
  irrational, 34
  irresponsible, 63-4, 121-4, 137-40
  Law of Choice and, 67-71
  lazy, 140
  lie, 145
  make excuses, 63-4
  manipulate people for support and power, 116-21
  manipulate people for sympathy and attention, 109-16
  motivations for responding to, 105
  negative effects of, 241-2
  never respond to with Getting and Protecting Behaviors, 246-7, 284-5
  of fate, 64-6, 127-8
  of fate, responding to, 293-4
  protecting ourselves from 242-3
  raise more victims, 149-50
  real meaning of what they say and do, 6-10
  responding to, 245-311, 276-83

Victims and acting like victims (cont.):
  responding to by describing what you're doing and choices available, 270-1
  responding to by giving what is needed and what can be given freely, 254-62, 285
  responding to by imposing consequences, 271-5
  responding to by listening to, 251-4, 285-6
  responding to by staying off the Field of Death, 275-6
  responding to by teaching them the truth about human behavior, 262-70
  responding to by telling them the truth about ourselves, 247-52, 287-8
  responding to by telling them the truth about them, 103-4, 133-5, 167-8, 196-7, 199-202
  responding to what they say, 297-308
  rightness of, 102-4, 106-7
  self-inflicted, 127-9, 294-6
  selfish, 43, 62-3
  special, 126-7
  spoiled, 140
  teaching children how to respond to, 306-8
  true, 25, 148
  vicarious, 119-21
  what they say, 80-4
  worthlessness, feelings of, 66-7

Waiting, victimhood and, 206
Walk in woods, metaphor, 309-10
Wedding vows, what we hear, 73
What people say and do (real meaning), 6-9, 46-9, 69
Woods, walk in, metaphor, 309-10
Workplace:
　angry customer in, 166-7, 284-6
　cost of victimhood in, 227-31
　discontented employee, responding to in, 286-8
　listening to victims in, 252-4
　Real Love in, 225-7
　unappreciated employee and critical boss in, 167-8
　victimhood in, 166-8, 206-7, 252-4, 283-8
Worthless, responding to people who feel, 295-6
Wounds, don't define us, 221-4
Wrong, victims cannot be, 106-7